Concepts of Physical Education:
What Every Student Needs to Know

Bonnie S. Mohnsen, Editor

Orange County Department of Education, Cosa Mesa, California

Published by the
**National Association for Sport and Physical Education
(NASPE)**
an association of the
American Alliance for Health, Physical Education, Recreation and Dance

NASPE Publications
1900 Association Drive
Reston, VA 20191-1599
(703) 476-3410
naspe@aahperd.org

Copy Editing: Carol A. Bruce
Graphic Design: Carol A. Bruce
Cover Design: Lisa Gillogly

Contents

Preface

Throughout the nation in recent years, educators and lay persons alike have called for educational reform. The need for change is imminent in order to circumvent the ever-increasing numbers of adolescents who continue to make poor lifestyle choices. What must students know and be able to do to be healthy, productive, and satisfied citizens in the twenty-first century? This question has guided the development of content standards in all the component disciplines of a comprehensive education.

The National Association for Sport and Physical Education (NASPE) took the lead in developing the definition of a physically educated individual and identifying the knowledge and skills needed to lead and enjoy a physically active lifestyle. The knowledge about physical activity and its benefits to a healthy lifestyle continues to expand. We have, therefore, renewed our interest in the Basic Stuff series, whose two editions have provided the scientific foundation for physical activity and performance in a ready to use and easy for students to understand format.

In the original project, the selection of information for the series was based upon its relevance to students in physical education programs. This time the filter for inclusion is the National Standards for Physical Education, which serve as a basis for determining the critical knowledge students must gain for healthy, productive, and satisfying life experiences.

Concepts of Physical Education: What Every Student Needs to Know provides the specific information about what must be taught so that students in grades K–12 can become physically educated individuals. Experts from the respective sub-disciplines have translated the latest research in biomechanics, exercise physiology, motor development, motor learning, social psychology, history, and aesthetics for delivery to students in relevant and meaningful ways. I would like to acknowledge these outstanding professionals for their contributions bringing the concepts supporting participation in physical activity to teachers and their students.

–Judith C. Young, Ph.D.
NASPE Executive Director

Chapter 1
Setting the Stage

By Bonnie S. Mohnsen

One of the most significant questions educators will face as they approach the year 2000 is what knowledge and experience high school graduates will need in order to live high quality lives in the twenty-first century. For physical educators, part of the answer can be found in the National Standards for Physical Education document. Those standards describe what a physically educated person should know and do. However, they do not provide the specific information about what must be taught so that students can become physically educated. This book, written for teachers, provides that information as it relates to students in grades K–12. It also provides instructional and assessment ideas to illustrate how the information can be addressed in K-12 physical education classes.

Before we can define the specific pieces of information (concepts) that students will need to live high-quality lives in the twenty-first century, we must look at some of the significant changes that occurred during the last century that will continue to accelerate after the millennium. Specifically, we must examine the trends in health, business, leisure pursuits, and education and their impact on physical education. This will include a look at the past work of the National Association for Sport and Physical Education's (NASPE) Outcomes Committee, National Standards Committee, and Basic Stuff Committee.

Health Trends

Life expectancy averages worldwide have increased during the last century. In the United States today, life expectancy is 77 years, and the number of individuals living past 100 is increasing weekly. Many futurists are predicting that children born today can expect to live into the twenty-second century. The quality of health care should continue to improve, and thus life expectancy should continue to increase. However, to be meaningful, increases in life expectancy must be matched with a quality of life and wellness that goes beyond simply being free from disease.

The Surgeon General's Report (U.S. Department of Health and Human Services 1996) concludes that people of all ages, both male and female, can substantially improve their health and quality of life by including moderate (at least 30 minutes most, if not all, days of the week) amounts of physical activity in their daily lives. In addition, the report recommends that "every effort should be made to encourage schools to require daily physical education in each grade and

---

Bonnie S. Mohnsen is coordinator, Physical Education and Integrated Technology, Orange County Department of Education, Cosa Mesa, California.

to promote physical activities that can be enjoyed throughout life" (p. 6). This recommendation is based on research that shows favorable attitudes toward physical education and physical activity are positively related to adolescent participation in such activity (Ferguson et al. 1989; Zakarian et al. 1994; Tappe et al. 1990). Thus, physical education plays an important role in society by instilling lifelong healthy habits in our youth.

Business Trends

In the late 1800s, with the advent of new technologies, America moved from an agricultural society to an industrial one (Davidow & Malone 1992). During the late 1900s, another transition occurred, this time from an industrial society to an information society. Today we have immediate access to vast amounts of information. And, with the "electronic superhighway," we are on the verge of another new transition, this time to a communication society.

In a communication society, everyone will be linked together. They will have immediate access to anyone, anywhere, and at any time. As society continues to change, businesses also will change.

Today's business leaders have a keen interest in how we are preparing students for a changing work force, since today's students will be the employees of tomorrow. In 1991, the Secretary's Commission on Achieving Necessary Skills (SCANS) identified five competencies that business leaders want from high school graduates (see Figure 1). Those competencies go a long way toward answering the question of what knowledge and experience young adults will need to live high-quality lives in the next century. The physical education curriculum contributes to all five competencies, and it has a direct relationship to Competencies 2, 3, and 4.

Competency 2, "works with others," is especially significant in view of our increasingly multicultural society. In such societies, beliefs differ dramatically and there are conflicting norms of behavior. In the physical education classroom, students learn the skill of cooperation along with other social skills. As Burrus, noted futurist has stated, "Many subjects that teach interpersonal skills, such as sports and music, are subjects that are being cut back at the present time, but shouldn't be" (p. 242).

Competency 3, "acquires and uses information," requires that we not only teach students how to access information, but also how to apply a filter so they acquire only the specific information they need. Knowledge currently doubles every year, and by the year 2020, information experts predict that knowledge will double every 70 days!

Physical educators must teach students how to find the information they need to plan valid and effective exercise, wellness, and activity programs. We are constantly bombarded with claims of "new" and "quick" solutions to weight and health issues, and students must be able to differentiate between those claims and effective programs.

Physical education addresses Competency 4, "understands complex interrelationships," in much the same way as it addresses Competency 2. For example, business leaders often send their upper level managers to team building seminars in order to learn to work more efficiently together. These seminars may include Outward Bound experiences, challenge courses (e.g., high ropes courses), or other types of physical challenge that require participants to work together to be successful. These are the same types of experiences that teachers provide in many of their classes!

Figure 1. What Businesses Want from High School Graduates

I. Resources: Identifies, Organizes, Plans, and Allocates Resources.
A. Time. Selects goal-relevant activities, ranks them, allocates time, and prepares and follows schedules.
B. Money. Prepares budgets, makes forecasts, keeps records, and makes adjustments to meet objectives.
C. Materials and Facilities. Acquires, stores, allocates, and uses materials or space efficiently.
D. Human Resources. Accesses skills and distributes work accordingly, evaluates performance, and provides feedback.
II. Interpersonal: Works with Others.
A. Participates as a Member of a Team. Contributes to group effort.
B. Teaches Others New Skills.
C. Serves Clients/Customers. Works to satisfy customers' expectations.
D. Exercises Leadership. Communicates ideas to justify position, persuades and convinces others, responsibly challenges existing procedures and policies.
E. Negotiates. Works toward agreements involving exchange of resources, resolves divergent interests.
F. Works with Diversity. Works well with men and women from diverse backgrounds.
III. Information: Acquires and Uses Information.
A. Acquires and Evaluates Information.
B. Organizes and Maintains Information.
C. Interprets and Communicates Information.
D. Uses Computers to Process Information.
IV. Systems: Understands Complex Interrelationships.
A. Understands Systems. Knows how social, organization, and technological systems work and operates effectively with them.
B. Monitors and Corrects Performance. Distinguishes trends, predicts impacts on system operations, diagnoses systems' performance and corrects malfunctions.
C. Improves or Designs Systems. Suggests modifications to existing systems and develops new or alternative systems to improve performance.
V. Technology: Works with a Variety of Technologies.
A. Selects Technology. Chooses procedures, tools, or equipment including computers and related technologies.
B. Applies Technology to Task. Understands overall intent and proper procedures for set-up and operation of equipment.
C. Maintains and Troubleshoots Equipment. Prevents, identifies, or solves problems with equipment, including computers and other technologies.

Reprinted from *What Work Requires of Schools: A SCANS Report for America 2000*, Secretary's Commission on Achieving Necessary Skills, 1991.

Leisure Pursuits

Trends in recreation are correlated with personal "habits, lifestyles, resource opportunities, and economic and social contexts" (Kelly 1987, p. iii). Thus, with the change from agricultural society, to industrial society, to information society came changes in the ways individuals used their leisure time. The increase in our use of technology has taken much of the physical labor (a natural source of physical activity) out of our work, and out of our daily lives as well. This has created a greater need for moderate to vigorous exercise pursuits.

It is interesting to note that, in the 1960s, futurists began to predict shorter work weeks and more leisure time. However, the reality is that it now takes two incomes for most families to maintain a middle class lifestyle, and that's an 80-hour work week per family (Popcorn 1992). In addition, people today spend a large amount of time traveling to work, watching television, and playing computer games (Kelly 1987). It is more important than ever that physical educators provide information on time management, stress reduction, and maximizing leisure time through moderate to vigorous activity.

Education Trends

Throughout the last several decades, the education community has strived to keep pace with the rapidly occurring changes in society. However, many educational leaders will argue that schools have, in fact, remained in the industrial age. For example, secondary students are moved from class to class throughout the day, much like a new product is moved from station to station along an assembly line.

Today, as we enter the communication age, futurists are beginning again to predict what "schools of the future" may look like. Thornburg (1992, p. 118) says that rather than have assigned classrooms, the school might become a huge resource center where students, teachers, and others could co-mingle, conduct research, discuss projects, and interact freely. The structure of classes and assignments would be provided through "telecomputing." This is a very different picture from what schools look like today. For starters, everyone at school would be there because they wanted to be. The school site would bustle with excitement and activity.

In Thornburg's view, schools would be more like museums, where students could exchange ideas and socialize with other students around the world. With this idea in mind, it is interesting to note what individuals from outside the education realm are saying about the future of education. Anglin (1991, p. 265), a computer designer, says that in addition to providing access to facilities that are not affordable on an individual basis—such as chemistry labs and gymnasiums—schools may become institutions whose most cherished aim is to deliver all of those services now considered of secondary importance: sports, art, choir, socialization, and individual attention.

The United States Department of Education's Educate America Act: Goals 2000 provides the roadmap for education. The American Alliance for Health, Physical Education, Recreation, and Dance (AAHPERD) along with NASPE, worked hard lobbying Congress to include physical education in the National Education Goals. (See Figure 2 for specific wording from Goals 2000 relating to physical education.)

Several trends that relate to effectively educating students for the 21st century emerge from both the National Education Goals and the current literature on educational reform. These include:

Figure 2. Goals 2000: Educate America Act–National Education Goals

1. All children in America will start school ready to learn.

2. The high school graduation rate will increase to at least 90 percent.

3. All students will leave fourth, eighth, and twelfth grades having demonstrated competency over challenging subject matter including English, mathematics, science, foreign languages, civics and government, economics, arts, history, and geography, and every school in America will ensure that all students learn to use their minds well, so they may be prepared for responsible citizenship, further learning, and productive employment in our nation's modern economy.

3B(iv). All students will have access to physical education and health education to ensure they are healthy and fit.

4. The nation's teaching force will have access to programs for the continued improvement of their professional skills and the opportunity to acquire the knowledge and skills needed to instruct and prepare all American students for the next century.

5. United States students will be the first in the world in mathematics and science achievement.

6. Every adult American will be literate and will possess the knowledge and skills necessary to compete in a global economy and exercise the rights and responsibility of citizenship.

7. Every school in the United States will be free of drugs, violence, and the unauthorized presence of firearms and alcohol and will offer a disciplined environment conducive to learning.

8. Every school will promote partnerships that will increase parental involvement and participation in promoting the social, emotional, and academic growth of children.

- There is equal access to instruction and information for all students.
- Teachers assume the role of facilitators of learning rather than disseminators of information.
- The approach to learning is interdisciplinary, to ensure the integration of important principles across the curriculum.
- The curriculum promotes lifelong learning.
- The curriculum emphasizes "how to learn" as opposed to "what to learn."
- The curriculum emphasizes critical thinking skills, creative thinking skills, decision making skills, and problem finding and solving skills.
- Instruction is meaningful for the learner.
- Students take responsibility for their own learning.
- Instruction emphasizes active learning, where students learn by doing.
- Learning is enhanced by the use of new technologies.
- Assessment measures student learning in performance-based settings, as it relates to predetermined standards of knowledge.

Such visions, goals, and assumptions are encouraging. However, forces exist that may point to a more cautious view of the future of education. Recent budget cuts have had a significant impact on education. As Milchrist (1995) says, "While reduced expenditures for education may account for immediate downsizing, a greater force, a restructuring of education at all levels, accounts for the major changes education is experiencing now and will be experiencing within the next decade."

While the trends listed previously paint a positive future for the education process, other groups predict a gloomier outcome. Their predictions include:

- Education as a private enterprise that is exempted from current rules, including those mandating equal access and providing for physical education.
- The use of "expert" teachers who are neither credentialed nor certificated.
- The downsizing of programs to the point where there is little depth left.

As we attempt to keep up with the changes in society, we also must keep up with the changes in education. We must be aware of the negative possibilities, and we must explore ways to educate parents and community members about how quality education relates to physical education programs.

On the national level, NASPE members have worked hard to keep physical education on an equal footing with the other subject areas. Several projects that lead to the development of the National Standards, and in turn, this book, are described in the following sections.

The Justification and Outcomes Projects

In the 1980s, NASPE began a long-term effort known as the Justification Project. Its purpose was to define the benefits of physical activity. This project resulted in two publications in 1986—*The Value of Physical Activity,* and *Physical Activity and Well-Being*—and began the long-term journey toward the National Standards. Also in 1986, NASPE appointed the Outcomes Committee to answer the question, "What should students know and be able to do?" related to physical education. The Outcomes Project culminated in the development of a definition of the physically educated person. This definition includes five major focus areas, and specifies that a physically educated person:

- Has learned skills necessary to perform a variety of physical activities.
- Is physically fit.
- Participates regularly in physical activity.
- Knows the implications and the benefits of involvement in physical activities.
- Values physical activity and its contribution to a healthful lifestyle.

This definition was expanded to 20 outcome statements, and then further defined with sample benchmarks for selected grade levels. The benchmarks provide an understanding of the type of content and learning required for each component of the definition. The work of the Outcomes Committee is presented in *Outcomes of Quality Physical Education Programs* (1992).

NASPE Content Standards

Following the publication of the *Outcomes of Quality Physical Education Programs,* NASPE leaders created the Standards and Assessment Task Force. Its charge was to develop assessment material for the outcomes document. The work of the task force, which began in the spring of 1992, reflected the national education reform movement. In the fall of 1992, the name of the committee was changed to the National Standards and Assessment Committee, and it was tasked with developing the National Content Standards for Physical Education.

The promotional brochure for the Standards states that the movement to clarify and establish important educational goals has provided the impetus and direction for much of the work of the Physical Education Standards and Assessment Task Force. To make the materials for physical education parallel to the materials being developed by other content areas, the identification of content standards and the further clarification of the content in physical education were undertaken before the issue of assessment was addressed.

The purpose of the document is to establish content standards for the physical education program that clearly identify what a student should know and be able to do as a result of a quality physical education program; and to establish teacher-friendly guidelines for assessment of the content standards.

The content standards in physical education identified in the 1995 document are:

1. Demonstrates competency in many movement forms and proficiency in a few movement forms.
2. Applies movement concepts and principles to the learning and development of motor skills.
3. Exhibits a physically active lifestyle.
4. Achieves and maintains a health-enhancing level of physical fitness.
5. Demonstrates responsible personal and social behavior in physical activity settings.
6. Demonstrates understanding and respect for differences among people in physical activity settings.
7. Understands that physical activity provides opportunities for enjoyment, challenge, self-expression, and social interaction.

Each of these content standards is further defined for kindergarten, second grade, fourth grade, sixth grade, eighth grade, tenth grade, and twelfth grade. Along with the definition of what that standard looks like at that grade level, there also are areas of emphasis and sample benchmarks. These standards represent a philosophy of physical education that goes beyond fitness or sport education into a comprehensive view of the subject area known as physical education. Figure 3 shows the definition, areas of emphasis, and sample benchmarks for Standard 5 at the kindergarten, fourth grade, eighth grade, and twelfth grade levels.

The Next Step

The next step in the process is to define the content that will allow students to accomplish the grade-level benchmarks and meet the National Standards. Although the standards are deliberately presented as broad-based demonstrations of learning, students will need specific baseline information in order to demonstrate them.

One example of identifying baseline information can be found in the book, *The Dictionary of Cultural Literacy* (Hirsch, Kett, and Trefil 1993). The authors attempted to define what a culturally literate individual must know to participate effectively in our society. Their errors were that they included too much information, they did not make the link to application for the reader, and they omitted information related to physical education, sport, and exercise. Perhaps this omission was due, in part, to our inability to communicate effectively to the general public the importance of physical education instruction.

The baseline information for physically educated people is derived from the subdisciplines of physical education, including aesthetics, biomechanics, motor development, exercise physiology, history, motor learning, psychology, and sociology. In 1981, in order to "encourage and support the idea that disciplinary knowledge about how and why the body moves is a worthwhile

Figure 3. Definition, Emphasis, and Benchmarks Related to National Standard 5:

Demonstrates responsible personal and social behavior in physical activity settings.

Twelfth Grade

Twelfth grade students demonstrate the ability to initiate responsible behavior, function independently, and positively influence the behavior of others in physical activity settings. They demonstrate leadership by holding themselves and others responsible for following safe practices, rules, procedures, and etiquette in all physical activity settings.

They act as a neutralizer in avoiding conflict or as a mediator in settling conflicts.

The emphasis for the twelfth grade student will be to:

• Initiate independent and responsible personal behavior in physical activity settings.

• Accept the responsibility for taking a leadership role and willingly follow as appropriate in order to accomplish group goals.

• Anticipate potentially dangerous consequences and outcomes of participation in physical activity.

Sample Benchmarks:

1. Sets personal goals for activity and works toward their achievement.
2. Encourages others to apply appropriate etiquette in all physical activity settings.
3. Responds to inflammatory situations with mature personal control.
4. Diffuses potential conflicts by communicating with other participants.
5. Creates a safe environment for their own skill practice.
6. Takes a supportive role in an activity.
7. Cheers outstanding performance of opponents as well as the "favored" team.

Eighth Grade

Students are beginning to seek greater independence from adults. They make appropriate decisions to resolve conflicts arising from the powerful influence of peers and to follow pertinent practices, rules, and procedures necessary for successful performance. They practice appropriate problem-solving techniques to resolve conflicts when necessary in competitive activities. Students reflect on the benefits of the role of rules, procedures, safe practices, ethical behavior, and positive social interaction in physical activity settings.

The emphasis for the eighth grade student will be to:

• Recognize the influence of peer pressure.

• Solve problems by analyzing causes and potential solutions.

• Analyze potential consequences when confronted with a behavior choice.

• Work cooperatively with a group to achieve group goals in competitive as well as cooperative settings.

Sample Benchmarks:

1. Identifies positive and negative peer influence.
2. Plays within the rules of a game or activity.
3. Considers the consequences when confronted with a behavior choice.
4. Resolves interpersonal conflicts with a sensitivity to rights and feelings of others.
5. Handles conflicts that arise with others without confrontation.
6. Finds positive ways to exert independence.

7. Tempers the desire to "belong" to a peer group with a growing awareness of independent thought.

8. Makes choices based on the safety of self and others.

9. Accepts a controversial decision of an official.

Fourth Grade

Students identify the purposes for and follow, with few reminders, activity-specific safe practices, rules, procedures, and etiquette. They continue to develop cooperation skills to enable completion of a common goal while working with a partner or in small groups. They can work independently and productively for short periods of time.

The emphasis for the fourth grade student will be to:

• Follow, with few reminders, activity-specific rules, procedures, and etiquette.

• Utilize safety principles in activity situations.

• Work cooperatively and productively with a partner or small group.

• Work independently and on task for short periods of time.

Sample Benchmarks:

1. When given the opportunity, arranges gymnastics equipment safely in a manner appropriate to the task.

2. Takes seriously his or her role to teach an activity or skill to two other classmates.

3. Works productively with a partner to improve the overhand throw pattern for distance by using the critical elements of the process.

4. Accepts the teacher's decision regarding a personal rule infraction without displaying negative reactions toward others.

5. Assesses his or her own performance problems without blaming others.

Kindergarten

Students begin to learn and utilize acceptable behaviors for physical activity settings. Focus is directed toward understanding safe practices as well as classroom rules and procedures. They begin to understand the concept of cooperation through opportunities to share space and equipment with others in a group.

The emphasis for the kindergarten students will be to:

• Apply, with teacher reinforcement, classroom rules and procedures and safe practices.

• Share space and equipment with others.

Sample Benchmarks:

1. Knows the rules for participating in the gymnasium and on the playground.

2. Works in a group setting without interfering with others.

3. Responds to teacher signals for attention.

4. Responds to rules infractions when reminded once.

5. Follows directions given to the class for an all-class activity.

6. Handles equipment safely by putting it away when not in use.

7. Takes turns using a piece of equipment.

8. Transfers rules of the gym to "rules of the playground."

From NASPE's *Moving into the Future—National Standards for Physical Education: A Guide to Content and Assessment,* 1995.

and appropriate aspect of the physical education curriculum" NASPE began publishing information from the Basic Stuff Project. That project drew upon information from the subdisciplines and identified key material that was deemed important for K-12 teachers and their students. The preface to the Basic Stuff booklets says:

> Many physical education teachers want to use and apply information particularly relevant to their teaching. It is not an easy task. The quantity of research alone would require a dawn to dusk reading schedule. The specialized nature of the research tends to make it difficult for a lay person to comprehend fully. And finally, little work has been directed toward applying the research to the more practical concerns of teachers in the field. Thus the burgeoning body of information available to researchers and academicians has had little impact on physical education programs in the field. (p. vii)

The project resulted in six informational booklets, with each booklet targeting a specific subdiscipline (exercise physiology, kinesiology, motor learning, psychosocial aspects of movement, humanities, and motor development). There also were learning experience booklets (early childhood, childhood, and adolescence) that provided examples of instructional activities teachers could use to introduce appropriate physical education concepts to the three age groups.

In 1987, three new booklets—*Basic Stuff in Action for Grades K-3, 4-8*, and *9-12*—replaced the learning experience booklets. The booklets contained sample lesson plans that showed teachers how to transfer the baseline information to their students. In 1995, the introduction of the Physical Education Standards created a need to update the Basic Stuff information. This book represents the results of that effort to redefine the significant content in physical education.

This Book

Like the original Basic Stuff Series, this new project asked leaders in the respective subdisciplines to review the current information and to summarize the most significant material in a form that allows K-12 teachers to share it with their students. In the Basic Stuff project, information was selected according to its relevance to students in physical education programs. This time, the filter for inclusion is the National Physical Education Standards and what students need to know to live "high quality lives" in the twenty-first century.

Chapters 2 through 8 of this book represent the seven subdisciplines (motor learning, biomechanics, exercise physiology, social psychology, historical perspectives, motor development, and aesthetics). Each chapter is organized as follows:

- Introduction to the subdiscipline.
- Importance of the subdiscipline.
- Link to and interpretation of the National Standards related to the subdiscipline.
- Significant subdiscipline concepts related to quality of life and the National Standards.
- K-12 sequence (every other grade) for the significant concepts.
- Lesson ideas.
- Assessment ideas.
- Resources for more information.

Chapter 9 pulls together the information presented in Chapters 2 through 8 and presents it in an integrated fashion. It answers the question, "What next?" It shows how to integrate the information from various subdisciplines and standards into learning experiences. And, it shows various ways in which the subdisciplines can be integrated into other subject areas to create an interdisciplinary approach.

Before we can apply the grade level concepts, instructional ideas, and student assessment ideas discussed in Chapters 2 through 8, we must identify a common language and knowledge base. The final sections in this chapter explain the concept selection process, instructional considerations, and assessment tools that are used throughout the book.

Concept Selection

The concepts included in the following pages align with and expand on the kindergarten, second grade, fourth grade, sixth grade, eighth grade, tenth grade, and twelfth grade benchmarks identified in the National Standards. However, instead of simply listing the standards, this book provides the critical concepts that must be addressed or learned by the students if they are to demonstrate their learning related to each of the standards.

Instructional Considerations

There are many ways that teachers can include cognitive concepts in the teaching of physical education. First and foremost, teachers must model the application of these concepts as they provide instructional experiences for students. Second, they must plan and provide specific learning activities that teach the concepts. Careful planning, based on the information contained in the concept and the various learning styles of the students in the class, will ensure that learning occurs.

One model to consider when developing activities for all students is Gardner's Theory of Multiple Intelligences. According to Gardner, there are currently eight identified areas of intelligence: linguistic intelligence, logical-mathematical intelligence, spatial intelligence, bodily-kinesthetic intelligence, musical intelligence, interpersonal intelligence, intrapersonal intelligence, and naturalist intelligence. Every individual has varying degrees of ability in each of these areas. When developing learning experiences, it is important for the teacher to consider each of the eight areas in order to provide learning opportunities that relate to the various capabilities (see Figure 4). Students can rotate through various learning stations or they may be allowed to select the one learning opportunity they feel is best suited to their strengths.

Assessment Tools

Assessment in K-12 education tends to fall into one of three major categories: traditional, alternative, and authentic. In the traditional approach, assessment is based on standardized motor skill tests for accuracy and distance; written tests on rules, history, and strategy; and physical fitness tests. Alternative assessment tools, as identified in the National Standards, include self-

Figure 4. Gardner's Multiple Intelligences

Linguistic—capacity to use words effectively

Logical-Mathematical—capacity to use numbers and reason effectively

Spatial—capacity to perceive the visual-spatial world accurately

Bodily-Kinesthetic—capacity to use bodies effectively

Musical—capacity to perceive musical forms accurately

Interpersonal—capacity to understand others effectively

Intrapersonal—capacity to understand themselves effectively

Naturalist—capacity to discriminate among living things

assessment, video analysis, open-ended questions, and focused journal writing. Authentic assessment takes this one step farther by requiring students to use alternative assessment tools to apply their learning to real-world situations.

In each chapter of this book, the author(s) includes ideas on how students can demonstrate their learning in relation to the standard or concept learned. These assessment ideas are based on the application of a number of different assessment tools and concepts, including checking for understanding, observation, reports, projects, role playing and simulations, student logs and focused journals, 30-second wonders, and written tests.

Checking for Understanding. With this quick technique, the teacher simply asks a question and then calls on several students to answer the question. It is important to query a heterogeneous group of students (low achievers, high achievers, boys, girls) in sufficient numbers to get an accurate reading of the students' cognitive understanding.

Observations. Observations can be done by the teacher, peers, or the students themselves. An observation requires a judgment to be made about a particular motor skill. When assessing performance based on observation, teachers use either a checklist or rubric (see following section on rubrics), or a simple counting system (e.g., number of serves in the court, number of free throws made). In some situations, students first assess themselves, then have a peer validate their assessment, and then have the teacher complete the assessment cycle by making the formal observation.

Reports. Reports are a commonly used assessment technique. Sometimes, they encompass several subject areas, providing an interdisciplinary assessment (e.g., the language arts teacher assesses the writing, and the physical education teacher assesses the content).

Projects (individual and group). Student projects take the report technique one step farther, and ask students to create products other than written reports. These products might take the form of videos, multimedia presentations, or oral presentations. Many students find projects intrinsically motivating, since they often can use skills that are associated with their primary intelligence. However, projects also can be very time consuming for students to do and for teachers to evaluate.

Role Playing and Simulations. Role playing and simulations provide students with the opportunity to respond as if they were in a real-life situation. They require students to use higher-level thinking and problem solving skills.

Student Logs and Journals. Student logs and journals are used to document perceptions, feelings, attitudes, and evidence of progress. Journal reflections are typically made at the end of each class, when students describe what they did, what they learned, what risks they took, and what they would change about their performance. In logs, on the other hand, students record levels of performance (number of sit ups, times for the mile run, etc.) or specific behaviors collected at regular intervals over a period of time.

Thirty-Second Wonders. The 30-second wonder is another quick assessment tool that can demonstrate whether students understand the concepts the teacher presented. The teacher simply asks a question and has each student write an answer on a piece of paper. Teachers can assess the answers to determine the lesson for the following day.

Written Tests. Written tests are typically used to assess cognitive understanding. They can include multiple choice, true/false, matching, fill-in-the blank, short answer, and essay questions. However, the recent shift has been to emphasize essay or open-ended questions. This is often referred to as going "beyond the bubble," indicating a shift from filling in a Scantron™ sheet to using cognitive and strategic problem solving skills.

Rubrics. A rubric is a scoring criteria that is used to assess student work. It provides a description of various qualitative levels of performance on a specific task or product. The rubric presents a criteria by which the quality of the final product is assessed. The rating can take the form of any number of scales, but a range of one through six, with six being ideal, or one through four, with four being ideal, is the most common. Initially, the teacher develops the rubric, but as confidence grows the development of rubrics becomes a joint effort involving teacher and students.

Portfolios. A portfolio is a permanent collection of a student's best work. It demonstrates progress toward identified standards. It is similar to an artist's portfolio, and can contain a variety of assessment tools. Most portfolios include a reflective essay in which the student comments on the portfolio. At the end of the year, the portfolio provides the teacher and the student with concrete information that can be used to discuss progress and to set goals for the next year.

Concluding Comments
This book is the most recent attempt to provide physical educators with up-to-date content that will assist students in becoming physically educated. As we move into the next seven chapters, it is imperative that readers challenge their existing assumptions about education in general and physical education in particular, and dare to create quality learning experiences that are relevant for the twenty-first century.

References

American Heart Association (1991). *Heart and stroke facts.* Needham, MA: Author.

Anglin, G. J. (Ed.). (1991). *Instructional technology: Past, present and future.* Englewood, CO: Libraries Unlimited, Inc.

Burrus, D. (1993). *Techno trends.* New York: Harper Business.

Carr, N. J. (Ed.). (1987). *Basic stuff series II.* Reston, VA: American Alliance for Health, Physical Education, Recreation and Dance.

Davidow, W. H., & Malone, M. S. (1992). *The virtual corporation.* New York: Harper Business.

Ferguson, K. J., Yesalis, C. E., Pomreh, P. R., & Kirkpatrick, M. B. (1989). Attitudes, knowledge, and beliefs as predictors of exercise intent and behavior in school children. *Journal of School Health, 59,* 112-115.

Franck, M. (1992). *Outcomes of quality physical education programs.* Reston, VA: National Association for Sport and Physical Education.

Gardner, H. (1985). *Frames of mind.* New York: Basic Books, Harper Collins.

Hirsch, E. D. Jr., Kett, J. F., & Trefil, J. (1993). The dictionary of cultural literacy. Boston: Houghton Mifflin.

Kelly, J. R. (1987). *Recreational trends toward the year 2000.* Champaign, IL: Management Learning Laboratories, Ltd.

Kneer, M. (Ed.). (1981). *Basic stuff series I.* Reston, VA: American Alliance for Health, Physical Education, Recreation and Dance.

Milchrist, P. A. (1995). *Future directions of university programs: Uncommon liaisons.* Paper presented at the Southwest AHPERD Convention, HI.

Popcorn, F. (1992). *The popcorn report.* New York: Harper Collins.

Rink, J. (1995). *Moving into the future—National standards for physical education: A guide to con-*

tent and assessment. Reston, VA: National Association for Sport and Physical Education.

Secretary's Commission on Achieving Necessary Skills (1991). *What work requires of schools: A scans report for America 2000.* Washington D.C.: U.S. Department of Labor.

Tappe, M. K., Duda, J. L., & Menges-Ehrnwald, P. (1990). Personal investment predictors of adolescent motivation orientation toward exercise. *Canadian Journal of Sport Sciences, 15,* 185-192.

Thornburg, D. D. (1992). *Edutrends 2010: Restructuring, technology and the future of education.* San Francisco, CA: Starson Publications.

United States Department of Health and Human Services, Public Health Services (1990). *Healthy people 2000: National health promotion and disease prevention objectives.* Washington DC: author.

United States Department of Health and Human Services (1996). *Physical activity and health: A report of the surgeon general.* Atlanta, GA: author.

Youth problems are frightening. (1988, September 13). *Deseret News.*

Zakarian, J. M., Hovell, M. F., Hofstetter, C. R., Sallis, J. F., & Keating, K. J. (1994). Correlates of vigorous exercise in a predominantly low SES and minority high school population. *Preventive Medicine, 23,* 314-321.

Chapter 2
Motor Learning

By Judith E. Rink

The National Standards for Physical Education, developed in 1995 by the National Association for Sport and Physical Education (NASPE), strongly support the concept that students should be prepared for a physically active lifestyle: Individuals who are physically active are healthier and lead more meaningful lives. The National Standards also call for a strong emphasis on learning concepts and principles that describe the learning and performance of motor skills. This intent is clearly described in Standard 2: Applies movement concepts and principles to the learning and development of motor skills.

What Is Motor Learning?

Motor learning is the study of change in the ability of a person to perform a skill that is inferred from improvement in performance over time as a result of practice or experience. First, like all learning, motor learning is inferred from behavior and represents a relatively permanent change in behavior. It is possible to observe performance and not be observing learning. Second, changes in behavior are attributed to experience or practice and not to changes in the organism (such as increased strength).

Why Is Motor Learning Important?

Teachers must be committed to the process and knowledgeable in the basic concepts of learning if students are to understand how to learn and why particular practices are important in their learning. This knowledge will help them be better learners today, and it will help them later in life when they choose to acquire new skills.

Adults who have a strong background in basic and fundamental movement patterns and who know how to learn new skills will be better prepared for an active life. Thus, at a minimum, students should understand the basic concepts that equip them to become independent learners of motor skills.

Linking Motor Learning to the National Standards

Motor learning concepts and principles can stand by themselves as content for physical education. Motor learning concepts and principles also can be integrated with other standards. This is particularly true of aspects of the following standards:

Judith E. Rink is department chair and professor, Department of Physical Education, University of South Carolina, Columbia.

- National Standard 1: Demonstrates competency in many movement forms and proficiency in a few movement forms.
- National Standard 4: Achieves and maintains a health-enhancing level of physical fitness.
- National Standard 6: Demonstrates understanding and respect for differences among people in physical activity settings.
- National Standard 7: Understands that physical activity provides opportunities for enjoyment, challenge, self-expression, and social interaction.

The National Standards do not intend that physical education become a classroom course in motor learning and motor control. Rather, the concepts and principles should be selected carefully, be developmentally appropriate for the age of the learner, and be integrated with physical activity. This is particularly true with motor learning concepts. It is their repetition through the program that will provide the reinforcement the student needs to learn them and to be able to transfer them to new learning experiences.

Selected Motor Learning Concepts

It is important for physical education teachers to understand and be able to apply the information contained in the textbooks on motor learning. While physically educated individuals do not need the same depth of understanding, it is important for them to grasp certain concepts if they are to be independent learners of motor skills. These ideas are organized around six major themes:

1. How do people get better at motor skills?
2. What is good performance?
3. What stages do individuals pass through to become proficient at motor skills?
4. What kind of practice facilitates learning?
5. How do individuals differ in learning a motor skill?
6. Will learning one motor skill help a person learn another motor skill?

Each of these themes is briefly developed in the next section. Critical student concepts that fall under each theme are listed in Table 1.

How Do People Get Better at Motor Skills?

Improvement in motor skills is usually the result of changes in growth and/or learning. As students grow bigger and stronger, many of their skills—particularly those requiring force production (jumping, throwing etc.)—will improve. However, the ability to improve the process characteristics (form) of a motor skill is not age or strength dependent. Learning might be described as a change in behavior that is the result of practice and experience in motor skills. Learning is inferred from performance, and it can only be measured indirectly.

For example, we infer that students have learned when they do well on an assessment of the product or product characteristics of a movement, and we infer that they have not learned when they do poorly. Because we are measuring performance, learning may or may not have occurred. We can measure learning by looking at performance after time has elapsed between practice and testing.

Short-term improvement in motor performance can be achieved without actual learning if the responses are not committed to long term-memory. This means that teachers might be able to elicit a good performance from a student who has not learned the skill and therefore will not be able to repeat it. When students have learned, performance becomes more consistent. Again, when we observe performance after a period of time has elapsed between practice and testing, we are more likely to see the degree of learning that has occurred. Once motor skills are committed to long-term memory, they will be retained for long periods of time. It should be noted here that continuous skills (riding a bike) are remembered for longer amounts of time than discrete skills (the tennis serve).

When we say that an individual learns a motor skill, we are really talking about several different kinds of change that take place as performance improves. The most obvious is the physical change that occurs with practice. The movement becomes more mechanically efficient and coordinated, the goal of the movement is accomplished to a greater extent, and the use of different muscle groups to accomplish the movement becomes more efficient. Cognitive change also is likely as skill develops. More skilled performers attend to different parts of the performance, can focus on how to use a skill, and have greater ability to correct their own performance.

What Is Good Performance?

There are two aspects to good performance. The first is the ability to correctly select what to do, and the second is the ability to execute that selection appropriately. For example, I may correctly select a drop shot in badminton, but I may not be able to execute that shot correctly. Or, I may be able to do a drop shot but may not select the appropriate time to use it. There also is knowledge involved in executing a motor skill. I may execute a motor skill according to the knowledge I have about how to do that skill, but my knowledge may be wrong.

When a performance is not good, it is important to know whether the problem is related to what was selected to do or how it was executed. Different kinds of skills put different demands on each aspect of performance. Skills that are performed in complex environments put more of an emphasis on what to do (response selection) than skills that are not performed in complex environments. Closed skills that must be performed with consistent form (e.g., gymnastics, diving) put more of an emphasis on correct execution.

There are several ways in which types of motor skills are differentiated, and these will affect what is learned and how it is learned. The most critical differentiation of motor skills is related to the continuum of closed and open skills. Closed skills are performed in stable and predictable environments. Gymnastics, diving, and the foul shot in basketball are all examples of closed skills. The environment in which the skill is performed is largely stable and predictable. Open skills are characterized by variable and unpredictable environments. The tennis forehand, the field goal shot in basketball, and the soccer pass all are examples of open skills. There also are some skills that are essentially closed skills but are performed in variable environments, such as those used in golf and bowling. For these skills, the performance must be adjusted to suit different situations.

Motor skills also are characterized as discrete skills, serial skills, and continuous skills. Discrete skills are single skills performed in isolation from other motor skills. Examples of discrete skills are the soccer penalty kick, the tennis backhand, the golf stroke, and the standing long jump. These skills are usually not performed with, or followed by, other skills. Serial skills are two or more different skills performed with each other, such as fielding a ball and throwing it, trapping a soccer ball and passing it, dribbling a basketball and shooting it, or performing a gymnastics dance routine. Most team sports require that players combine two or more complex skills in a serial fashion. Continuous skills are two or more repetitions of the same skill, such as dribbling in basketball or soccer.

Good performance of serial and continuous skills requires that the performer link movements together in a smooth fashion. Preparation for the next movement actually occurs during the previous movement. Consider, for example, going from a handstand into a forward roll, or fielding and throwing a ball. If I am going to go into a forward roll after a handstand, I will have to make adjustments to both the handstand and the forward roll. How I field a ball and come up from it is determined in large part by the kind of throw I need to make. Players actually prepare for the throw while they are fielding. In serial skills such as the dribble, one movement prepares for the next.

It is important to determine how the links between skills should be made and to practice movements in sequence. Sports such as soccer, where many skills are performed in a serial fashion, require players to practice many different combinations of skills (i.e., receive an aerial ball, dribble and pass, receive a ground ball, dribble and shoot).

Good performance for open skills requires the performers to adapt their performance to the open environment. For instance, basketball players must make a decision about what to do based on their opponents' and their teammates' positions and abilities. They also must adjust their movements to the demands of different situations. The more skilled individuals are able to choose appropriate responses and execute those choices in complex and changing environments.

What Stages Do Individuals Pass Through To Become Proficient at Motor Skills?

An individual must pass through three stages to become proficient at a motor skill (Fitts & Posner 1967):

• *Stage 1.* This is the verbal-cognitive stage. At this point, the individual is trying to figure out how to do the skill and is generating beginning attempts. The emphasis here is on "what to do." Performance is very inconsistent, and attention demands are very high. For instance, a beginning volleyball player trying to do a forearm pass is likely to have a facial expression that shows extreme concentration. He or she also is likely to misjudge the timing and point of contact of the ball, resulting in a lack of control. This player is not able to deal with what may be happening with teammates or opponents, and may be completely unaware of their movements.

• *Stage 2.* This is the motor stage of learning. The emphasis here is on trying to perfect the motor response. Learning continues to involve cognitive processes of performance. Consistency improves. Performers begin to attend to other environmental aspects of performance. A good example of this stage of development is the basketball player who can make some defensive adjustments in the dribble to accommodate the movements of an offensive player, but who cannot quite take his or her eyes off the ball. At this level, most adjustments to the environment are made very much at a conscious level of awareness.

• *Stage 3.* This is the automatic stage. At this point, movement responses flow. There is little cognitive involvement, and the level of performance is consistently high. Performers at this stage can function in highly complex environments such as games. They can focus on what to do without having to think about how to do it. The soccer player moving into scoring position can focus on where teammates and opponents are located on the field and can anticipate their movements without having to worry about dribbling, passing, or shooting skills.

What Kind of Practice Facilitates Learning?

Practice is the most critical variable in learning a motor skill. The literature tells us that the quality of practice (degree to which the response resembles the "appropriate" response) is related to learning. Practice alone does not produce learning; the practice must be of high quality. If you consistently practice something in an incorrect manner, you most likely will learn it incorrectly. The type of skill to be learned and the skill level of the learner will determine what type of practice is appropriate.

Learning in motor skills is best measured with retention tests—tests that measure performance after a period of time has elapsed. When you can perform a skill several days after practicing it, then you can say you have learned the skill.

Blocked, Random, and Variable Practice. The terms blocked, random, and variable practice refer to the degree of drill-like repetition in the practice. In the initial stages of learning a motor skill, blocked practice (repeating the same skill in the same way) has merit. Stage 1 learners are trying to get the idea of the skill. There is value in repetition because it helps develop consistency. For example, there may be merit in practicing the movement of the tennis forehand until the process characteristics that describe good performance become part of the action.

After the initial stages of learning, open skills should be practiced under variable conditions (same skill, different conditions) that gradually take on the characteristics of the conditions of the game or performance (e.g., dribbling stationary, dribbling with other players, dribbling with a passive defense, dribbling with an active defense). The intent is to encourage processing during the learning stages. Rote drill does not encourage processing, and it does not work for movements that must be adapted to continuously changing environments.

For more advanced learners, random practice of different skills may have merit. Random practice in volleyball might include the forearm pass, the serve, and the overhead pass or spike in random order.

Transfer of Practice. Transfer of practice is the degree to which practice in one situation will be helpful in another situation. The manner in which a skill is practiced should relate as closely as possible to the manner in which it will be used in a game or performance. Skills that are practiced in simple conditions and then used in a complex game are likely to break down because there is no transfer from the practice to the setting in which they are used.

A typical example of the lack of transfer is the volleyball forearm pass that is practiced from partner tosses and then must be used in a game. In a game, the forearm pass is executed from a serve, usually coming at great speed and height. Practice from a partner toss does not even begin to approach game conditions

Whole Versus Part Practice. A critical practice decision concerns whether it is better to practice a skill as a whole or to break down the skill into its component parts. Most skills should be practiced as a whole when possible. This is particularly true of skills that have a great deal of flow quality or those that are normally performed at fast speeds (e.g., back handspring). When it is important to practice a part (such as the toss for the tennis serve), the whole skill should be put together as soon as possible. Very complex skills (e.g., tennis serve), and dangerous skills (e.g., giant swing on the high bar) may benefit from practice of parts in initial stages, but also should be practiced as a whole as soon as possible.

Amount of Practice. Generally speaking, the more a person practices the better they will become at a motor skill. This is particularly true if the practice is good. Good practice encourages students to process what they are doing and to have an accurate plan for how to execute the skill. However, learning can occur in practice even though performance has decreased. This means that learning can occur even though the performer may be tired. Open skills take longer to develop than closed skills, and therefore require more practice as well as practice under varied conditions.

Speed-Accuracy Trade Off. There are many skills that require both speed and accuracy to be performed effectively. The tennis serve, for example, must be placed in the opponent's court accurately. It also is more effective if it is done at a high speed. For most skills, however, accuracy decreases as speed increases. If good performance requires both speed and accuracy, there may be merit in slowing the skill initially. However, it is important that opportunities for practicing skills at high levels of force also be provided. The demand for accuracy can then be increased gradually. If too much pressure for high levels of accuracy is put on beginning players they will not develop the skills necessary to produce high levels of speed.

Kinesthetic Awareness. Internal feedback for a movement can be developed by calling attention to the feeling of a movement and learning to attend to its different stimuli. Kinesthetic awareness plays a significant role in closed skills (e.g., gymnastics, swimming, ballet, diving, golf), and can be major contributor to consistent levels of performance. The performer who has developed a high level of kinesthetic awareness of a skill can learn to detect errors and will have immediate access to internal feedback.

Skills Requiring Balance. Establishing a visual focal point during a skill requiring balance can improve the skill. This is most evident in balance beam events in gymnastics, where the end of the beam serves as a visual focus. Establishing a visual focus point also is useful in skills such as spins and turns in dance or skating.

Attention Issues. Readiness to perform, alertness, and the arousal level of the performer relate to the attention a performer is paying to a motor response. Alert performers can respond more quickly, and the level of excitement produced during performance of a motor skill can have a direct effect on that performance. The degree of arousal is affected by a performer's cognitive, emotional, and physiological involvement in a motor response.

Most motor learning theorists acknowledge that performance will be affected if a performer does not have a high enough level of arousal. It also is true that a performance can be negatively affected by too high a level of arousal. When the psychological arousal level for a performer produces both psychological and physical discomfort, the performer is said to be experiencing anxiety. Finding the optimum level of arousal for a particular individual and helping that performer to exert some control over his or her own state of arousal is an important function of teaching and coaching. In addition, different activities require different arousal levels. For example a complex eye-hand coordination task (e.g., shooting a basket, walking on the high rope of a ropes course) may require more attention than a gross motor skill (e.g., jumping).

The kind of motor skill that is being performed and the ability level of the performer also can affect the level of arousal. To a point, an increased arousal level can improve the performance of gross motor skills that are executed quickly. Skills that require finer motor control or a high degree of decision making are adversely affected by high arousal. Beginners are adversely affected by anxiety in most motor performance situations. Sport psychologists have spent a great deal of time working with the idea of arousal, particularly as it relates to the elite performer.

Feedback. Information on feedback comes from both the motor learning literature and the literature on working with more applied settings. Most of the time, feedback is reinforcing. Prescriptive feedback, which informs the learner about how to change in order to improve performance, is generally preferable to negative feedback, which gives information on what not to do. Feedback is usually divided into knowledge of results (KR—what happened to the object/how far he or she jumped) and knowledge of performance (KP—the process characteristics of the movement). Learners who are denied access to knowledge of results are more apt to focus on knowledge of performance. In some cases, teachers and coaches have prevented knowledge of results (hitting into a net in golf, bowling without pins) to help students focus on knowledge of performance.

Beginning learners who have not established consistent motor skills probably cannot use feedback to improve performance. When feedback can be used, it is best to keep it specific. For example, if a learner is asked to focus on the step into a throw, the initial feedback should focus on the step into the throw.

How Do Individuals Differ in Learning a Motor Skill?

Different people have different qualities that make them more suited to one activity than another (e.g., gymnasts are small, basketball players are tall, football players are big). Unlike body type, some characteristics—such as interest and motivation to perform a particular activity—can be changed or improved. There is no such thing as "general motor ability." What we normally refer to as "athletic ability" is in actuality many different abilities—reaction time, multi-limb coordination, dynamic balance, visual acuity etc.—that are necessary for good performance. While potential in motor ability may be genetically based, experience and practice also play a role.

Different characteristics may be required to learn a skill and to perform it at a high level. Students who move quickly through the initial stages of learning a motor skill may not necessarily be the ones who will become more skilled over time—they may just be faster learners.

Will Learning One Motor Skill Help a Person Learn Another Motor Skill?

Motor learning theorists refer to the transfer of learning from one skill to another as skill to skill transfer. And, such transfers can be either positive or negative. The closer one skill is to another, the more likelihood of transfer. For example, there are some aspects of tennis that transfer positively to racquetball (ball tracking, anticipating the rebound of the ball, etc.), and some aspects that do not transfer positively (e.g., wrist action). Transfer can be facilitated by directing attention to similar skills and to what you want to transfer (e.g., ready position, force production). At high levels of performance, however, all skills become sport specific.

Placing Motor Learning Concepts in the Curriculum

If motor learning concepts are to be integrated into the physical education program, decisions must be made about where those concepts should be placed. Table 1, which begins on page 28, shows a placement at different grade levels. The grade levels were chosen to be consistent with the grade levels used in the National Standards. The concepts were designed to be consistent with National Standard 2 (applies movement concepts and principles to the learning and development of motor skills), as this standard relates to concepts of motor learning. The motor learning concepts were placed by grade level to correspond with the benchmarks and emphases described in National Standard 1 (demonstrates competency in many movement forms and proficiency in a few movement forms).

The twelfth grade exit goal is for students to be able to apply these concepts independently to the learning of motor skills. Students must have many examples of a concept in order to develop it to this level. If concepts are developed experientially throughout the entire program, students are more likely to use them independently.

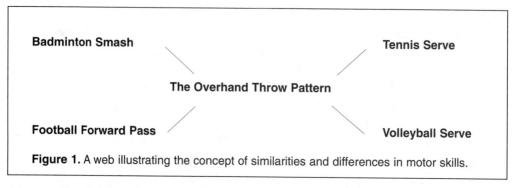

Figure 1. A web illustrating the concept of similarities and differences in motor skills.

Integrating Motor Learning Concepts into Instruction

The first responsibility a teacher has is to determine what concepts will be included in the curriculum and at what grade levels each will be taught. The second responsibility of the teacher is to determine how the concepts will be included in the program. It also is important that the teacher model good practice as well as provide specific learning experiences.

The last chapter of this text looks at ideas related to integrating physical education content with other academic areas. This discussion draws heavily on the types of integration described by Fogarty (1991). Fogarty's work also is useful for conceptualizing ways in which teachers can integrate motor learning concepts into their physical education instruction. Threading, webbing, sequencing, and immersion all are integration methods.

Threading the Concepts into Your Existing Framework

Using a threaded method of integration, the teacher determines which concept(s) should be integrated into the existing curriculum. (See Example 1.) Threading does not require the teacher to add more units and it does not require a great deal of program time. It requires a long-term perspective and careful integration of content. The more similar concepts are reinforced by threading them throughout the curriculum, the more likely they will be used. Most of the concepts identified in this chapter can benefit from being threaded into a succession of units.

Teachers determine when students have learned a concept by assessing the degree to which they use it in their independent work. This means that if students are free to design their own practice, and the practice does not use the concepts identified, they have not yet learned them to the necessary level.

Webbing Content Around a Concept

Another useful way to integrate motor learning concepts into the curriculum is to use a variety of activities to teach them, or to web content around a concept like a spider web. Figure 1 illustrates a potential web for the concept that there are similarities and differences in motor skills. Knowing the similarities will help students learn new skills that have similar fundamentals.

Example 2 provides an elementary and a secondary example of webbing. In each of these examples, the teacher has identified a concept he or she believes is critical to learning how to learn motor skills, and has developed opportunities to use and practice that concept across the physical education curriculum. Experiencing the concept across different skills and activities (in these cases many sports) serves to reinforce the idea that the concept can be generalized and increases the possibility that it will be used in new experiences.

Sequencing Content To Teach a Concept

Sequencing content to teach a concept involves identifying those content areas that can best be taught in close proximity to each other to ensure transfer of the concept from one content area to another (e.g., teaching racket sports as a unit or sequence of units). Another example would be teaching several invasion games in sequential units (e.g., soccer, basketball, lacrosse) and emphasizing the related concepts. Elementary teachers who discuss the principle of "giving" to receive an object and then teach catching, landing from heights, trapping, and collecting skills with objects are using sequencing. If they also draw their students' attention to how information about one skill can be used to learn another they are teaching the concept of transfer as well.

The Immersion (Project) Approach to Concept Development

The immersion approach (Fogarty 1991) is more commonly known as the project approach. Teachers design a project that requires students to explore a given concept over an extended period of time. Example 3 illustrates how the immersion approach can be used at both the elementary and the secondary levels. The technique capitalizes on student interests and incorporates other skills in developing a project. The drawback of this approach is that it is quite time consuming. And, because projects are individualized, they are more difficult to assess.

Assessing Student Learning

Students should be able to use motor learning concepts in class to improve their own performance and out of class to learn new skills. If they can answer the following questions when they leave high school, they can be considered physically educated:

> You want to learn how to play a new sport or activity, and have obtained a book on how to play the sport. For the sport or activity of your choice identify:
> A. What constitutes good performance.
> B. What stages are you likely to go through as you learn this sport.
> C. What kind of practice for this sport will help you improve.
> D. What kind of potential you have for good performance in this sport.
> E. What other sports or activities are likely to require the same kinds of skills as this activity and therefore be positively influenced by your learning this sport.

It is important for teachers to use assessment techniques that can assess what students have learned. Many of these techniques are described in detail in *Moving into the Future: National Standards for Physical Education* (NASPE 1995).

Checking for Understanding. One of the most useful methods for determining whether students understand a concept is to ask the group and check the responses of several students. Example: What kind of skill is this? What does that mean for the kind of practice that we should be doing?

Thirty-Second Wonders. Have each student write the answer to a quick question on a piece of paper. Example: This is the first time you have practiced this skill. What should you be trying to do?

Notebook Assessment. Many teachers have students record information in a notebook at the end of each lesson. Teachers can use these notebooks to determine student understanding of concepts or to help students reflect on their personal experience in leaning a skill. Example: What other sport activities that you enjoy are likely to be affected positively by what we learned today?

Peer Observation. Peer observation requires one student to make a judgment about the performance of another. It is particularly useful for assessing the degree to which students use cues and concepts of practice to improve their performance. Example: As your partner is playing, assess the degree to which he or she makes good choices about what to do. For now do not worry about whether or not your partner is able to execute those choices effectively.

Student Logs and Journals. Student logs and journals are useful ways to individualize instruction and involve students in their own learning processes. Logs and journals are usually kept over a long period of time. Logs generally focus on recording performance. Example: Make daily entries in your log that record your performance in archery unit. Student journals are generally more reflective. Example: In your daily entries, describe your performance and how you felt about your progress.

Student Projects. Student projects provide useful learning experiences as well as good opportunities for assessment. However, they usually take more time to complete. Example: Choose a new skill and design a learning program. Include practice schedules.

Written Tests. The written test is a useful way to assess the degree of knowledge a student has about a subject. It is important that written tests be designed to assess the specific level of knowledge the student is expected to have. For example, if a test measures whether students can *identify* a concept when the teacher wants to know whether the student can *apply* the concept, it is not a useful test. Example: Identify the three stages of learning a motor skill and describe what a learner is likely to look like at each stage.

Concluding Comments

Many of the concepts discussed in this chapter may seem like common sense to physical educators, but that is not necessarily the case with students and the public. Many adults continue to believe that the ability to play sports is a talent you are born with, and that they are not capable of participating in sports at a level that would be enjoyable. Many adults continue to use rote practice to improve open skills, and give no thought to practicing skills in combinations. In short, they do not know how to approach their own learning.

Physical educators who teach motor learning concepts are providing students with the ability to learn new activities as adults. And students who are prepared to learn have skills that can serve them for a lifetime.

Example 1. Threading Motor Learning Concepts into the Curriculum

Elementary School Example: Second Grade
Concept: Two or more skills done together are called serial skills. They are combined correctly when they flow smoothly from one to another without any breaks.
The content area the teacher is working with is combining locomotor actions. As part of the planned experiences for this part of the curriculum, students will combine locomotor movements on small equipment (hurdles, low boxes, and hoops) into a sequence. The teacher has decided to thread the concept that combined skills are called serial skills and are performed well when the transitions between the movements are smooth. The teacher focuses instruction on how to make the transitions smooth and assess the degree to which students have knowledge of good transitions and can execute good transitions.

The teacher has decided to thread the concept of serial skills and smooth transitions into work with fielding and throwing a ball. Students are reminded that fielding and throwing are serial skills, and that it is important to make the transitions between these movements smooth. Students explore how they can make the transitions smooth.

Each time the teacher teaches serial skills, he or she reintroduces the idea of what a serial skill is and what constitutes good performance. The potential for students to transfer the concept of serial skills into new experiences increases with the amount of reinforcement threaded throughout the curriculum.

Secondary School Example

Concept: Good performance requires a performer to select a correct movement response and to execute it correctly

The activity the teacher is working with is badminton. As part of the planned experiences for this unit, the teacher will work with net game offensive and defensive strategies. The teacher has decided to thread the concept that there are two parts to performance in a strategy: the decision, and the execution of the decision.

Part way through the unit, the teacher videotapes the play of students and asks them to analyze their play. As part of this analysis, students determine whether their errors were a problem with their choice of what to do (their intent) or the manner in which they executed what they did. Students then make a list of those problems on which they need to work. They divide their list into problems with choosing a strategy and problems executing a strategy.

The teacher threads this concept through all of the sports that are included in the curriculum, increasing the potential that students will be able to use the concept to learn new sports independently.

Example 2. Webbing a Concept into the Curriculum

Elementary School Example: Fourth Grade

Concept: Feedback that informs the learner on how to improve performance is usually the best kind of feedback.

The teacher has decided to teach students how to give good feedback as an important concept. She also has decided it is important for students to experience the concept in a variety of settings. She has therefore webbed the concept of transfer to work during the next several days in ball handling skills, gymnastics, and dance. For each lesson, students will work in pairs and the focus will be on giving their partner good feedback.

The first lesson is on throwing, something the students have worked on previously. The teacher provides each student with a checklist of the cues that they have been using, and has several students demonstrate for the group while the others assesses their performance. After each student has demonstrated his or her overhand throw, the teacher asks the others to determine what the performer needs to do to improve the performance and how they would say it to this person if this person were their partner. The teacher stresses positive feedback— information on what the performer can do to improve. The teacher then sends the students off to work with their partners. At the end of the class, students discuss their feelings about the quality of the feedback they were given with their partners.

The teacher does the same thing in subsequent lessons in gymnastics and dance. She uses skills the students have been working on so they can focus on the feedback they are receiving. After the series of lessons on giving good feedback, the teacher turns to other parts of the curriculum. The teacher uses peers to give feedback to students on a regular basis, and continuously reinforces this work.

Secondary School Example

Concept: Good performance of closed skills should result in practice and performance that is done the same way each time.

The teacher has chosen to assign a few days at the end of the school year to the development of this concept. He or she has identified all of the closed skills that students have learned during their basketball, volleyball, badminton, archery, and bowling units, and has set up stations around the gym where each of these skills can be practiced.

After identifying and developing the concept with several examples, the teacher asks each student to rotate through each of the stations. At each station, students must identify the important cues for the skill. Each student then has the opportunity to practice the skill 10 times with a peer observer. The peer observer identifies aspects of performance from trial to trial that are not consistent—including preparation and what the student does following performance—and gives feedback. After students have had an opportunity both to perform and to be an observer, they may move on to the next station.

Example 3. The Immersion (Project) Approach to Teaching Motor Learning Concepts

Elementary School Example: Fifth Grade

Concept: Fundamental skills change according to how they are used

The teacher has decided that this concept is important for students in the middle elementary grades to learn before they deal with the important discriminations involved in open and closed skills. He or she has chosen a project approach. Students are to take a fundamental locomotor or manipulative skill and demonstrate how that skill changes in different environments. Students may choose from several options:

1. Cut out pictures of people using the skill and describe what characteristics the skill would have in this environment (walking with another person, walking on the beach, and walking in a crowd; or, throwing a ball to a person who is close and throwing a ball to a person who is far away).

2. Videotape themselves or another person using the skill in different environments and describe how the skill changes in those environments.

3. Describe different environments in which they think the skill is used and what is important in that environment.

Secondary School Example

Concept: Individuals pass through different stages of learning to become proficient at motor skills.
The teacher wants students to be able to identify the stages through which they pass as they become proficient in a motor skill. Students may do this by teaching a skill to a peer, younger sibling, or younger friend. They also may do this project with themselves as the learner. Students are encouraged to choose a skill that does not require a great deal of time in which to develop proficiency.

Students must identify the stages of learning and provide a videotape and descriptions of the learner at the different stages. The final project report should include:

1. An introduction describing the stages of learning through which individuals pass as they are learning a motor skill.

2. Videotape of the learner at the stages of learning described in the first part of the report.

3. Descriptions of the learner at different stages of learning.

The project should result in at least a three-page report describing the conditioning for the activity. The teacher should collect the reports, share the best ones with the class, and spend a class session comparing and contrasting the conditioning for different activities and sports. Students who are interested in a particular sport or activity should be provided with access to the reports for those activities or sports.

Secondary School Example

Concept: Different skills require different kinds of practice, and different stages of learning require different kinds of practice.
The teacher wants students to be able to set up their own practice schedule for a skill of their choice. The student must:

1. Identify the skill and the type of skill for which they will develop a practice schedule, and list the implications for practice.

2. Identify the stage of development that they are in with the skill they have chosen, describe how they have determined their stage of development, and list the implications for practice.

3. Develop a six-week practice schedule for the skill they have chosen that is consistent with the above ideas.

4. Implement the practice schedule.

5. Assess performance at the beginning, and after several days without practice at the end of the project, to determine the degree of improvement that has taken place.

The teacher should assess and approve the first three steps before students begin practice. At the end of the six-week period, students should share with each other the procedures they used and the results they achieved.

Table 1. Critical Student Concepts, K–6

Kindergarten	Second Grade	Fourth Grade	Sixth Grade
Motor Learning Concept I: How do people get better at motor skills?	*Motor Learning Concept I: How do people get better at motor skills?*	*Motor Learning Concept I: How do people get better at motor skills?*	*Motor Learning Concept I: How do people get better at motor skills?*
Practice makes you better at motor skills.	Practice makes you better at motor skills.	Practice makes you better at motor skills.	People who have more experience and practice at motor skills perform better.
	Some people are better at motor skills because they have had more experience.	Some people are better at motor skills because they have had more experience.	You will get better at some skills when you grow and are stronger.
		You will get better at some motor skills as you get bigger and stronger.	
Motor Learning Concept II: What is good performance?	*Motor Learning Concept II: What is good performance?*	*Motor Learning Concept II: What is good performance?*	*Motor Learning Concept II: What is good performance?*
You are good at a motor skill when you perform the skills with the correct cues (form), e.g., hopping.	Your are good at a motor skill when you perform the skills with the correct cues (form), e.g., steps into a jump.	You are good at a motor skill when you perform the skills with the correct cues (e.g., throwing, basketball chest pass).	Game strategy is a decision of what to do in a competitive situation. Some strategies are correct but executed poorly.
	Knowing how to perform a skill will help you learn that skill.	Knowing how to perform a skill will help you learn that skill.	The game strategy you select is related to what your teammates do and what your opponents do.
	Two or more skills (serial) are combined correctly when they flow smoothly from one skill to another without any breaks (e.g., running into a jump).	Two or more skills (serial) are combined correctly when they flow smoothly from one skill to another without any breaks (e.g., gymnastics sequence, dribbling	Open skills are performed in unpredictable and unstable environments and should be practiced in variable conditions.

Table 1. Critical Student Concepts, K–6

Motor Learning Concept III: What stages do individuals pass through to become proficient at motor skills?

When you first begin to learn a motor skill you will not be good at it.

Assessment should be considered in terms of improvement.

Skills need to be modified when they are performed in a continuous fashion. These are continuous skills (e.g., traveling while dribbling a basketball).

Good performance of open skills requires a performer to adapt performance to an environment (e.g., modifying a forward roll to meet the size of the mat , or performance to a partner).

Motor Learning Concept III: What stages do individuals pass through to become proficient at motor skills?

When you first begin to learn a motor skill you will not be good at it.

Assessment should be considered in terms of improvement.

You can do a motor skill more consistently when you become better at it.

and passing a basketball).

Skills need to be modified when they are performed in a continuous fashion. These are continuous skills (e.g., two forward rolls in a row).

Good performance of open skills requires a performer to adapt performance to an environment (e.g., dribbling a soccer ball at slow and fast speeds while dodging other people).

Motor Learning Concept III: What stages do individuals pass through to become proficient at motor skills?

When you first begin to learn a motor skill you will not be good at it.

Assessment should be considered in terms of improvement in process and/or product.

You can do a motor skill more consistently when you become better at it.

You can begin to concentrate on other parts of performance after

Motor Learning Concept III: What stages do individuals pass through to become proficient at motor skills?

You can begin to concentrate on other aspects of performance after you gain some consistency in the skill itself.

In the last stage of learning a motor skill the skill becomes automatic.

Good practice improves learning.

Table 1. Critical Student Concepts, K–6

Motor Learning Concept IV: What kind of practice facilitates learning?	Motor Learning Concept IV: What kind of practice facilitates learning?	Motor Learning Concept IV: What kind of practice facilitates learning?	Motor Learning Concept IV: What kind of practice facilitates learning?
The more practice, the more learning.	The more practice, the more learning.	The more practice, the more learning. ...you gain some consistency in the skill itself (e.g., having a defender in the basketball dribble).	Practice that promotes processing of how to do the skill is better practice.
	Skills requiring balance can be improved with a visual focal point (e.g., any inverted balance).	Skills requiring balance can be improved with a visual focal point (e.g., inverted balance, walking on a balance beam).	Knowledge of accurate cues can increase performance.
	Feedback that informs the learner on how to improve performance is usually the best kind of feedback (e.g., partner feedback on the overhand throw).	Feedback that informs the learner on how to improve performance is usually the best kind of feedback (e.g., partner feedback on a dance routine).	Skills should be practiced in conditions that are game like and performance like as much as possible.
		Good practice improves learning.	Do not practice "parts" of skills or sequences of movement for too long without putting them in the "whole."
			Practice skills at the correct speed as much as possible.

Table 1. Critical Student Concepts, K–6

Motor Learning Concept V: How do individuals differ in learning a motor skill?	*Motor Learning Concept V: How do individuals differ in learning a motor skill?*	*Motor Learning Concept V: How do individuals differ in learning a motor skill?*	*Motor Learning Concept V: How do individuals differ in learning a motor skill?*
Everyone is at a different level in learning a motor skill and can learn to perform at a level that is personally satisfying.	Everyone is at a different level in learning a motor skill and can learn to perform at a level that is personally satisfying.	Everyone is at a different level in learning a motor skill and can learn to perform at a level that is personally satisfying.	Motor performance can be increased by improving physical abilities (health related, motor, and fitness) and motivation to learn.
	It is okay to be a beginner.	It is okay to be a beginner.	
Motor Learning Concept VI: Will learning one motor skill help a person learn another?	*Motor Learning Concept VI: Will learning one motor skill help a person learn another?*	*Motor Learning Concept VI: Will learning one motor skill help a person learn another?*	*Motor Learning Concept VI: Will learning one motor skill help a person learn another?*
Some skills are used in many different activities (e.g., throwing).	Some skills are used in many different activities (e.g., throwing, jumping).	Some skills are used in many different activities (e.g., throwing, jumping).	The more closely related one skill is to another the more likely the transfer of learning (e.g., throwing a variety of objects)
	Striking with implements has many similarities to striking with your hand.	Throwing a large ball has some characteristics that are similar to throwing a small ball and some characteristics that are different than throwing a smaller ball.	

Table 1. Critical Student Concepts, 8–12

Eighth Grade	Tenth Grade	Twelfth Grade
Motor Learning Concept I: How do people get better at motor skills?	*Motor Learning Concept I: How do people get better at motor skills?*	*Motor Learning Concept I: How do people get better at motor skills?*
You will get better at some skills when you grow and are stronger.	Different skills require different physical abilities that can be developed through training programs (e.g., flexibility in gymnastics, strength for skills requiring force production abilities, cardiorespiratory ability in basketball agility and reaction time).	Short-term improvement in motor performance can be achieved without learning if the practice is not long enough for learning to be stored in long-term memory.
Different skills require different physical abilities that can be developed through training programs (e.g., flexibility in gymnastics, strength for skills requiring force production abilities, cardiorespiratory ability in basketball agility and reaction time).	Motor skills that are learned well enough to be stored in long-term memory are kept for a long time.	
Motor skills that are learned well enough to be stored in long-term memory are kept for a long time.	Short-term improvement in motor performance can be achieved without learning if the practice is not long enough for learning to be stored in long-term memory.	
Motor Learning Concept II: What is good performance?	*Motor Learning Concept II: What is good performance?*	*Motor Learning Concept II: What is good performance?*
Game strategy is a decision of what to do in a competitive situation. Some strategies are correct but executed poorly.	When performance is not effective the problem may be the choice of the response or the execution of the response.	Open skills look different when performed in different environments.

Table 1. Critical Student Concepts, 8–12

The game strategy you select is related to what your teammates do and what your opponents do.	Good performance of closed skills should result in practice and performance that is done the same way each time.	Learning is assessed after a break between practice and testing.
When performance is not effective the problem may be the choice of the response or the execution of the response.	Some closed skills are performed in different environments.	
Good performance of closed skills should result in practice and performance that is done the same way each time.	Open skills are performed in unpredictable and unstable environments and should be practiced in variable conditions.	
Some closed skills are performed in different environments.	Different skills require different physical abilities that can be developed through training programs (e.g., flexibility in gymnastics, strength for skills requiring force production abilities, cardiorespiratory ability in basketball agility and reaction time).	
Open skills are performed in unpredictable and unstable environments and should be practiced in variable conditions.	Motor skills that are learned well enough to be stored in long-term memory are kept for a long time.	
Movement sequences, routines, and combinations of skills should have as their goal smooth flow from one movement to the other.	Learning is assessed after a break between practice and testing (retention).	
Preparation for a subsequent movement occurs in the previous movement.	Movement sequences, routines,	

Table 1. Critical Student Concepts, 8–12

Motor Learning Concept III: What stages do individuals pass through to become proficient at motor skills? In the first stage of learning a motor skill you should seek to get a clear idea of how to do the skill and should be able to describe what you should be doing. In the second stage of learning a motor skill you should work toward consistent performance. In the third stage of learning a motor skill your responses should be automatic. Difficult motor skills never reach 100 percent reliability.	and combinations of skills should have as their goal smooth flow from one movement to the other. Preparation for a subsequent movement occurs in the previous movement. *Motor Learning Concept III: What stages do individuals pass through to become proficient at motor skills?* In the first stage of learning a motor skill you should seek to get a clear idea of how to do the skill and should be able to describe what you should be doing. In the second stage of learning a motor skill you should work toward consistent performance. Complexity can be added gradually to stage two learning. In the third stage of learning a motor skill your responses should be automatic. Difficult motor skills never reach 100 percent reliability.	*Motor Learning Concept III: What stages do individuals pass through to become proficient at motor skills?* Complexity can be added gradually to stage two learning.

Table 1. Critical Student Concepts, 8–12

Motor Learning Concept IV: What kind of practice facilitates learning?	*Motor Learning Concept IV: What kind of practice facilitates learning?*	*Motor Learning Concept IV: What kind of practice facilitates learning?*
Practice that promotes processing of how to do the skill is better practice.	Practice that promotes processing of how to do the skill is better practice.	Deliberate practice is good practice.
Knowledge of accurate cues can increase performance.	Knowledge of accurate cues can increase performance.	Kinesthetic awareness of the body plays a major role in the development of some closed skills, and it can be developed.
Skills should be practiced in conditions that are game like and performance like as much as possible.	Skills should be practiced in conditions that are game like and performance like as much as possible.	
Do not practice "parts" of skills or sequences of movement for too long without putting them in the "whole."	Do not practice "parts" of skills or sequences of movement for too long without putting them in the "whole."	
Practice skills at the correct speed as much as possible.	Practice skills at the correct speed as much as possible.	
High arousal level may increase performance of gross motor skills and decrease performance of fine motor activities.	Mental practice can increase performance at higher skill levels.	
	Kinesthetic awareness of the body plays a major role in the development of some closed skills, and it can be developed	

Table 1. Critical Student Concepts, 8–12

Motor Learning Concept V: How do individuals differ in learning a motor skill?

Motor performance can be increased by improving physical abilities (health related, motor, and fitness) and motivation to learn.

Motor Learning Concept VI: Will learning one motor skill help a person learn another?

The more closely related one skill is to another the more likely the transfer of learning (e.g., tennis serve and overhand throw).

Motor Learning Concept V: How do individuals differ in learning a motor skill?

Motor performance can be increased by improving physical abilities (health related, motor, and fitness) and motivation to learn.

Individuals can improve performance by increasing their ability in prerequisite skills.

Motor Learning Concept VI: Will learning one motor skill help a person learn another?

The more closely related one skill is to another the more likely the transfer of learning (e.g., ready position in badminton and tennis).

Some aspects of one sport will negatively transfer to another (e.g., wrist action in tennis and badminton), while some aspects will transfer positively.

Motor Learning Concept V: How do individuals differ in learning a motor skill?

Individuals can improve performance by increasing their ability in prerequisite skills.

Motor Learning Concept VI: Will learning one motor skill help a person learn another?

Some aspects of one sport will negatively transfer to another (e.g., wrist action in tennis and badminton), while some aspects will transfer positively.

How Can I Learn More?

Carr, N. (Ed.). (1987). *Basic stuff series II.* Reston, VA: AAHPERD.

Christina, R. N., & Corcus, P. M. (1988). *Coaches guide to teaching sport skill.* Champaign, IL: Human Kinetics Publishers.

Gould, D. (1992). The arousal athletic performance relationship: Current status and future directions. In T. S. Horn (Ed.), *Advances in sport psychology* (pp. 119-142). Champaign, IL: Human Kinetics Publishers.

Kneer, M. (Ed.). (1981). *Basic stuff series I.* Reston, VA: AAHPERD.

Magill, R. (1993). *Motor learning concepts and applications.* Madison, WI: Brown and Benchmark.

Schmidt, R. (1991). *Motor learning and performance.* Champaign, IL: Human Kinetics Publishers.

References

Fogarty, R. (1991). *The mindful school: How to integrate curricular.* Palentine, IL: IRI/Skylight Publishing.

Fitts, P., & Posner, M. (1967). *Human performance.* Belmont, CA: Brooks-Cole.

NASPE. (1995). *Moving into the future: National content standards for physical education.* St. Louis, MO: Mosby YearBook.

Glossary

Arousal level: a state of excitability and readiness of the physical, cognitive, and emotional systems.

Blocked practice: repetitive practice of the same skill over a period of time.

Closed skills: motor skills that are performed in an environment that does not change or that changes very little (e.g., archery).

Continuous skills: skills that are repeated one after another (e.g., basketball dribble) and do not have a clearly defined beginning and end.

Discrete skills: skills that are performed unconnected to other skills (e.g., volleyball forearm pass) and have a clear beginning and end.

Feedback: information that is given to the learner about performance (internal or external); can be knowledge of performance (KP) or knowledge of results (KR).

Kinesthetic awareness: awareness of movement and the position of the body in space provided by the body's sensory perception systems.

Chapter 3
Motor Development

By Kathleen Williams and V. Gregory Payne

A class of seventh graders is working at a series of physical activity stations. Students set their own goals for the number of sit-ups and push-ups they can do; they time each other running one mile around the school track; they practice a series of stretches to improve their overall range of motion. As you observe, it is clear that some students barely finish the activities, even though they appear to be trying their hardest. They can only do a couple of sit-ups; they must stop frequently and walk on the track; even with your help and periodic reference to illustration cards, they cannot seem to remember the stretches. Most of the students appear to be motivated. So why are their abilities all so different?

Among other things, you are watching differences in *development*. Within this group of students, you see youngsters who have not yet entered puberty and others who have nearly completed their adolescent growth spurts. There are dramatic differences in strength, size, level of coordination, and cognitive development. There are differences in *motor development*.

What Is Motor Development?

Motor development is a process that includes both experience (like practice and instruction) and an individual's current physical, cognitive, emotional, and social status. The motor development process causes changes in motor behavior across the entire lifetime (Williams et al. 1994). An important misconception about development is that change occurs automatically. Viewing change in motor skills from a developmental perspective means that skills do not just appear; they do not simply "mature" at certain ages. Few people would say they think development "just happens," but many of us act as though that were the case.

Asking all third graders to perform the same skill or series of skills assumes all third graders are the same. It implies that being in the third grade equates to having certain abilities and capabilities. We need only look at a class of third graders to know this is not the case. Few, if any, of the children in a single class will look or act the same. Individuals who lag are simply behind their same-aged peers; their movements are less efficient than others. Individuals differ developmentally, and developmental change does not occur automatically during maturation. Nor does it occur as errors in the way a person performs a movement are corrected. Performance dif-

Kathleen Williams is associate professor, Department of Exercise and Sport Science, University of North Carolina at Greensboro. V. Gregory Payne is professor, Department of Human Performance, San Jose State University, San Jose, California.

ferences are not performance errors. Change occurs as a result of the interplay between inherited potential, current status, and experiences that occur during our lives. Skill level is judged on a continuum, from least to most efficient. Where we fall on that continuum is a result of the interactive process called development.

Why Is Motor Development Important?

Understanding and accepting that change is developmental results in a different perspective than that often assumed by teachers. First and foremost, it assumes students (whatever their age) will not be able to learn the same things at the same time, or at the same rate. Teaching and learning from a developmental perspective assumes that learners are at different places in their motor, cognitive, emotional, and social development. Where they are in each domain will affect their ability to change at any point in time. Some students will be stronger, others will be more flexible; others might have more knowledge about a skill or have a longer attention span.

There are other important differences, too. When you have a developmental perspective, you understand that motor skills change in qualitative and sequential ways. For example, two students at the same age may be able to kick a ball an equal distance, but their movement form may differ dramatically. One may use a very inefficient movement pattern, but be very strong. The other may use a more efficient pattern, but have less muscular strength. This means that a teacher must look at how and why a skill is performed a certain way. He or she must help each learner to progress from where they are. The stronger student needs help to use a more efficient pattern, resulting in an even longer kick. The other student needs help in becoming stronger or in using his or her strength more efficiently.

The seventh graders described in the beginning of this section struggle with the activity stations. A prepubertal boy may have insufficient arm strength to complete a series of push-ups. An inactive, postpubertal girl with poor eating habits may have gained excessive body fat, making it difficult to raise her trunk off the floor during sit-ups. Other youngsters may lack the motivation or cognitive sophistication to translate illustrations of stretches to their own performance. Each student demonstrates a different level of development, and teachers must address these differences. More important, teachers need to know when someone is not ready to change, and whether that lack of readiness is due to a lack of strength that may simply take more time (growing bigger), a lack of cognitive understanding of the teacher's instructions, or from some other factor that inhibits change.

Waiting can be a very difficult thing for teachers or students to do. Sometimes, however, it is important to simply back off or try something different. Maybe more practice on the fundamentals might help. Maybe more individual or small group practice is key, or maybe it is time to do something entirely different for a while. It is important for teachers and their students to understand that each person will change at his or her own rate. That rate is determined in part by level of maturity, but experience in a positive learning environment also is important.

Linking Motor Development to the National Standards

Standard 2 of the National Standards relates directly to developmental perspective:
* Applies movement concepts and principles to the learning and development of motor skills.
    Two other standards relate to accepting that individuals are different:
* Demonstrates understanding and respect for differences among people.
* Demonstrates competency in many movement forms and proficiency in a few movement forms.
Examples of these standards are illustrated in the major motor development concepts that follow.

Selected Motor Development Concepts

Change Is Sequential and Takes Time

One of the characteristics of motor development is its sequential nature. The way most five-year-olds throw or kick is very different from the effective patterns we often observe in high school students or adults who play recreationally. The change from the five-year-old effort to that of the adult occurs in many small, sequential steps over the years. Even the way we rise from a chair is marked by gradual, sequential changes from our first attempts at sitting independently through the adaptations observed in the elderly. Developmental sequences describe the course of that change.

What Is a Developmental Sequence?

For motor skills, developmental sequences are the series of changes that occur from when a skill first emerges to when it reaches its most mechanically efficient state. That may mean it is first observed in a very young child (e.g., walking or running), or not until much later, as in a sport–specific skill like catching a ball in lacrosse. Regardless of when the action first emerges, however, a series of specific and sequential changes will then occur until the skill reaches its most advanced, or mechanically efficient, form.

Several developmental sequences may be needed to describe a single motor skill, because changes in each part of the body may occur at different rates. Roberton and Halverson (1984) describe movement components that divide the body into separate joint actions. Together, they make up its total action. Table 1 shows two developmental sequences for the hop, for example.

Movement components in hopping are the actions of the arms and the legs, which together comprise the integrated action of hopping on one foot. For the arm action, five developmental levels are described; there also are four levels of leg action. The earliest arm actions involve responses to a loss of balance, first in a flailing action, and somewhat later as a more orderly pattern where the arms almost seem to act like wings (Level 2). The wing–like action of the arms appears to be a way of controlling balance and the speed of movement. By the time a young hopper reaches intermediate levels of development, there is little concern about balance. Now, the arm action

---

Table 1. Developmental Levels Within Movement Components for Hopping

Leg Action
Step 1. Momentary flight.
Step 2. Fall and catch; swing leg inactive.
Step 3. Projected takeoff; swing leg assists.
Step 4. Projection delay; swing leg leads.

Arm Action
Step 1. Bilateral inactive.
Step 2. Bilateral reactive.
Step 3. Bilateral assist.
Step 4. Semi-opposition.
Step 5. Opposing assist.

Note. For a description of the actions within each developmental level, see Halverson & Williams, 1985.

serves to propel the hopper forward with increasingly efficient effort (Levels 3 through 5).

Four changes are detailed for the legs. At the most primitive level (Level 1), the hopper barely gets off the ground, and is able to complete only one or two hops. With time and practice, strength and balance improve and the second developmental level emerges. Here, fatigue or boredom may be the primary determinants of the number of hops completed. At this level, the swing leg is stationary; it is not used to project the hopper forward. At the most advanced levels (Levels 3 and 4), the swing leg is moved forward and back through an increasing range of motion, again demonstrating increased efficiency.

Developmental sequences within movement components have been devised for many fundamental motor skills. Fundamental skills are the building blocks of more complex actions such as sport–specific skills (Wickstrom 1983). Throwing is a fundamental skill that is incorporated into the sport-specific field and throw used in softball or baseball. Fundamental skills include throwing, catching, running, and jumping. They are of primary interest to physical education teachers, and they also are used by physical therapists or physicians in rehabilitation settings (VanSant 1990).

But, fundamental skills comprise only a small part of teaching physical education or of rehabilitating a patient. In fact, in traditional physical education settings, most teachers expect their students will be fairly proficient at these skills by the end of elementary school. At that point, it becomes important to help children begin to learn the more complex skills that relate to specific games and sports. These are called sport-specific skills (Wickstrom 1983). They require adaptation and modification of fundamental skills to a specific game.

For example, serving a tennis ball uses the general overarm pattern used in throwing, but it differs in several ways: The ball is struck rather than thrown, and a relatively long implement (a racket) is used. To be considered a "good" serve, the ball must land within the legal boundaries of the appropriate service court. Therefore, many adaptations must be made to the fundamental pattern of overarm throwing to meet the requirements of a tennis serve. As with fundamental skills, a novice tennis player's performance will differ dramatically from that of a professional or even proficient player's performance.

Are there developmental sequences for sport-specific skills, too? Only in the last several years have researchers begun to examine this question. And, the answer appears to be "yes." Six components and developmental sequences are associated with the tennis serve. Seven movement components have been identified for the vertical cradle in lacrosse. This means that learning to play sports requires attention to the principles of development, just as building fundamental skills does. Sports players pass through developmental levels as they become increasingly proficient.

What Is More Important—Form or Result?

There are other reasons to describe developmental sequences for fundamental and sport-specific skills. First, as sequences of change have been identified we have learned that many motor skills take longer to reach their most advanced levels than we previously thought (Halverson, Roberton & Langendorfer 1982). Early texts that described changes in motor behavior suggested that many fundamental skills were "established" (Sinclair 1973) or that children were "skillful" (Zaichkowsky, Zaichkowsky, & Martinek 1980) by age five or six. Much of this research was based on quantitative aspects of the skill, like how far a ball was thrown, or how fast a certain distance was covered. Little attention was paid to what the movement looked like.

Recall the sequences for hopping. A teacher could ask a five-year-old child to hop continuously for as long as possible (a typical test). Using both arms to pump forward and back simultaneously (an intermediate developmental level), and a swing leg that moved through a limited range of motion (Level 3), the child might make 15 hops before losing balance. Based only on the outcome of the test, that child would be judged a proficient hopper (McCaskill & Wellman 1938). Based on movement form, however, the child would be judged to have intermediate skill. The two types of information tell a slightly different story, and should be considered together to see the full movement picture.

Another reason to describe developmental sequences for motor skills is so we can assess student progress. Students could be pre-and post-tested individually to determine whether their level of skill had changed during an instructional unit. Informal assessment could be made throughout a unit to determine if a student was demonstrating any improvement.

A less obvious, but equally important use of developmental sequences is to examine how performance is influenced by a specific task: Do task requirements result in use of different movement patterns, depending on the developmental level of the performer? Different types of factors can influence performance in different ways.

Individual Qualities. There are three categories of factors that are important to remember: First are the specific qualities of an individual performer. These qualities include strength, size, or level of cognitive development. Our earlier example of two students kicking a ball demonstrates this point. One kicker was stronger than the other, and even though his form was poor, he could kick the ball as far as a more advanced, but physically weaker student. Students who are less cognitively sophisticated than others may have difficulty understanding specific offensive or defensive placements on a playing field.

Environmental Factors. The environment also affects the way a task is performed. Environmental factors include temperature and playing surface, and in many cases are difficult or impossible for teachers to control. Slam-dunking a basketball on the moon would be very different than on Earth. Basket heights could be increased dramatically in the low gravity environment found there! On Earth, teachers only have to worry about whether or not to go outside during threatening weather.

Instructional Requirements. The third category—instructional requirements, or game rules—is most important to teachers because it is related to the task itself. Instructional requirements include the teacher's directions to students and the equipment that is provided. For example, playing a game of hopscotch would require a very different hop pattern than hopping as fast as possible across the gym. The equipment provided to students also is of critical importance. Rackets or bats that are too long or heavy are not only difficult to swing, but they also can result in developmental regression. That is, students might demonstrate developmentally less advanced patterns than they could if the equipment was suited to their size or strength.

The rules of games also dictate how skills are performed. In volleyball, for example, there are specific rules governing how contact can be made with the ball. In college and professional football, tackling methods are modified regularly to help protect players from injury.

Consider the interface between what the teacher asks of the student and the student's current developmental level. The game of hopscotch does not require the performer to use developmentally advanced actions, while hopping as fast as possible does. What if the performer's only option is to hop using relatively primitive actions? Attempting to hop fast may result in frustration and embarrassment when one student consistently finishes last. A fifth grader who cannot perform a legal volleyball set also may be ridiculed if the team loses too many points due to illegal contact with the ball. It is the teacher's responsibility to understand what a task requires and what the students are capable of doing (e.g., when is a relatively primitive action the only one a child can perform, and when is that all the task requires).

How Does Cognitive Development Help Some People Perform Better Than Others at Certain Skills?

Years ago, Benjamin Bloom (1956) categorized objectives in education. In his educational taxonomy, Bloom established three major domains—cognitive, affective, and psychomotor— beneath which all educational objectives would be clustered. Bloom's domains also are useful for categorizing various elements involved in the study of human development.

The cognitive domain focuses on the intellectual aspects of human development. The affective domain emphasizes the social-emotional aspects of development. Rather than focusing on young students' changing ability to ponder math problems or spelling words (cognitive skills) we attend to their self-esteem, what they think about themselves, and how they interrelate with other students in class. The psychomotor domain pertains more specifically to motor development. The fundamental and sport-specific skills described in the previous section are part of the psychomotor domain. All voluntary movements—like walking, writing, or playing a musical instrument—are included here.

Most motor development experts would agree that Bloom omitted one important area of human development—the physical domain. Often clumped into the psychomotor domain, physical changes clearly constitute a separate development category. This addition to Bloom's domains enables us to discuss bodily changes—including increases or decreases in percent of body fat or muscle mass, changes in flexibility, or cardiovascular or muscular endurance—as a separate issue.

Bloom's domains, along with the physical domain, provide an excellent means for categorizing areas of study within human development. However, while these categories can be simply and clearly defined, we must remember that they also are artificial. We can easily begin to imagine a student at her desk completing math problems. She "clicks" into the cognitive domain. When a fellow student approaches and greets her, she "clicks" into the affective domain, and then into the psychomotor domain just before running out to the playground for recess. Obviously, this is an inaccurate characterization of human behavior.

All of the domains are functioning and interacting all the time. When a permanent, or even subtle change occurs in one domain, a modification is likely to occur in the others. For example, many of us have experienced an increase or decrease in percent of body fat, which is a physical change. Remember how it changed your self-esteem (affective), or your movement (psychomotor) ability? In the following sections, we will look at the relationship between motor development and other areas of human behavior, including the cognitive, social-emotional, and physical domains.

Cognitive and Motor Development. The strong emphasis that has been placed on cognitive development over the years may be a result of work by Jean Piaget. Piaget, originally a biologist, developed his clinical method of collecting data by observing his own children. He used a question and answer system to gain insight into how children think. Gradually, he composed the most carefully detailed and most widely known explanation of any aspect of human development (Payne & Isaacs 1995).

Piaget observed four sequential stages in cognitive development:
1. Sensorimotor–Birth to 2 years.
2. Preoperational–2 to 8 years.
3. Concrete Operational–8 to 11 years.
4. Formal Operational–11 to 12 years.

The ages Piaget set for each stage are intended to be guidelines. Nevertheless, most children are thought to follow the stages in order (Piaget 1952).

1. Sensorimotor Stage. Note that the word "motor" is imbedded in the name of this stage, indicating the importance that Piaget placed on human movement in intellectual development. In this stage, Piaget proclaimed that the infant "thinks by bodily movement." For example, initial efforts to reach out, grasp, and hold a toy provide opportunities for problem solving that facilitate cognition. Of particular importance in this stage is the child's interaction with the environment: It is instrumental in shaping cognitive function. Movements such as reaching, grasping, creeping, crawling, and eventually walking play a major role in the child's ability to experience, interact with, and learn about his or her environment.

Piaget also acknowledged the importance of reflexes during the first few months of life. While these movements are involuntary, infants initially learn to stimulate their own reflexes, creating a series of gratifying, repetitive movements. For example, the sucking reflex is generally observed during the first several weeks following birth. Babies may accidentally stimulate their own reflex and enjoy the feeling. After a few accidental touches, they learn to voluntarily stimulate their own sucking reflex. While the reflex remains involuntary, a new behavior has emerged.

As they progress through infancy, more and more voluntary movement evolves. Infants gradually learn to modify their movements through experimentation. Once a new behavior is created, the infant repeats it over and over, something Piaget referred to as a circular reaction. They also "discover" their hands and arms, and experiment with eye-hand coordination and early reaching and grasping. As the first year passes, infants gradually become more aware of their own environment and expand their exploration. They also begin to combine movements to create completely new behaviors. Toward the latter part of the first year, they begin to apply past modes of behavior to new situations. This ability is enhanced by a rapidly expanding movement repertoire, including more efficient locomotion in the form of creeping, crawling, and then walking. The cognitive ability of anticipation also emerges. The infant begins to understand that when someone rolls a ball, he or she can roll it back.

During the first half of the second year, the young child actively explores and experiments. Locomotion plays an important role in helping the child explore the environment and learn from that exploration. Despite these new intellectual capabilities, the child still possesses limited ability to ponder future or upcoming events. Interacting with others becomes increasingly important as the child seeks help in problem solving. Piaget thought this indicated a child's increased understanding that people and things are separate from self. This awareness shows a clear relationship between cognitive and social development. Motor development is integral, because movement is necessary to actively seek social interactions.

At this time, children also spend more time thinking about their own movement, a climax of Piaget's first stage of development. Throughout this first stage, the child's interaction with the environment has been facilitated by improving abilities in locomotion and manipulation. Concepts like trajectory, velocity, direction, texture, and weight become increasingly clear intellectually as a result of the child's manipulation of objects. In short, this first stage is characterized by "thinking with the body," and is gradually replaced by "thinking with the mind." As a result, children can ponder the past via better recall capabilities and consider the future via better anticipation skills.

2. Preoperational Stage. Piaget's second major stage of cognitive development lasts from age two to five, and is characterized by improved use of symbols, leading to improved language skill. Language skill is the most important characteristic of this stage of development. The rapid development of language skills may be related to similarly improving movement abilities. By this time, the child has well developed locomotor skills. The increasing ability to move about results in increased opportunities to interact with the environment. Greater mobility plays a role in the emergence of many new cognitive skills.

Pretend play was another area of emphasis for Piaget. Children role play and use props as symbols for real life objects and reconstruct past events or events they would like to see happen. This form of play contributes to social as well as cognitive development, and uses movement as a medium. Thus, once again motor development is an important contributor to intellectual development.

The term "preoperations" was selected because most children are capable of limited logical thought at this time. Piaget believed the preoperational child's thinking was flawed in a number of other ways. For example, at this stage, children tend to think of inanimate objects as animate (e.g., trees may come to life or express emotions). They also tend to attribute cause and effect simply, because two events happen simultaneously.

Perhaps the most serious flaw in preoperational thinking is the child's narrow perspective. This narrow perspective and the child's inability to decenter thinking from one aspect of a problem to another hampers the ability to solve problems. These limitations also lead to an inability to conserve, a term Piaget attributed to knowing that specific properties of an object or a substance remain unchanged even when the appearance has been rearranged. A classic example of conservation is Piaget's ball of clay test. When a clay ball is rolled into a sausage shape, most preoperational children will say the clay weighs more, even though they saw that no clay was added. This is a result of the inability to focus on more than one aspect of a problem simultaneously, or to decenter attention.

The inability to decenter attention has obvious implications for motor development. Imagine the detailed problem solving or strategic abilities we expect of children around this age in youth sports. Many children have difficulty understanding that passing the ball to a teammate is a good way to score a goal. They focus primarily on how much fun it is to run and kick as they move down the field. Unfortunately, rather than understanding their intellectual limitations, we become frustrated as we expect too much too soon.

3. Concrete Operational Stage. The concrete operation stage lasts from about 7 to 11 years of age. Piaget thought this stage emerged with the improved ability to conserve and decenter attention. While the declining degree of egocentrism is important, there are still cognitive limitations. Children are unable to consider events that are unreal, unimaginable, or hypothetical.

Nevertheless, intellectual ability improves as children begin to demonstrate concepts like reversibility or seriation. Reversibility is the ability to reverse a thought process. This is demonstrated by another of Piaget's classic tests: If a concrete operational child rolls three balls of different colors through a tube, he or she can predict the sequence of exit at the other end. If the child is then asked to roll the balls back through the tube without changing the order, the concrete operational child also can successfully predict the outcome. Preoperational children cannot do this.

Seriation is another skill that illustrates the improving cognitive ability found at this stage. Seriation is the ability to place objects or even concepts in a series based on such characteristics as length or size. It is the ability to understand the relationships between objects in a series. If a child is shown three colored balls of increasing size, he or she can explain that the red ball is bigger than the blue, and the blue is bigger than the green. From that information, the child also would know that the red is bigger than the green. Seriation is another cognitive skill that appears to be influenced by a child's interaction with the environment, again reinforcing the importance of movement.

4. Formal Operational Stage. Piaget's final stage of cognitive development—formal operations—has its onset in early to mid-adolescence. Piaget noted that not all people achieve this level of cognitive ability, however. He believed formal operations to be domain or area specific. That is, you can exhibit formal operational qualities in one area, but concrete operational thought in others. For example, a basketball player might be able to think abstractly about offensive or defensive floor positions, but may find singles tennis strategies problematic.

For those who reach the formal operations level, hypothetical thought emerges. They can consider propositions that are not reality based. Furthermore, formal operators can understand and consider several aspects of a problem simultaneously. This ability has obvious implications for motor performance. Imagine the numerous decisions a quarterback makes when he prepares to receive a snap in football. To perform optimally, he must remember the snap count while carefully considering the defensive alignment in relationship to the play that he called. At the same time, he must check his team to assure that they are all properly aligned, while remembering his responsibility when the ball is snapped. Clearly, anything less than formal operational thought would severely hamper the quarterback's ability to function.

Formal operators also are capable of what Piaget called hypothetical-deductive reasoning. This is a process of systematically thinking about a problem and its potential solutions. It is rational, logical, and abstract thinking that enables one to ponder hypothetical ideas. As Piaget noted, this form of thinking can have a dramatic emotional effect on young adolescents. They may become more idealistic as they think about perfect energy sources or world peace. Changing ideals can affect social interrelationships, decisions about peer group involvement, and, indirectly, choices concerning participation in movement activities. At this developmental level, an adolescent can begin to think about the positive consequences of lifelong physical activity and fitness.

Information Processing. Piagetian developmental stages are only one way cognitive development can be viewed. Other researchers have looked at cognitive development from a different perspective, called information processing (Payne & Isaacs 1995). They study what and how things are remembered across the lifespan. In one system, memory is divided into short and long-term structures. Short-term memory is the ability to recall recently learned information (within the past few seconds or minutes). Long-term memory is the ability to recall information that was learned days or even years ago. Both forms of memory improve throughout childhood and adolescence, as children become more adept at employing strategies like rehearsal and grouping. They can arrange, rearrange, and tag information for easy retrieval.

As we age, short and long-term memory remain remarkably intact. This dispels the myth that general memory declines as senility develops during later adulthood (Payne & Isaacs 1995). Another form of memory—secondary memory—shows some decline with increasing age. Secondary memory is similar to short-term memory, but differs in that a form of interference or distraction exists. For example, if you are introduced to a new person, then immediately diverted into a conversation, how well can you recall the person's name after a few seconds?

A second area of concern involves information retrieval speed. Children and older adults have been found to require more time to process information. Thus, certain types of problem solving may be more difficult, or may take longer for these groups than for younger adults. The reason for this phenomenon is still unclear, and probably differs for the two age groups. Young children may become more efficient in their search for information, while older adults may experience decline due to degeneration of the central nervous system. Declines in retrieval speed also may be related to increased amounts knowledge. The more knowledge one has to sort through, the longer it takes to find the desired information (Payne & Isaacs 1995). Regardless of the cause, a slowing in mental processing can affect our ability to perform movement activities that require quick information retrieval and decision making. Thus, as intellectual ability declines, so may some forms of movement performance.

The relationship between movement and intellectual development also is illustrated in extensive research on reaction time and aging. While reaction time often is viewed as an indicator of movement ability, psychologists study it because of the role it plays as a marker for central nervous system integrity. Knowledge about reaction time and age can yield valuable information concerning our mental processing speed. Investigators have found that reaction times improve during the childhood years. We react fastest in our 20s, and then beginning around age 40, a gradual decline begins.

Responding to a situation often involves making a decision about how to respond. The greater the number of potential responses, the longer people of all ages require to decide. More interesting, perhaps, is the research that has focused on the effect of consistent involvement in physical activity on the reaction time decline observed with aging. Researchers grouped older and younger participants by their level of physical activity. While younger adults still performed better on measures of reaction time, physical activity level appeared to be integral in reducing the amount of decline (Spirduso 1995). These findings are supported by more current investigations that placed older adults in physical activity programs and found the increased activity levels prevented the slowing of reaction time. These results demonstrate the relationship between cognitive development and movement activity.

How Does Interacting with Others in Movement Activities Help Learning?

Socialization is a process whereby we learn who we are and how we are attached, socially, to our world. The most important means by which socialization occurs is through interaction with other people. We use such modes as observation, modeling, trial and error, inference, and behavior modification to gradually become "socialized." This process starts early in life and continues throughout the lifetime. Socialization affects our motor development and the decisions we make about human movement. Conversely, motor development also affects the socialization process.

Socialization and the interactions between social and motor development begin immediately after birth, and are generally somewhat predictable. For the first few months of life, babies look, cry, and smile to initiate social contact. They have limited ability to seek out social interaction, and are dependent upon others to approach them. Once someone does approach, the baby can interact by exchanging visual looks or touches. The baby also can express dissatisfaction by crying when someone leaves.

During the first three months of life, babies learn to distinguish between people. Soon thereafter, with rapidly improving locomotor abilities, infants can initiate social interaction by creeping or crawling to those with whom they want to socialize. They also can interact manually by exchanging touches, hugs, and caresses. Thus, gradually improving motor abilities enhance a baby's opportunities for social interaction.

During infancy and early childhood, the family is the primary socializing agent. It plays a major role in the choices children make concerning movement activity as family members' approval or disapproval of movement choices provide reinforcement. Other socializing forces are television, baby sitters, and—increasingly—preschools.

Play, which is almost always dominated by some form of movement activity, is also a major socializing force during this time. Play is defined as being movement oriented, pleasurable, and usually spontaneous and voluntary (Garvey 1990). As infants, we are content to have someone jostle, lift, cuddle, or tickle us. Until approximately two and one-half years of age, play is primarily solitary, since two children may not interact during play even though they are seated side by side. With advancing social abilities, children become capable of parallel play. Though still characterized by minimal social interaction, children up to about three and one-half years show an awareness of each other by exchanging glances and even an occasional toy. They may even copy each other, although significant interactions are not likely. At approximately four and one-half years, children will engage in associative play. As the name implies, more interaction occurs between children as they readily interact and exchange toys. No group goal or purpose is evident during associative play. During the early school ages, around five years, children begin to display cooperative play. Group goals become evident through games or activities. Leaders begin to emerge during cooperative play (Cratty 1986).

Play is facilitated by improved social skills. Play also enables children to practice these skills in a variety of increasingly complex forms, and it includes the social skills involved in competition and cooperation. As social skills become increasingly complex, play enables more complex movement behaviors to emerge. Conversely, improving movement behaviors enables more complex forms of play and social interaction to occur.

An important effect of movement activity and motor development during childhood occurs in the area of self-esteem, or the value we place on ourselves. Gruber (1985) found children involved in physical education or directed play situations generally had better self-esteem than other children. In addition, Gruber found that children who were emotionally disturbed, mentally challenged, or economically disadvantaged showed the greatest improvements. Those who showed the greatest gains through involvement in physical activity were those who needed it most. These children felt more important when involved in programs of motor enrichment that were led by qualified and supportive professionals.

Different groups predominate as important socializing forces during childhood and adolescence. Toward the end of early childhood, school becomes a significant socialization factor, and the roles played by teachers and coaches are particularly important. For many children, these influences become so powerful that they may overtake the family as the most prominent socializing agent. During late childhood and early adolescence, the peer group becomes another powerful socializing force. Peer groups are characterized by being highly transitory. They change from week to week, or even day to day. The peer group at school may be different from the peer group at home or at team practice. Wherever the location, peers help shape decisions about dress, speech, behavior, and of course, decisions about participation or non-participation in movement activities.

For those youths who participate in sport at a young age, team play becomes another important socializing force. The family and peers influence choices made about sports. Team involvement teaches us to work toward group goals while we learn to subordinate individual preferences. Concepts like division of labor become increasingly clear as youngsters still express some of the egocentrism common during childhood. They learn that each team member has an individual responsibility for achieving the group goal. Sharing those responsibilities is the most effective way to achieve the goal. They learn to be gracious winners and humble losers. And, those who do not actively work toward accomplishment of their task may find themselves ridiculed, while those who show exceptional achievement may be praised.

The interaction between social and motor development goes well beyond childhood and adolescence. As evidenced by the exercise-aging cycle (Berger & Hecht 1989), physical activity decreases throughout adulthood. According to *Healthy People 2000* (USDHHS 1992), only 10 percent of our population exercises three or more times per week at a level that would improve cardiovascular endurance. Twenty-five percent of the population participates in no leisure time physical activity at all. Inactivity, of course, contributes to physiological changes like increased body fat and decreased strength, flexibility, and cardiovascular endurance. These changes can affect self-esteem and increase stress, anxiety, and depression. The downward cycle continues, resulting in even less physical activity. As we become even less active, more severe physiological changes like heart disease, arthritis, osteoporosis, and other hypokinetic diseases become more prevalent.

The tendency of many adults to be inactive seems to be influenced by sociocultural factors. Three of the most influential factors often occur early in adulthood. For most Americans, we leave school, go to work, marry and have children in our twenties. While these factors affect all adults differently, a common tendency is for us to become less physically active in conjunction with these events.

A number of other sociocultural influences also occur throughout adulthood. These include empty nest syndrome (when children reach an age at which they are mature enough to leave home), retirement, and the death of a spouse. Most of us become increasingly sedentary with each successive event. For that reason, as we age we commonly see decreases in cardiac output, vital capacity, muscle mass, connective tissue elasticity, and nerve conductivity. We also see increases in physiological factors like blood pressure, total blood cholesterol, and osteoporosis.

To further complicate the situation, our society holds low expectations for adults regarding their involvement in movement. Even those adults who choose to maintain a physically active lifestyle may encounter some problems. Research results (Ostrow, Jones, & Spiker 1981) indicate that barriers to exercise exist for the elderly: They are cautioned to "be careful." These barriers may be greater than those inherent in sex stereotyping and likely contribute to a decline in participation.

The sociocultural factors discussed in this section can have life threatening consequences. As much as 50 percent of the physiological decline associated with aging may be related to lifestyle choices rather than to the aging process (Berger & McInman 1993). In short, we can overcome much of the decline common in adulthood. For example, Barry, Rich, and Carlson (1993) studied frail elderly nursing home patients who were placed on an exercise program. They showed increased work and oxygen capacity, bone density, flexibility, muscle strength, and coordination. They also lowered their resting heart rates, total cholesterol, and blood pressure. Perhaps even more important, they improved their mental outlook while reducing loneliness, idle time, anxiety, depression, and appetite.

How Does Your Physical Make–Up Influence Your Performance?

Earlier in this chapter, we focused on the importance of the task and the "fit" between it and the developmental level of the performer. We also said that performance was influenced by certain person-related factors, like strength or body size. How do these characteristics change over the course of childhood and adolescence? How do the physical changes that occur as we grow older influence the way we perform?

Body Proportions. Throughout our lives, we continually undergo internal and external physical and physiological change. One of the most dramatic changes that occurs is in the way our bodies are laid out—in our body proportions (see Figure 1). At birth, we have a relatively large head, representing approximately 25 percent of our total body length. In contrast, our legs make up only about one-third of that length. The trunk accounts for the remaining 45 percent of our total length.

No wonder babies do not walk! Their large heads, long bodies, and short legs make them ill-suited for upright locomotion. By the time a child begins school, the head makes up about 15 percent of the total height, while the legs comprise nearly 40 percent of that height. Although their proportions are not yet adult-like, a young child's body is much more suited to running, jumping, and throwing. Additional proportional changes continue throughout childhood and

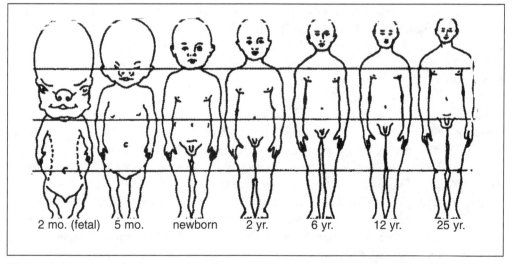

| 2 mo. (fetal) | 5 mo. | newborn | 2 yr. | 6 yr. | 12 yr. | 25 yr. |

Figure 1. Changes in body proportions from two months post-conception to 25 years. (Redrawn from H. Eckert. (1987). *Motor Development.* Indianapolis, IN: Benchmark Press. Originally appeared in C. M. Jackson (1928). *Some aspects of form and growth.* In W .J. Robbins, S. Brody, A. G. Hogan, C. M. Jackson, & C. W. Green (Eds.), *Growth.* New Haven, CT: Yale University Press.)

adolescence, although they are less dramatic. There is a spurt in leg length at adolescence, but most of the increase in height during late adolescence and early adulthood comes from growth in the length of the trunk (Malina & Bouchard 1991).

There are virtually no differences in the body proportions of boys and girls during childhood. This lack of gender difference before puberty is only one of many areas of similarity, and it supports the idea that children should not be separated by gender during these years. There are clear differences in body proportions (and many other areas) following puberty, however. Then, young women have relatively longer trunks and shorter legs than young men of the same height.

Increases in height cease for most individuals sometime between age 20 and 25. Later, particularly after age 40, many adults actually become shorter. These changes begin slowly, then accelerate to approximately one inch per decade beginning around age 60. Compression of the cushioning disks between the vertebrae contribute to this height decline, as well as increased forward curvature of the thoracic spine (called kyphosis). Many older women suffer small compression breaks of the vertebrae, resulting from osteoporosis, which contributes to even shorter stature. While decreases in height are not likely to cause problems for most people, the reasons for them can. Compression of the disks between the vertebrae may result in less flexibility of the trunk, making twisting or turning movements more difficult. Kyphosis compresses the chest and lungs, making breathing more difficult. The fractures associated with osteoporosis can result in further decline.

Skeletal Development. At birth, our skeleton consists largely of cartilage, the relatively flexible material that makes up the ears and nose. Over the course of the next 20 years, the cartilage is gradually replaced with much harder, bony material. The process of laying down bony material is called ossification, and it begins about two months after conception. That is when ossification centers appear within the shafts of long bones like the humerus or femur. After birth, new centers appear at the ends of these bones, and account for their increased length and the accompanying increase in stature.

Typically, females are ahead of males in terms of skeletal age. For example, the growth plates in an adolescent female's humerus fuse at around 15.5 years; for males, growth does not cease until around 18 years (Haywood 1993). Once the growth plates fuse, the bone no longer increases in length. The longer period over which males grow contributes to their generally taller stature than females.

This longer period of growth also has the potential to result in serious injury. On the one hand, breaks of the bone shaft generally heal rapidly. An injury to the area of the growth plate can be serious, however, and can result in malformation or premature cessation of growth. These types of injuries are rare, but can occur as a result of contact sports like football.

Although ossification of the skeleton is largely complete by age 19 or 20, the reabsorption and replacement of bone goes on continuously throughout our lives. The rate of reabsorption is roughly equal to its replacement until women reach their 30s and men reach their 50s (Gabbard 1992). Then, the rate of reabsorption exceeds the rate of bone replacement.

Women tend to lose bone faster than men. This loss is associated with declines in estrogen levels as women approach and pass through menopause. The loss of bone can be extensive and serious. Women tend to lose .75 to 1.0 percent of their bone mass per year after age 30. The rate of loss increases to 2 to 3 percent per year by menopause. By age 70, many women have lost 25 to 30 percent of their bone mass, while men have lost only 12 to 15 percent. Excessive bone loss is called osteoporosis, and leads to increased risk of fractures. On average, women are at a four times greater risk of fractures after menopause than are men of the same age.

Treatment of osteoporosis includes hormone replacement therapy for post-menopausal women, along with calcium supplements and weight bearing exercise. Weight bearing exercise, like walking or jogging, seems to stimulate the processes that help to maintain and even add to bone density. For older women, some sort of weight bearing activity is important for strengthening the head of the femur and the vertebrae of the spinal column. It is the head of the femur that often breaks, resulting in the need for hip replacement. The small, often undetected breaks of the spinal vertebrae contribute to the loss in stature and kyphotic posture described earlier.

The threat of osteoporosis and potentially crippling fractures can seem very far away for teens and pre-teens. There is some indication, however, that women who lead active lives and consume calcium-rich food have reduced risk for severe bone loss, regardless of their age.

Muscular Development and Strength. Most of the growth that occurs in muscle fibers is due to hypertrophy, or an increase in size (Haywood 1993). As muscle fibers grow, they increase in length and diameter. During childhood, there are small gender differences in the characteristics of muscle that slightly favor boys. Differences are larger following adolescence, when muscle mass approaches 54 percent of a man's body weight, but only about 45 percent of a woman's. Interestingly, gender differences are most marked in the upper body, and are much smaller in the legs.

Strength is the ability to exert force against a resistance. The more something weighs, for example, the greater the force that must be applied in order to move it. Increased muscle mass often is associated positively with increased strength. While the size of the muscle is important, it is only one factor in determining the strength of an individual. Another aspect of strength is the ability to recruit motor units. A motor unit is the number of muscle fibers attached to a single motor neuron. Some motor units consist of a neuron and many fibers, like in the back. Where fine control of movement is necessary, motor units consist of a neuron and just a few fibers, like in the eyes or fingers. A person who is able to recruit more of the available motor units will be able to exert greater force than someone who recruits only a few. When assessing strength and changes in strength it is important to consider whether the changes are related to increased muscle mass, increased efficiency in recruitment, or both.

Studies of children and older adults suggest it is a combination of increased mass and the ability to recruit those fibers that results in increases in strength. Several investigators (discussed in Haywood 1993) found that peak weight velocity (a rough indicator of muscle mass increase) occurs six months to two years before peak strength gain. This lag suggests that children need time to learn to coordinate the recruitment of muscle fibers beyond the period of maximum growth. This means there might be lag time between the adolescent growth spurt and improved performance of actions that require strength. People often talk about the "awkwardness" of adolescence. Perhaps the process of learning to effectively recruit muscles contributes to this condition.

Fiatarone and colleagues (1990) found that older adults also gain strength through a combination of increased muscle mass and more efficient recruitment. Before this study, some researchers presumed that strength gains in the elderly might simply be a matter of helping them "re-learn" to recruit muscle fibers efficiently. Fiatarone placed a group of frail 90-year-olds on an eight-week strength training program, resulting in increased muscle mass in many participants. The most important findings, however, were that strength could be increased and quality of life improved. Average strength gains were 174 percent, and some participants no longer needed to use walking aids following strength training.

Cardiorespiratory Development. At birth, the left ventricle of the heart is smaller than the right ventricle. It grows very rapidly, however, and quickly attains adult proportions (Haywood 1993). Throughout the remainder of childhood, the entire heart grows gradually until the adolescent growth spurt. There also are changes in heart rate and the oxygen carrying capacity of the blood. At birth, the average heart rate is approximately 140 beats per minute (bpm). This rate drops dramatically to around 100 bpm by year one, and it continues to decline throughout childhood. Slight gender differences appear at around age 10, when girls' heart rates remain 3 to 5 bpm higher than those of boys. By late adolescence, resting heart rate averages 76 bpm for girls and 72 bpm for boys (Malina & Bouchard 1991).

Oxygen carrying capacity of the blood is related to the number of red blood cells and the amount of hemoglobin they contain. Forty to 45 percent of an adult males' blood volume is composed of red blood cells; it is 38 to 42 percent for women. At birth, the blood is about half red blood cells, but this percent declines rapidly after only a couple of months. Then, the percentage of red blood cells increases through adolescence for boys and through childhood for girls. The result of this gender difference is that boys have more red blood cells than girls, and therefore, greater oxygen carrying ability. These differences have been attributed to differences in body mass and muscle mass (Malina & Bouchard 1991).

Physical Fitness and Motor Development. Only about one-half of the young people from 12 to 21 years in America participate regularly in any vigorous physical activity. Nearly 25 percent do not exercise vigorously at all. Unfortunately, the percentage of inactive children and adolescents increases with age. Despite the bleak statistics, however, many school districts require students to undergo physical fitness testing once or twice a year. This testing may include some or all of the components of physical fitness, including cardiorespiratory endurance, muscular strength and endurance, flexibility, and body composition.

There is evidence that vigorous activity can positively influence components of physical fitness in adults. How does physical training influence these factors, especially in children and adolescents?

Before examining the specific influence of training on fitness factors, it is important to note that many of these factors change with age whether training occurs or not (Payne & Isaacs 1995). For example, resting heart rate declines and maximum oxygen uptake increases throughout childhood and adolescence. Because these types of changes are used as indicators of improvements in fitness, it is unclear and difficult to determine whether prepubescent children benefit from cardiovascular training regimes.

In many of the studies performed, the amount of improvement in maximum oxygen uptake is no greater than would be assumed to occur through typical biological growth. Scientists have suggested that prepubescent children (at least those tested in the available investigations) may be well trained already. It is not that all children and young adolescents are well trained; it may be that children who participated in the investigations performed to date do not represent typical children in that age group. Certainly, more testing is needed.

Muscular strength is another important component of physical fitness. In general, strength has been demonstrated to improve across childhood and adolescence (Haywood 1993). These improvements can be attributed to two separate processes. Muscle mass may increase, or an individual's ability to use his or her muscles may improve. That is, in the latter case, the individual is better able to recruit those muscle fibers necessary to produce a certain force.

As with cardiovascular measures, it is unclear whether additional training produces many strength improvements beyond those that occur through physical maturation. We discussed the relationship between muscle mass and recruitment earlier. Of course, while improvements in muscular strength might have inherent importance for children, adolescents, and young adults (especially as they affect body image or self-esteem), it also is important to know whether they might influence performance in games and sports. Unfortunately, this research is yet to be done.

Flexibility, or joint range of motion, is another important component of physical fitness. The difficulty here is that flexibility is very specific. Being flexible in one part of the body does not necessarily mean a person is flexible in other parts of the body. Despite this joint-specific flexibility, the most widely used test is the back saver sit-and-reach test of hamstring and lower back range of motion. The sit-and-reach has been the focus of most test batteries because so many Americans suffer from chronic low back pain.

In general, there are age-related improvements in flexibility, favoring females, across the childhood years. In a number of studies (reported in Payne & Isaacs 1995), the improvements have been demonstrated to continue through late adolescence (between 15 and 18 years). Other studies, however, report decline beginning as early as age 10. The general consensus is that gradual decline continues throughout adulthood.

We noted the low level of vigorous activity among Americans earlier in this chapter. In addition to poor performance on cardiovascular, muscular strength and endurance, and flexibility components of fitness, sedentary lifestyles often result in individuals who are overweight. This component of physical fitness is known as body composition, and is comprised of the relative proportions of fatty tissue and lean body mass (primarily muscle and bone). The relative proportion of lean body mass is important because of the positive relationship between it and high levels of physical fitness. Because of the problem with obesity, however, we often hear more about the relative proportion of fatty tissue in body composition.

Health problems associated with obesity include coronary heart disease, diabetes, and strokes. Interestingly, there is no real consensus on what constitutes obesity (Payne & Isaacs 1995). An individual may be considered obese based on societal expectations or average population data. Whatever definition is used, obesity is a growing problem in the United States. More than 25 percent of American children are considered obese, a figure that has doubled in the past 30 years. Although there is not a direct correlation between obesity in childhood and adulthood, the longer a child remains obese the more likely he or she is to become an obese adult. For example, 41 percent of those who are obese at age 7 to 10 become obese adults, and 63 percent of obese adolescents age 10 to 13 remain obese as adults.

Because so many components of physical fitness change as a result of biological maturation, the utility of fitness testing has been questioned (Whitall 1992). Even if teachers focus specifically on the elements of fitness, it is unclear whether training has much impact. Because so little time is allotted to physical education, this time might be better spent teaching children motor skills and fostering a positive attitude toward lifelong involvement in activity.

What Happens to Performance as People Grow Older?

We are all growing older. Many researchers and writers have adopted the term "aging" to refer to changes occurring at the upper end of the lifespan, and we will use the term in that way here.

We looked at several biological aspects of aging in the previous section. One might get the impression from that section that we decline as we grow older, and there is little we can do about it. However, there are many things we can do to forestall or delay the effects of aging. There are even lifestyle changes that elementary and high school students can use to delay the effects of aging!

People are living longer than ever before. At the turn of the century, the average life expectancy was around 47 years, with females outliving males by approximately 2 years. By 1990, our life expectancy had increased to between 70 and 80 years. Now, the average man is expected to live to about 72 years, and the average woman to 79 years (National Center for Health Statistics 1990). Approximately 12 percent of the American population is over 65 years of age. This older segment of the population will continue to grow rapidly as post-World War II baby boomers pass 50 and look toward retirement.

Some older adults continue to participate in sport and fitness activities, and many perform extremely well. There are many examples of the physically elite elderly (Spirduso 1995), like the 83 year old who completed the Boston Marathon in just under six hours. These individuals are the exception rather than the rule, however. For many older adults, maintaining an active lifestyle that enables them to live independently and participate in their community is a primary goal. Therefore, much of the research related to activity and aging has focused on activities of daily living (ADLs). ADLs include activities typically associated with independent living, such as bathing, dressing, and shopping.

Independent locomotion in older adults is an ADL that has been widely investigated. Many investigations focus on how the walking gait of older adults differs from younger adults. Early investigations resulted in consistent findings: Older adults take shorter steps, use a slower velocity, and spend longer time in two-footed support (Murray, Kory & Sepic 1970).

More recent investigators found that some of these so-called differences might be related to walking speed instead of increased age. Older adults generally walk more slowly than younger adults. If walking speed is equated across ages, however, many differences disappear. That is, shorter steps with longer time spent in support seem related to walking speed rather than increased age. Thus, while older adults may move more slowly than younger adults, they often retain many characteristics of younger movers. Of special importance is the fact that healthy older adults can use a range of walking speeds. What is not entirely clear is why they tend to move more slowly. A number of factors have been linked to the age-related changes in gait. Among them are health status, balance, muscular strength, and self-confidence.

Many elderly persons have health concerns that are unique to growing older, like arthritis, osteoporosis, cardiovascular disease, or Parkinson's disease. The health status of the elderly is a problem for researchers because any of these diseases can affect motor performance. There was little documentation of current health status in much of the early research with older adults. Healthy adults were mixed with less-than-healthy adults. That lack of experimental control makes it impossible to separate true age-related declines from those attributable to health concerns.

The balance of older adults also declines. Clinical balance tests, such as the functional reach, are used to document declines throughout adulthood. In this test, participants stand with arms extended forward, and then lean as far as they can without taking a step. Tests like the functional reach can be administered easily by physicians or physical therapists, and they provide a measure of balance ability that is roughly comparable to that provided by more technologically sophisticated techniques.

Others used more sophisticated techniques and found that one reason balance declines with age is that muscle activation patterns change. When balance is disturbed in younger people, the muscles closest to the floor contract first, followed by those farther up the body. When older adults responded to an action similar to having a rug pulled from under their feet, the muscles of the legs often contracted simultaneously, or in the wrong order. Many older adults fall in response to having their balance disturbed, where younger adults are able to regain their balance.

Falls are common in older adults. In fact, fall-related injuries and illnesses are the leading cause of death in persons over age 65 (Sattin 1992). An estimated 230,000 hip fractures occur each year, most resulting from falls. Falls and fall-related injuries result in billions of dollars of health care costs per year.

Currently, there are many research groups studying intervention techniques aimed at preventing falls. Some techniques include a component of balance training. For example, participants may stand on one foot, with and without support, or perform heel-to-toe walking.

Reversing the decline in balance is only one component of a program of fall prevention, however. Improvements in strength, such as those discussed previously, also are important. In particular, weak ankle muscles have been found to contribute to the risk of falling. Many intervention studies include some form of weight training as part of a fall prevention program. How improved strength affects balance is unclear. The research is consistent, however, in reporting a lowered risk of falling when strength training is used.

A final component of fall prevention relates to confidence. That is, are the elderly afraid they might fall? Research (Gill, et al. 1994) has demonstrated that how older people feel about their ability to perform is an important factor in discriminating fallers from non-fallers.

Placing Motor Development Concepts in the Curriculum

The concepts outlined in the previous sections are important for all students to learn. Table 2 summarizes the main concepts and outlines placement of each at grade levels that correspond with the National Standards (1995).

Integrating Motor Development into Instruction

It is one thing to determine what motor development content is important for students to know. It is quite another for teachers to integrate that content into their instruction. These concepts also should be modeled throughout the class. They should be incorporated in a developmentally appropriate fashion for students. The examples in the box on pages 67–68 show how the critical concepts presented previously might be introduced and developed within elementary and secondary school curricula.

Assessing Student Learning

The concepts outlined in the previous section are aimed at helping students to improve their motor skills and to understand the lengthy (and sometimes frustrating) process of change in motor skill development. According to the National Standards, students should be able to apply the concepts described to their learning of motor skills.

It is important for teachers to check their students' learning of motor development concepts in the same ways they assess the learning of motor skills. Following are some ways that students knowledge might be assessed. The list is not intended to be exhaustive, and teachers are encouraged to add their own ideas.

Table 2. Critical Student Concepts, K–6

Kindergarten	Second Grade	Fourth Grade	Sixth Grade
Motor Development Concept I: Change is sequential and takes time.	*Motor Development Concept I: Change is sequential and takes time.*	*Motor Development Concept I: Change is sequential and takes time.*	*Motor Development Concept I: Change is sequential and takes time.*
Change in motor skills occurs gradually over many years.	Change in motor skills occurs gradually over many years.	Change in motor skills occurs gradually over many years.	There is a specific sequence of changes that occurs as people become better movers.
	Getting better at motor skills requires lots of practice.	Getting better at motor skills requires lots of practice.	Some people pass through developmental sequences more quickly than others.
	Bigger, stronger people may be better at some skills due to their size.	Bigger, stronger people may be better at some skills due to their size.	Practice should be set up from simple situations to increasingly more complex ones to adjust for changes in motor performance.
		People who look different as they move are not better or worse; they are more or less advanced in their skills.	
Motor Development Concept II: What is more important—form or result?	*Motor Development Concept II: What is more important—form or result?*	*Motor Development Concept II: What is more important—form or result?*	*Motor Development Concept II: What is more important—form or result?*
Some people look better than others when they perform, even though the results are not very good.	Some people look better than others when they perform, even though the results are not very good.	Some people look better than others when they perform, even though the results are not very good.	Better movement results are produced by improving movement form.
Other people's form is not very good, but the result is usually good.	Other people's form is not very good, but the result is usually good.	Other people's form is not very good, but the result is usually good.	Putting two or more skills together sometimes results in a temporary decline in form and results.
	It is better to focus on movement form. The outcome will improve as form improves.	It is better to focus on movement form. The outcome will improve as form improves.	

Table 2. Critical Student Concepts, K–6

		Putting two or more skills together sometimes results in a temporary decline in form and outcome.	
Motor Development Concept III: How does cognitive development help some people perform better than others at certain skills?	*Motor Development Concept III: How does cognitive development help some people perform better than others at certain skills?*	*Motor Development Concept III: How does cognitive development help some people perform better than others at certain skills?*	*Motor Development Concept III: How does cognitive development help some people perform better than others at certain skills?*
People may differ cognitively even though they are the same age.	People may differ cognitively even though they are the same age.	People may differ cognitively even though they are the same age.	Performing complex skills depends on the interaction of cognitive, social-emotional, motor, and physical abilities.
	Students at different levels of cognitive development may understand instructions for performing motor skills differently.	Students at different levels of cognitive development may understand instructions for performing motor skills differently.	*Many players at this age may need concrete instructions regarding how to perform specific skills or playing strategies.*
		Performing complex skills depends on the interaction of cognitive, social-emotional, motor, and physical abilities.	
Motor Development Concept IV: How does interacting with others in movement activities help learning?	*Motor Development Concept IV: How does interacting with others in movement activities help learning?*	*Motor Development Concept IV: How does interacting with others in movement activities help learning?*	*Motor Development Concept IV: How does interacting with others in movement activities help learning?*
Sharing equipment helps partners get better at movement skills.	Sharing equipment helps partners get better at movement skills.	Working together helps partners get better at motor skills.	Practice with increasingly complex interactions among teammates and opponents can help a person become a better player.
	Working together helps partners get better at motor skills.	Movement skill development influences social skill development and vice versa.	

Table 2. Critical Student Concepts, K–6

Motor Development Concept V: How does your physical make up influence the way you perform?	*Motor Development Concept V:* How does your physical make up influence the way you perform?	*Motor Development Concept V:* How does your physical make up influence the way you perform?
People may differ physically, even though they are the same age.	People may differ physically, even though they are the same age.	Physical differences (taller, stronger) contribute to motor skill differences.
A person who is less developed physically will not perform a skill requiring that physical attribute as well as someone who is more developed.	Physical differences (taller, stronger) contribute to motor skill differences.	During the adolescent growth spurt, more time may be necessary to adjust motor patterns to rapidly changing body dimensions.
	Sometimes people who are more advanced physically demonstrate better movement results.	Equipment should be selected because it matches one's physical make-up.
	A person who is less developed physically will not perform a skill requiring that physical attribute as well as someone who is more developed.	There are virtually no differences between boys and girls in body proportions throughout childhood.
	Equipment should be selected because it matches one's physical make-up.	

Small group practice helps people "work out" problems with skills and strategies to fit into the bigger game.

Movement skill development influences social skill development and vice versa.

Activity choices are related to those of friends and family.

Table 2. Critical Student Concepts, K–6

Motor Development Concept VI: What happens to performance as people grow older?	*Motor Development Concept VI: What happens to performance as people grow older?*	*Motor Development Concept VI: What happens to performance as people grow older?*	Some children begin puberty earlier than others, resulting in dramatic physical differences between same-aged individuals.
Regular participation in physical activities enhances skill development.	Regular participation in physical activities enhances skill development.	Regular participation in physical activities enhances skill development.	During their pubertal growth spurt, children will have more endurance and may be stronger than others.
Regular participation develops positive health habits.	Learning many different motor skills gives people more choices for movement as they grow older.	Learning many different motor skills gives people more choices for movement as they grow older.	*Motor Development Concept VI: What happens to performance as people grow older?*
		Learning individual, team, and fitness skills helps people to stay healthier as they grow older.	Participating in regular physical activity helps to delay or minimize the effects of aging-related diseases.
		Learning to enjoy motor skills when young helps people to enjoy them as they grow older.	A variety of different activities are necessary to maintain a high level of function throughout life.

Table 2. Critical Student Concepts, 8–12

Eighth Grade	Tenth Grade	Twelfth Grade
Motor Development Concept I: Change is sequential and takes time.	*Motor Development Concept I: Change is sequential and takes time.*	*Motor Development Concept I: Change is sequential and takes time.*
There is a specific sequence of changes that occurs as people become better movers.	Practice should be set up from simple situations to increasingly more complex ones to adjust for changes in motor performance.	Simple performance strategies should be practiced before more complex ones.
Some people pass through developmental sequences more quickly than others.	Experience in many different situations is necessary to become a better mover.	Individuals who have had more practice and experience will have better skills than individuals with less practice and experience.
Practice should be set up from simple situations to increasingly more complex ones to adjust for changes in motor performance.	Simple performance strategies should be practiced before more complex ones.	Practice should simulate the setting in which play will occur.
Experience in many different situations is necessary to become a better mover.		
Motor Development Concept II: What is more important—form or result?	*Motor Development Concept II: What is more important—form or result?*	*Motor Development Concept II: What is more important—form or result?*
Putting two or more skills together sometimes results in a temporary decline in form and outcome.	Movement efficiency is important and may differ from person to person.	When combining several skills, better movement form generally leads to a better movement result.
Movement efficiency is important and may differ from person to person.	When combining several skills, better movement form generally leads to a better movement result.	Changes in movement result may not be matched exactly or immediately by changes in movement form.

Table 2. Critical Student Concepts, 8–12

Motor Development Concept III: How does cognitive development help some people perform better than others at certain skills?	Changes in movement result may not be matched exactly or immediately by changes in movement form.	*Motor Development Concept III: How does cognitive development help some people perform better than others at certain skills?*
Performing complex skills depends on the interaction of cognitive, social-emotional, motor, and physical abilities.	*Motor Development Concept III: How does cognitive development help some people perform better than others at certain skills?*	As adolescents pass through developmental stages (to concrete and formal operations) they become capable of more advanced cognitive and motor skills.
Some players will begin to understand and perform according to complex strategies and rules.	As adolescents pass through developmental stages (to concrete and formal operations) they become capable of more advanced cognitive and motor skills.	Students with advanced cognitive skills and experiences are able to perform activities that involve more complex strategies, such as offenses and defenses.
	Some players will begin to understand and perform according to complex strategies and rules.	Players who demonstrate advanced cognitive skills in one type of game may or may not have these skills in another game (for example, they may understand complex skills in field or

Table 2. Critical Student Concepts, 8–12

Motor Development Concept IV: How does interacting with others in movement activities help learning?	*Motor Development Concept IV: How does interacting with others in movement activities help learning?*	*Motor Development Concept IV: How does interacting with others in movement activities help learning?*
Practice with increasingly complex interactions among teammates and opponents can help a person become a better player.	Cooperation among teammates is important, even when competing.	Cooperation among teammates is important, even when competing.
Small group practice helps people "work out" problems with skills and strategies to fit into the bigger game.	Observing more skillful teammates and opponents can help a person become more skillful.	Observing more skillful teammates and opponents can help a person become more skillful.
Activity choices are related to those of friends and family.	Not everyone is able to compete at the same level of skill.	Not everyone is able to compete at the same level of skill.
Playing group or team activities/games can teach a person about cooperation and competition.		team games and they may not in court or individual games).

Table 2. Critical Student Concepts, 8–12

Motor Development Concept V: How does your physical make up influence the way you perform?	Motor Development Concept V: How does your physical make up influence the way you perform?	Motor Development Concept V: How does your physical make-up influence the way you perform?
Physical differences (taller, stronger) contribute to motor skill differences between people.	Improvement of physical aspects through training (e.g., strength training) can help improve motor skills and emphasize physical attributes.	Individuals may be better suited to some activities than others, based on their physical attributes.
During the adolescent growth spurt, more time may be necessary to adjust motor patterns to rapidly changing body dimensions.	People with different physical attributes may be better suited to play different activities or different positions in an activity.	Individuals may be better suited to playing some positions than others, based on their physical attributes.
Young adults already past their growth spurt may be able to use longer or heavier equipment (e.g., rackets, bats) to improve their force or power.	Young adults already past their growth spurt may be able to use longer or heavier equipment (e.g., rackets, bats) to improve their force or power.	After their pubertal growth spurt, children can benefit from physical training programs.
During their pubertal growth spurt, children will have more endurance and may be stronger than others.	After their pubertal growth spurt, children can benefit from physical training programs.	

Table 2. Critical Student Concepts, 8–12

Motor Development Concept VI: What happens to performance as people grow older?

Participating in regular physical activity helps to delay or minimize the effects of aging-related diseases.

A variety of different activities is necessary to maintain a high level of function throughout life.

Motor Development Concept VI: What happens to performance as people grow older?

Participating in regular physical activity helps to delay or minimize the effects of aging-related diseases.

A variety of different activities is necessary to maintain a high level of function throughout life.

Females who participate in vigorous regular exercise can lessen the effects of age-related diseases like osteoporosis.

Motor Development Concept VI: What happens to performance as people grow older?

Participating in regular physical activity helps to delay or minimize the effects of aging-related diseases.

A variety of different activities is necessary to maintain a high level of function throughout life.

Females who participate in vigorous regular exercise can lessen the effects of age-related diseases like osteoporosis.

Participation in at least moderate levels of activity for 30 minutes most days of the week is important to maintain adequate fitness throughout one's adult years.

Integrating Motor Development into Instruction

Elementary School Example: Grade 4
Concept: Change in motor skills occurs gradually over many years.
Teachers model this concept by clearly acknowledging differences among their students without assigning values regarding the "correctness" of their skills. They also have students monitor their own motor skill performance over time. For example, using the overarm throw, student are assessed (by the teacher or a peer using a performance rubric and a target) at the beginning of the school year, and once a month throughout the year.

After each assessment, students review their progress (both form and outcome) and that of the group members. The teacher steers students away from discussions that lean toward comparing one student to another. Students advance at their own rate, and the important thing is self-improvement through practice over time.

Elementary Example: Grade 2
Concept: It is better to focus on movement form. The outcome will improve as form improves.
All too often, teachers use outcome measures to evaluate performance simply because they are easier to collect. This leads students to believe that the result is the most important thing and can lead to the development of poor form. As discussed in previous sections, however, movement form is an important part of skill. Movement components like the ones presented for hopping shown in Table 1 may be too complex for these students. Instead, movement components can be used as guides for developing age-appropriate criterion sheets.

In hopping, for example, swinging the non-support leg through an increasing range of motion is critical; alternating or oppositional use of the arms and legs is most efficient. Students are taught to look for the amount of arm and leg swing performers use as they hop across a gym. Additionally, they can encourage their partner to incorporate a greater range of motion in their movements. At the conclusion of the lesson, students are asked about the focus of the lesson. Students come to realize that the expected result will follow once they have developed the proper form.

High School Example: Grade 10
Concept: People with different physical attributes may be better suited to play different activities or different positions in an activity.
During a volleyball unit, teams meet to decide who will set and who will spike. Students discuss similarities and differences between players and which differences might be exploited to improve play. Throughout the discussion, students consider skill, strength, height, previous experience, and the desire to play a certain position.

It is important for the teacher to explain that professional sports are full of examples of athletes who are successful despite their lack of certain attributes, such as size. For example, Mugsy Bogues is a successful basketball player, and Doug Flutie played professional football. Both were considered too small to play their positions. What other attributes did they have that helped them be successful?

Middle School Example: Grade 6

Concept: A person's activity choices are related to those of friends and family.

Students are provided with a grid that lists a variety of physical activities. Across the top of the grid students write their name, the names of their friends, and the names of their family members. For homework, students survey their friends and family to determine their three favorite physical activities. The next day in class, students share their favorite physical activities and compare their favorites with those of their friends and family. The class, as a whole discusses whether the concept, "A person's activity choices are related to those of friends and family," is true, based on the data they collected.

Middle School Example: Grade 8

Concept: Young adults already past their growth spurt may be able to use longer or heavier equipment to improve their force or power.

Students select a bat from several different sizes and practice batting. At some point during the lesson, the teacher prompts students to switch to another bat. A discussion of how performance changed follows. In this situation, the teacher clearly acknowledges that some students will be more comfortable with a lighter bat, and some with a heavier bat. Frequently, however, such choices are not possible once "the game" is introduced.

Teachers may consider helping students modify their games to suit their needs. Smaller, weaker, or less developmentally advanced students may play a game of whiffle ball, while another group uses a pitcher and a modified softball. Over time, and in an environment where developmental differences are accepted, these two activities are viewed as simply two different versions of the same game.

High School Example: Grade 12

Concept: Participation in regular physical activity helps to delay or minimize the effects of aging-related diseases.

The focus of our motor activity is likely to change as we grow older. Most people become more interested in lifetime pursuits like tennis or golf, and fitness activities like aerobics or jogging. And, it is important to help students begin to develop attitudes that favor a lifetime pattern of activity.

 Studies show that most Americans know they should be active, despite increasing levels of inactivity. Teachers should structure activities that are fun, so students will continue to participate. Simultaneously, teachers should work with students to help them to understand that learning to get better can be hard work and can take time, but if they persist it can pay off.

Journal writing can help students focus on their future. Students complete the following statements in terms of physical activity levels:

• I am now 20, and I am actively involved in...
• I am now 30, and I am actively involved in...
• I am now 40, and I am actively involved in...
• I am now 50, and I am actively involved in...
• I am now 60, and I am actively involved in...
• I am now 70, and I am actively involved in...

Students must consider developmental changes as they complete each of these statements.

Student Notebooks/Journals. Teachers set aside 5 to 10 minutes at the end of class for reflection. During this time, students can make journal entries. Younger students might draw a picture of the day's activities or illustrate their response to some question. Older students could draw or verbalize their experiences. Sample prompts include:

- Describe what your motor pattern looked like as you _____. Can you describe what another student looked like?
- How did you perform _____ compared with someone else in the class? Describe the differences and the similarities.
- Look at your description of how you performed _____ at the beginning of the unit. How does it compare with your current performance? Have you gotten better? How? What factors do you think helped you improve?

Peer/Small Group Observations. In pairs or small groups, students observe each other doing a skill or activity. They compare how each participant performed. They tell or show other students something that will help them get better. Each person in the group must say at least one thing.

Essay. Students watch a sports/dance event (whatever is being taught in class). They focus on physical differences, skill differences, strategy differences, or offensive/defensive differences (the teacher will choose, depending on what is appropriate). Students will write a short paper describing how the more skilled athletes differ from members of their class.

Project. The teacher provides the students with a brief case study. This could be a verbal presentation for younger students and a reading assignment for older students. The case could focus on one of the major concepts outlined. It could involve problem solving (e.g., helping someone set up an activity or exercise program to get better at a skill or game). The teacher could break the class into small groups or lead a whole-class discussion aimed at solving the problem presented in the case.

Concluding Comments

Motor development consists of changes in motor behavior that occur across the lifespan and the processes that underlie and drive those changes. Some change is slow to occur, and some change occurs more slowly in some people than others.

In this chapter we have highlighted many of the important motor changes that occur, and considered how they are affected by social, cognitive, and physical changes. It is important to remember that these changes occur as part of an interactive process between the current status of the individual and the environment in which he or she moves. And finally, we have noted that development takes time—lots of time—and perhaps the teacher's most important job is to help students of all ages to be patient in the face of slow and gradual change.

How Can I Learn More?

The following references will help you to learn more about motor development across the lifespan:

Clark, J. E., & Whitall, J. (1989). What is motor development? The lessons of history. *Quest, 41*, 183-202.

Gallahue, D. L., & Ozmun, J. C. (1995). *Understanding motor development: Infants, children, adolescents, adults* (3rd ed). Dubuque, IA: Brown and Benchmark.

Haywood, K. M. (1993). *Life span motor development.* (2nd ed.). Champaign, IL: Human Kinetics.

Malina, R., & Bouchard, C. (1991). *Growth, maturation, and physical activity.* Champaign, IL: Human Kinetics.

National Association for Sports and Physical Education. (1995). *Moving into the future: National standards for physical education: A guide to content and assessment.* St. Louis, MO: Mosby.

Payne, V. G., & Isaacs, L. D. (1995). *Human motor development: A lifespan approach.* Mountain View, CA: Mayfield.

Roberton, M. A., & Halverson, L. E. (1984). *Developing children–Their changing movement.* Philadelphia, PA: Lea & Febiger.

Spirduso, W. W. (1995). *Physical dimensions of aging.* Champaign, IL: Human Kinetics.

Thomas, J. R. (1997). Motor behavior. In J.D. Massengale and R.A. Swanson (Eds.), *The history of exercise and sport science.* Champaign, IL: Human Kinetics.

United States Department of Health and Human Services, Public Health Service. (1992). *Healthy people 2000: National health and disease prevention objectives.* Boston: Jones and Bartlett.

The President's Council on Physical Fitness and Sports. (1996). *Physical activity and health: A report of the surgeon general.* Pittsburgh, PA: Superintendent of Documents.

Williams, K., Barrett, K., Clark, J., French, K., Langendorfer, S., & Whitall, J. (1994). *Looking at physical education from a developmental perspective: A guide for teaching.* Reston, VA: NASPE.

References

Barry, H. C., Rich, B. S. E., & Carlson, R. T. (1993). How exercise can benefit older patients: A practical approach. *The Physician and Sportsmedicine, 21*(2), 124-140.

Berger, B. G. & Hecht, L. M. (1989). Exercise, aging, and psychological well-being: The mind-body question. In A. C. Ostrow (Ed.), *Aging and motor behavior.* Indianapolis, IN: Benchmark.

Berger, B. G., & McInman, A. (1993). Exercise and the quality of life. In R. N. Singer, M. Murphy, & L. K. Tennant (Eds.), *Handbook of research on sports psychology.* New York: Macmillan.

Bloom, B. S. (1956). *Taxonomy of education objectives: Handbook I: Cognitive domain.* New York: McKay.

Cratty, B. J. (1986). *Perceptual and motor development in infants and children* (3rd ed.). Englewood Cliffs, NJ: Prentice-Hall.

Fiatarone, M., Marks, E., Ryan, N., Meredith, C., Lipsitz, L., & Evans, W. (1990). High intensity strength training in nonagenarians. *JAMA, 263*, 3029-3034.

Gabbard, C. (1992). *Lifelong motor development.* Dubuque, IA: W. C. Brown.

Garvey, K. (1990). *Play.* Cambridge, MA: Harvard University Press.

Gill, D., Kelley, B., Williams, K., & Martin, J. (1994). Stair climbing and physical activity in older adults: Preliminary report on psychological factors. *Research Quarterly for Exercise and Sport, 65*, 367-371.

Gruber, J. (1985). Physical activity and self-esteem development in children: A meta-analysis. *The Academy Papers, 19*, 30-48.

Halverson, L. E., Roberton, M. A., & Langendorfer, S. (1982). Development of the overarm throw: Movement and ball velocity changes by seventh grade. *Research Quarterly for Exercise and Sport, 53*, 198-205.

Halverson, L. E., & Williams, K. (1985). Developmental sequences for hopping over distance: A pre-longitudinal screening. *Research Quarterly for Exercise and Sport, 56*, 37-44.

Haywood, K. M. (1993). *Life span motor development* (2nd ed.). Champaign, IL: Human Kinetics.

Malina, R., & Bouchard, C. (1991). *Growth, maturation, and physical activity.* Champaign, IL: Human Kinetics Pub.

McCaskill, C. L., & Wellman, B. (1938). A study of common motor achievements at the preschool age. *Child Development, 9*, 141-150.

Murray, M., Kory, R., & Sepic, S. (1970). Walking patterns of normal women. *Archives of Physical Medicine and Rehabilitation, 51*, 637-650.

National Association for Sport and Physical Activity. (1995). *Moving into the future: National standards for physical education: A guide to content and assessment.* St. Louis, MO: Mosby.

National Center for Health Statistics (1990). *Advance data from vital and health statistics: Numbers 31–40.* Washington, DC: Author.

Ostrow, A. C., Jones, D. C., & Spiker, D. D. (1981). Age role expectations and sex role expectations for selected sport activities. *Research Quarterly for Exercise and Sport, 52*, 216-227.

Payne, V. G., & Isaacs, L. D. (1995). *Human motor development: A lifespan approach.* Mountain View, CA: Mayfield.

Piaget, J. (1952). *The origins of intelligence in children* (Margaret Cook, Trans.). New York: International Universities Press.

Roberton, M. A., & Halverson, L. E. (1984). *Developing children–Their changing movement.* Philadelphia: Lea & Febiger.

Sattin, R. (1992). Falls among older persons: A public health perspective. *Annual Review of Public Health, 13*, 489-508.

Sinclair, C. (1973). *Movement of the young child: Ages two to six.* Columbus, OH: Merrill.

Spirduso, W. W. (1995). *Physical dimensions of aging.* Champaign, IL: Human Kinetics.

United States Department of Health and Human Services, Public Health Service. (1992). *Healthy people 2000: National health and disease prevention objectives.* Boston, MA: Jones and Bartlett.

VanSant, A. (1990). Life-span development in functional tasks. *Physical Therapy, 70*, 788-798.

Wickstrom, R. (1983). *Fundamental motor patterns* (3rd Ed.). Philadelphia, PA: Lea & Febiger.

Whitall, J. (1992). Elementary school physical fitness. *Teaching Elementary Physical Education, 3*, 14-15.

Williams, K., Barrett, K., Clark, J., French, K., Langendorfer, S., & Whitall, J. (1994). *Looking at physical education from a developmental perspective: A guide for teaching.* Reston, VA: NASPE.

Zaichkowsky, L. D., Zaichkowsky, L. B., & Martinek, T. (1980). *Growth and development: The child and physical activity.* St. Louis, MO: Mosby.

Glossary

Affective domain: an aspect of human development that emphasizes the social and/or emotional changes through life.

Cognitive domain: an aspect of human development that emphasizes the intellectual changes through life.

Concrete operational stage: generally occurring from about 7 to 11 years of age, the third major stage in Piaget's theory of cognitive development where development is characterized by an improving ability to decenter one's attention though still lacking an ability to consider events which are unreal, unimaginable, or hypothetical.

Developmental perspective: a point of view that assumes that learners are at different levels in their motor, cognitive, emotional, social, and physical development and that their developmental status will affect their ability to change.

Developmental sequence: the series of changes that occur from when a skill first emerges to when it reaches its most mechanically efficient state.

Formal operational stage: generally beginning at early to mid-adolescence, the fourth major stage of Piaget's theory of cognitive development where development is characterized by an improving ability to think abstractly or hypothetically while simultaneously pondering multiple aspects of a problem.

Motor development: a process that includes both experiences (like practice and instruction) and an individual's current physical, cognitive, emotional, and social status, and leads to changes in motor behavior across the entire lifespan.

Ossification: beginning about two months after conception, the process of laying down bony material in the human body.

Physical domain: an aspect of human development that emphasizes bodily change through life.

Play: a movement-oriented, pleasurable activity that is usually inherently unproductive, spontaneous, and voluntary.

Preoperational stage: generally occurring from about two to seven years of age, the second major stage in Piaget's theory of cognitive development where development is characterized by improved use of symbols, language development, and pretend play.

Psychomotor domain: an aspect of human development that emphasizes changes in human movement through life.

Sensorimotor stage: generally occurring from about birth to two years of age, the first major stage in Piaget's theory of cognitive development where one is characterized as "thinking by bodily movement."

Socialization: a process whereby we learn who we are and how we are attached, socially, to our world, including any way that we gather information about society and learn to live in that society.

Strength: the ability to exert force against a resistance.

Chapter 4

Biomechanics

By Susan J. Hall and Gail G. Evans

At what angle of release should a ball be thrown for maximum distance? What movements can contribute to the development of lower back pain? Why does a properly thrown boomerang return to the thrower? Why are some people unable to float? The answers to all of these questions are rooted in the scientific field of biomechanics. In this chapter, we will look at biomechanical concepts as they relate to safe and effective movement in exercise, sport, dance, and daily living. These concepts are an important part of the cognitive foundation for a physically educated person, and an understanding of basic biomechanical principles can enhance the experience of acquiring or maintaining a physically active lifestyle.

What Is Biomechanics?

Biomechanics is a multidisciplinary field of study that involves biologists and zoologists, biomechanical and biomedical engineers, orthopedic, cardiac, and sports medicine physicians, dentists, physical therapists, exercise scientists, and physical educators. All of these very diverse groups of professionals have an interest in the mechanical aspects of biological organisms.

Researchers interested in human biomechanics have studied a wide variety of topics. Using computer analysis of films or videotapes, biomechanists have studied performers who range in ability from physically challenged to elite. They have studied many movement forms—including dance, aquatics, gymnastics, individual and team sports, outdoor and leisure pursuits—as well as safety and rescue activities. Sport biomechanists also are concerned with reducing the number of sport injuries by eliminating dangerous practices and improving sport equipment and apparel. And, there are important clinical applications for biomechanics research. Physical therapists regularly analyze the biomechanics of patients' walking gaits and other movements to monitor progress toward rehabilitation. Prosthetists work to improve the biomechanical aspects of artificial limbs and implants.

Occupational biomechanics deals with prevention of work-related injuries and improvement of working conditions and worker performance (Chaffin & Andersson 1991). It such considers questions as how much weight an individual of a given strength can safely lift on a repetitive basis, what keyboard designs may help minimize the likelihood of carpal tunnel syndrome, and at what height and angle to best position implements that will be manipulated by assembly line workers.

Susan J. Hall is a professor at the University of Texas at El Paso. Gail G. Evans is professor, Department of Human Performance, San Jose State University, San Jose, California.

Relevant biomechanical considerations include human motion: how fast a movement is executed, how much space a movement requires, and whether movements are coordinated.

The study of biomechanics also involves analysis of force, including muscle force that produces movements and enables the throwing and kicking of balls, as well as impact force that may cause injuries. Experienced teachers are well aware that factors such as joint range of motion and movement speed directly influence the amount of force that is generated by a moving arm or leg. Physical education teachers at all levels rely on visual observations of movement biomechanics to provide appropriate learning cues.

Why Is Biomechanics Important?

A solid understanding of biomechanical principles is important for the physical educator because this knowledge is intimately linked with effective teaching and learning of motor skills. And, while the physically educated person need not be as knowledgeable about biomechanics as the physical education teacher, understanding basic biomechanical principles is important for anyone interested in movement skills.

Linking Biomechanics to the National Standards

The biomechanical concepts comprise important cognitive components of the first two National Physical Education Standards compiled by NASPE in 1995. These include:

- National Standard 1: Demonstrates competency in many movement forms and proficiency in a few movement forms.
- National Standard 2: Applies movement concepts and principles to the learning and development of motor skills.

An understanding of basic biomechanics is also relevant to several of the other National Standards, including:

- National Standard 3: Exhibits a physically active lifestyle.
- National Standard 4: Achieves and maintains a health-enhancing level of physical fitness.
- National Standard 6: Demonstrates understanding and respect for differences among people in physical activity settings.

Selected Biomechanics Concepts

In this section, we will consider biomechanics concepts that are related to the National Standards.

What Is Force?

Where should a ball be hit when executing a floater serve in volleyball? What determines whether a push can cause a heavy piece of furniture to move? Why is it easier to open a door when pushing on the door knob rather than in the center of the door? The answers to these questions all center around the nature of force.

A force may be thought of simply as a push or a pull. Each force can be characterized by its magnitude or size, its direction, and the point at which it is applied. Although we tend to notice the forces acting on our bodies only in injury-related situations, forces act continually upon us during daily activities. The forces of gravity and friction enable us to walk and manipulate objects in predictable ways when internal forces are produced by our muscles. When we participate in sports activities we apply forces to balls, bats, racquets, and clubs. We absorb forces from impacts with balls when we catch them, and with the ground or floor when we walk and run.

The Effects of Force. There are two potential effects of force. The first is acceleration, or the change in velocity of the object to which the force is applied. The more massive or heavy the object, the smaller the acceleration will be. The second effect is deformation, or change in shape. When a racquetball is struck with a racquet, the ball is both accelerated (put in motion in the direction of the racquet swing) and deformed (flattened on the side struck).

Net Force. Since a force rarely acts in isolation, it is important to recognize that what we see and feel are effects of what is called the net force. The net force is the vector sum of all the acting forces on a body. Thus, it represents the size and direction of all acting forces. The magnitude and direction of the net force determines the speed and path of motion of the body experiencing the net force. When the forces acting on an object are balanced, or cancel each other out, there is no net force and no resulting motion. If two people simultaneously apply equal and opposite forces on the two sides of a swinging door, for example, the door will not move.

The effect of a net force on the resulting motion of a body depends not only on the size and direction of the force, but also on the point at which the force is applied. A body's center of gravity is the point around which its weight is balanced. When a pencil is balanced horizontally on an extended finger, the pencil's center of gravity is positioned directly above the finger. When a net force is directed through a body's center of gravity, the resulting motion of the body will be along a straight line in the direction of the force. If a net force is directed through any point other than the body's center of gravity, the body will also rotate as it moves in the direction of the force. To execute a floater serve in volleyball with no spin, the server applies force directly through the center of the ball, which is the ball's center of gravity. To produce spin on a ball, we would apply force away from the center of the ball.

Torque. Torque, which may be thought of as rotational force, is the product of a force and its moment arm. A moment arm is the shortest distance between the force's line of action and the body's center of rotation (see Figure 1). The size of the force and the size of the moment arm

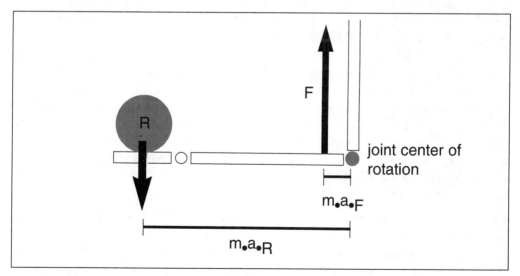

Figure 1. Schematic representation of the arm and hand, with the hand supporting a resistance. Muscle torque at the elbow is the product of muscle force (F) and muscle moment arm (m.a.F). Resistance torque at the elbow is the product of the resistance (R) and resistance moment arm (m.a.R). Motion at the joint is in the direction of the net torque.

contribute equally to torque. A heavy door can be pushed open with minimal effort by applying force at the farthest possible distance (moment arm) from the hinges.

Equilibrium. When all acting forces and torque on a body are balanced (there is no net force or net torque acting), the body is said to be in a state of equilibrium. A body in equilibrium may either be motionless or moving at a constant speed along a straight path. A body's tendency to remain in equilibrium is known as its inertia. A body's inertia is proportional to its mass, with heavier objects having more inertia than lighter objects. For example, the more weight discs that are loaded onto a barbell positioned on the floor, the greater the barbell's inertia, and the more difficult it is to disturb its equilibrium.

Reaction Force. When one body exerts a force on a second body, the second body exerts a reaction force of equal size and opposite direction. When we catch a ball, our hands apply a force to the ball that reduces its velocity to zero. During the catch, the ball applies a force of equal size to our hands. When we walk or run, our feet apply force to the ground and the ground applies reaction force to our feet.

How Is Force Effectively Generated?

Why do skilled tennis players position the serving arm so far behind the body during the "back scratch" or preparatory phase of the serve? Why are muscles "stronger" when the body is in certain positions? The answers to these questions are related to the body's ability to generate force.

Muscle Tension. There are approximately 434 muscles in the human body. About 150 of these muscles control body movements and posture, and the others are responsible for activities such as eye control and swallowing. When a muscle produces force, it does so by developing tension, a pulling force. A tensed muscle pulls on the bones to which it is attached. Because each muscle can only apply force in one direction, muscles are arranged in functional pairs that pull on bones in opposite directions. For example, tension in the quadriceps muscle group on the anterior thigh extends (straightens) the knee, and tension in the hamstrings on the posterior thigh produces flexion (bending) at the knee.

Although muscles can only pull on bone, several things can happen when a muscle is tensed. When a tensed muscle shortens, the attached bones are moved closer together and there is motion of one or more body segments (i.e., forearms, thighs, hands, feet). Muscles also can develop tension without any change in length. When body builders pose they tense muscles on opposite sides of the body segments so the effects of the muscle forces developed are neutralized and no motion occurs. A tensed muscle also can lengthen. Lowering a barbell from shoulder height to waist height involves lengthening of the elbow flexor muscles at the same time that tension is produced to control the movement of the barbell. The terms used to describe decrease, increase, and no change in the length of a tensed muscle are concentric, eccentric, and isometric.

Effects of Muscle Tension. Several factors influence the resulting effect of muscle tension on motion of the body segments. A major factor is the magnitude or amount of tension developed. We produce large magnitudes of muscle tension during a forceful motion. Because muscles that are large in cross section are stronger than muscles that are smaller in cross section we tend to use larger muscles and to recruit more muscles for tasks requiring large amounts of force. Thus the large, powerful gastrocnemius is called to action during a maximal vertical jump, but only smaller muscles—such as the underlying soleus—are intermittently active to control postural sway when we stand.

An equally important influence on the outcome of muscle tension development is the moment arm of the muscle force (see Figure 1). Muscles within the human body produce torque at joints. This is the product of muscle force and muscle moment arm, or the distance from the muscle force's line of action to the center of rotation at the joint. Torque causes rotation of a body segment at a joint. A muscle's strength is essentially the amount of joint torque it can produce. As the angle at a joint such as the elbow changes, the moment arms of the muscles crossing the elbow also change. Change in muscle moment arm translates directly into change in the muscle's ability to generate joint torque. Isokinetic resistance machines are designed to provide variable resistance through a joint's range of motion that matches the changing torque-generating potential of the muscle groups involved.

Joint Movement. Whether movement occurs at a joint in response to torque produced by a muscle depends on the magnitude of the resistance torque at the joint (see Figure 1). A resistance torque is the product of a resistance force and its moment arm with respect to the joint center. Resistance forces can be applied by external loads, such as a weight held in the hand, the weights of the body segments, and opposing muscles. Motion at a joint occurs in the direction of the net torque. Because most of the muscles of the human body attach relatively close to the joints they cross, muscle forces must typically be much larger than resistance forces to generate a net joint torque that causes motion.

Effect of Muscle Stretch. Muscle length is another factor that influences the torque produced by a muscle at a joint. A muscle's ability to produce force increases when the muscle is slightly stretched. Thus, a stretch fosters subsequent forceful shortening of the muscle. This phenomenon promotes effective muscular force development in many sport activities. Baseball pitchers, football quarterbacks, javelin throwers, and water polo players all place the anterior shoulder muscles in eccentric stretch during arm "cocking" immediately before forceful throwing. The same action occurs in muscle groups of the trunk and shoulders at the peak of the backswing of a golf club or a baseball bat, and during the "back scratch" position of the tennis serve or the badminton clear shot. During walking and running, the cyclic stretching of the gastrocnemius and the soft tissues of the arches of the foot also acts to store and return elastic energy.

How Is Force Effectively Matched to Motor Skill Requirements?

Why do baseball players "choke up" on the bat to execute a bunt? Why do expert dart throwers move at just one joint during the throw? Why do elite gymnasts tend to be of short stature and slight build?

Although muscular strength is an important asset for many sports, strength alone does not always translate into skillful performance. Effective movement during sport, exercise, dance, and daily activities also is dependent on factors such as movement speed, range of motion, the weight and length of the body segments, the number and coordination of the body segments involved, and the anthropometric characteristics of the body.

Movement Speed and Range of Motion. When an athlete swings a bat, club, or racket, the faster the angular velocity of the swinging implement, the greater the amount of force that will be delivered to the ball at impact when other factors are equal. The larger the range of motion—or distance through which the motion occurs—the greater the potential for building angular velocity. This is true for both swinging sport implements and moving human body segments. A volleyball player uses a large arm range of motion to generate high angular velocity and deliver a large force to a spiked ball, but uses a much smaller range of motion and angular velocity to dink the ball over a block.

Weight and Length. Other factors to consider are the weight and length of the swinging bat, club, racket, or body segment. If other related factors are the same, a heavier implement or body segment will produce more force than will a lighter version of the same implement or segment. The same is true for a longer implement in comparison to a shorter one. In brief, it is the distance between the center of rotation of the swinging implement and the point at which the ball is struck that influences the velocity of the struck ball. This distance between the center of rotation and a given point of interest on a rotating body is known as the radius of rotation (see Figure 2).

Other factors being equal, the longer the radius of rotation for striking a ball, the greater the amount of force transferred to the ball. For this reason we use longer clubs (woods) for longer shots in golf and shorter clubs (irons) for shorter ones. Likewise, we tailor the length of the radius of rotation of moving body segments to the force requirements of the activity. A water polo player uses an entire extended arm to throw a long pass, but may use only forearm motion for a short toss. A skillful baseball pitcher uses considerable trunk rotation, making the center of rotation the spine, rather than the shoulder, to maximize the radius of rotation for delivery of the ball.

Number of Moving Segments and Coordination. The greater the force requirements of the motor skill, the larger the number of body segments that are likely to be involved. This makes sense for two reasons: increasing the number of moving segments increases the amount of body mass involved in force production, and the more segments that are involved, the longer the potential radius of rotation between the major joint center of rotation and the point of force application. To impart a large force to a ball, a server in tennis strikes the ball with the arm fully extended to maximize the ball's radius of rotation.

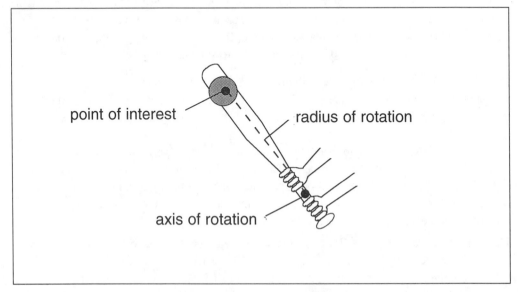

Figure 2. The radius of rotation is the distance between the center of rotation of a rotating body and a point of interest (in this case, the point of contact with a ball).

Motion of more than one body segment brings into consideration another important factor that affects effective delivery of force during motor skill execution. This is the timing and sequencing of joint motions, or coordination. Although coordination is a highly complex neuro-muscular phenomenon, two general observations may be made about the coordination of skill-ful movements. Skillful execution of ballistic activities such as throwing and kicking involves a sequential progression of segment motions, beginning with the more proximal (and larger) seg-ments and ending with the more distal (and smaller) segments. Alternatively, skillful execution of activities such as weight training, that require control of a heavy resistance object, tend to involve simultaneous joint motions.

Anthropometric Considerations and Body Position. People vary considerably in anthropome-try (height, weight, the shapes of body segments, etc.). We typically associate basketball play-ers with large height, gymnasts with small height and slight build, and football players with large body mass. Although diet and training certainly influence body weight and, to some extent, the shapes of the body segments, body size and shape is a function of genetic makeup. Although people of average anthropometric characteristics have the potential to participate in a wide range of sports, dance, and other physical activities, it is clear that some characteristics provide advan-tages for selected activities. As discussed previously, a body's inertia, or resistance to change in state of motion, is proportional to body mass. For this reason, people with large body masses tend to excel at activities where a large amount of stability is desirable. Playing the offensive line in football is an example. Alternatively the small body mass and short height of most gym-nasts are assets, since both height and mass contribute to what is called moment of inertia, or resistance to rotation. Rotation is easier with both shorter height and smaller body mass.

Although most adults do not have the anthropometric characteristics to excel at either playing the line in football or doing gymnastics, we can all manipulate body position to our advantage in other sports. Other factors being equal, we can enhance body stability by lowering our center of gravity (bending the knees), increasing the size of our base of support (widening the stance) in the direction of force resistance, and leaning in the opposite direction of any force to be resisted (lean-ing into an oncoming force or away from a pulling force). We also can improve our ability to rotate the body during a forward roll or a dive by assuming a tightly tucked position.

Fast movements of body segments can be facilitated by keeping them as close to the major center of rotation as possible. Good sprinters, for example, swing their legs forward with the knees in near maximum flexion, keeping the lower leg and foot as close to the center of rotation at the hip as possible. In throwing motions, a large amount of flexion at the elbow during the "cocking" phase allows forward motion with maximum speed, since the forearm and hand are positioned close to the center of rotation at the shoulder. Similarly, spins and twists executed by dancers, ice skaters, gymnasts, and divers are more efficient when the limbs are held close to the axis of rotation of the body.

How Is Force Effectively Applied to Projectiles?

What is the optimal angle of release for throwing a softball for maximum distance? Where along its flight path does a curve ball actually curve? How does spin affect the rebound of a ball served in tennis? The answers to these questions are related to the ways in which force is applied to the projected ball.

A projectile is a body that is moving through the air and subject only to the forces of gravity and air resistance. Projectiles include not only balls, Frisbees, boomerangs, javelins, and falling acorns, but also the human body during the performance of a jump or dive. In the absence of air resistance, the flight path or trajectory followed by a projectile is predetermined by the force of projection. When force is applied to project a body into the air, the magnitude, direction, and point of application of the applied force all exert potentially significant influences on the resulting flight path of the body.

Projection Speed. Typically of greatest importance is the magnitude of the applied force, which influences projection speed. Other related factors being the same, it is projection speed that determines the overall size of the trajectory. Successful shot, discus, javelin, and hammer throwers possess the muscle strength and power necessary to apply a large force to the implement.

Projection Angle and Relative Projection Height. The angle at which a body is initially projected determines the shape of the trajectory in the absence of air resistance. The flight path of a body projected at an angle between 0 and 90 degrees is a smooth, symmetrical curve, with left and right halves forming mirror images of one another when projection and landing heights are the same.

When the goal of projection is to achieve maximum horizontal distance, the optimum projection angle varies with what is called the relative projection height. The relative projection height is the difference between projection and landing heights. A football punted from a height of four feet that falls to the playing field has a relative projection height of four feet. A soccer ball kicked from the field and landing on the same field has a relative projection height of zero. When the relative projection height is zero, the optimum angle of projection for achieving maximum horizontal distance is 45 degrees. When projection height is higher than landing height, however, the optimal angle for projecting something for maximum distance is less than 45 degrees.

Performance Considerations. It is important to recognize that, because of human body biomechanics, there are often tradeoffs among projection speed, angle, and height. During a throw for maximum distance, for example, it is advantageous to maximize release height, since greater release height translates to longer flight time and greater distance. It would be a mistake, however, to release the ball at too large an angle of projection, since this would serve to shorten the distance achieved.

When the projectile is the human body during a jumping event, there also is a potential tradeoff between projection angle and projection speed. In the long jump, since take off and landing heights are the same, the theoretically optimum take-off angle is 45 degrees. Yet the take-off angles actually measured for elite long jumpers range from only 18 to 27 degrees (Hay 1986). This is because in order to achieve a 45 degree take-off angle, researchers estimate that jumpers would also decrease their horizontal speeds going into the jump by about 50 percent, resulting in much poorer performance (Hay 1986).

What External Forces Influence Motion?

Why is it difficult for some people to float? Why does a golf ball have dimples? How can a ballet dancer standing on one toe be perfectly balanced? The answers to these questions have to do with the actions of external forces.

Gravity. Gravity is an external force that is always present on earth. The force of gravity accelerates all bodies vertically toward the surface of the earth at a constant rate of about 9.8 m/s^2.

Our body weights are the product of our masses (physical matter) and gravitational acceleration. Astronauts on the surface of the moon experience much lighter body weights because, although their body masses are the same as on earth, there is less gravitational acceleration on the moon.

It is important to recognize that gravitational acceleration is constant and that it acts equally on all bodies, regardless of their size, shape, or mass. Neglecting aerodynamic factors, this means that objects dropped from the same height fall at the same speed.

Buoyancy and Floatation. Buoyancy is an external force that can counteract the force of gravity. Buoyant force acts vertically upward. The size of the buoyant force acting on a body in the water is proportional to the amount of body volume submerged beneath the surface of the water. Of course, when a person is in the water, gravitational force continues to act. A person is able to float only if he or she has sufficient body volume to generate a buoyant force greater than or equal to body weight. (In the presence of these two opposing vertical forces, the action of the net force produces either floating or sinking.) Individuals who have difficulty floating typically have high ratios of lean body mass to fat, or relatively high body weights relative to their body sizes. One simple strategy for improving the ability to float is to hold a large breath of air in the lungs, thereby increasing body volume with a negligible addition of body weight.

Resistance Forces. Several types of external force act to slow the motion of moving bodies. One such force is friction, a force that acts opposite the direction of motion or intended motion at the interface between two surfaces in contact. Friction increases with the roughness or interactivity of the surfaces in contact and with the amount of force pressing the surfaces together (often the weight of an object sitting on a surface). The magnitude of friction varies, being greatest just before motion is initiated and least after motion occurs.

Although friction can sometimes be a nuisance, as when we are trying to rearrange heavy pieces of furniture in a room, it also can be very useful. Without friction, for example, our feet would slide out from under us each time we tried to take a step. A great deal of sports equipment is designed to optimize the amount of friction generated. This is true not only of athletic shoes designed for specific sports and even for different playing surfaces, but for racket, bat, and club grips, for the gloves used in many sports, and for the tires used in different types of cycling competitions.

It is useful to remember that the nature of both surfaces affects the size of the frictional force. The friction between the soles of a pair of leather shoes and a sidewalk may provide excellent traction when the sidewalk is dry, but very poor traction when the sidewalk is icy. Likewise, whereas ballet shoes are constructed to provide the proper amount of friction for sliding and pivoting on a smooth wooden floor, they would not provide proper traction on surfaces such as concrete or asphalt.

Frictional force is dramatically reduced for rolling motions as compared to sliding motions, and when a layer of fluid is present between the surfaces in contact. Within the human body, the layer of fluid present at synovial joints reduces the amount of friction present to only about 17 to 33 percent of that produced by a skate on ice under the same load (Brand 1979).

A resistance force known as drag also opposes the motion of bodies moving through fluids and through air. Drag increases with factors such as the roughness and area of the body's surface, the relative speed of the body moving through the fluid, and the density and viscosity of the fluid. Streamlining of body shape, alternatively, serves to reduce drag. In speed-related sports such as swimming, skiing, skating, and cycling, athletes wear tightly fitting apparel made of ultra-smooth fabrics and assume crouched (streamlined) body positions to reduce drag. The dimples on a golf ball are carefully designed to produce a streamlining effect of the air flow around the ball during its flight. During swimming, the generation of waves by the swimmer is also a source of drag that increases with up and down motion of the body in the water. Swimming pool lane lines are engineered to dissipate wave action.

Lift and the Magnus Effect. Lift is another force that can affect the motion of bodies moving through both air and water. Although the term "lift" suggests upward movement, lift is directed perpendicular to the relative fluid flow and can be oriented in any direction. Objects that are shaped like a foil are capable of generating lift (see Figure 3). The special shape of the foil creates a difference in pressure on the top and bottom that creates a force directed toward the foil's flat side. Lift increases with the velocity of the foil relative to the fluid, the fluid density, and the surface area of the flat side of the foil.

A swimmer's hands sufficiently resemble a foil shape when viewed from a lateral perspective that as the hands slice rapidly through the water they generate lift forces directed toward the palm. Lift is an important contributor to propulsion in a number of swimming strokes, particularly the breast stroke (Schleihauf 1979).

When a projectile is shaped and oriented such that it generates lift in the upward direction, the result is a longer trajectory and greater horizontal distance. The shapes of the discus, football, Frisbee, and boomerang are sufficiently foil-like that they generate lift when properly oriented with respect to the relative air flow.

Balls can generate lift by spinning. Like lift generated by a foil, the spinning action of a ball creates a difference in pressure on opposite sides which produces a force in the direction in which the spin was imparted. This force, known as the Magnus effect, is what causes curve balls to curve and tennis serves hit with top spin to drop. The path of a spinning ball is a smooth arc. Magnus effect also affects rebound from a horizontal surface. A ball with top spin rebounds on a lower trajectory, and a ball with back spin rebounds on a higher trajectory as compared to the same ball without spin.

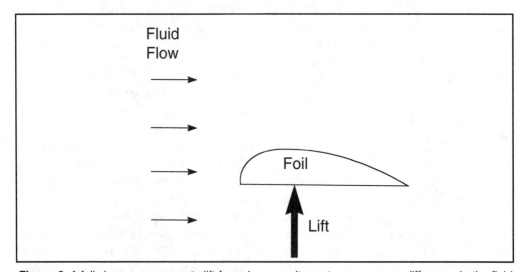

Figure 3. A foil shape can generate lift force because it creates a pressure difference in the fluid on the curved and flat sides of the foil.

What Biomechanical Concepts Are Important for Safe Participation in Everyday Activities?

Why is the old adage, "lift with your legs and not with your back," not necessarily good advice? Should exercises that are taxing to the lower back muscles be avoided? When is it appropriate to perform fast, ballistic exercises? The answers to these questions are based on biomechanical concepts.

Lifting and Carrying. Because lifting and carrying even light objects can place an added load on the spine, understanding the biomechanical factors that contribute to spinal loading can help prevent back pain or injury. When the body is in an upright position, body weight, the weight of any load held in the hands, and tension in the spinal ligaments and muscles all contribute to compression on the spine.

When a load is held in front of the body, tension in the spinal muscles increases. These muscles must produce enough torque to balance the torque generated by the load to prevent the body from toppling forward. To minimize the work that must be performed by the back muscles during lifting and carrying, the load should be positioned close to the body.

For this same reason, workers have been advised to "lift with the legs and not with the back." This translates to maintaining the trunk in a relatively upright position when lifting an object from the floor. The benefit of this style of lifting is that it minimizes the flexor (forward leaning) torque generated by the trunk that must be counteracted by the spinal extensor muscles. Leg lifting is often impractical, however, because of the awkward nature of the task or simply because it is more physiologically taxing than back lifting (McGill & Norman 1993).

It may, in fact, be more important to focus on biomechanical factors other than use of the legs during lifting. One alternative is to maintain a normal curve in the lower back, rather than allowing the lumbar spine to flex (sag forward) during a lift (McGill & Norman 1993). This enables lumbar extensor muscles to better control the load and helps to even the force distribution on the spine.

Other research-based advice is to avoid lateral flexion—or side bending—and twisting during lifting. Other factors being equal, researchers have estimated that compression on the L4/L5 vertebral joint is nearly doubled with side bending, and more than tripled with twisting as compared to flexion (McGill & Norman 1993). These increased loads appear to be due to tension development in antagonist trunk muscles (McGill 1992). Asymmetrical left-right loading of the trunk also should be avoided because of the increased load on the spine due to side bending torque (Drury et al. 1989, Mital & Kromodihardjo 1986).

Another factor that has been shown to affect spinal loading is body movement speed. Lifting in a very rapid or jerking fashion dramatically increases the forces acting on the spine, as well as tension in the spinal muscles (Hall 1985). This is one of the reasons that resistance training exercises should normally be performed in a slow, controlled fashion.

Exercising. Protecting the lower back should be a priority when exercising. This does not imply, however, that the back muscles should not be exercised. In fact, weakened back and abdominal muscles are known to be predisposing factors for lower back pain.

To avoid injury, it is particularly important that back exercises be performed in a slow, controlled fashion. Those exercises involving lumbar hyperextension also should be stopped before the end of the range of motion is reached (Liemohn 1993). Sit-up type exercises should always be performed with the hips and knees in flexion, with the trunk elevated no more than approximately 30 degrees. This ensures that the abdominal muscles are exercised without involvement of the hip flexors. Over-development of the powerful hip flexor muscles can promote exaggerated lumbar lordosis, which predisposes the individual to lower back pain.

All exercises performed for strength development should be performed in a slow and controlled fashion. This minimizes the development of momentum of the resistance, thus promoting involvement of the working muscles throughout the range of motion. It also minimizes the likelihood of injury derived from accidentally exceeding a joint's normal range of motion.

In accordance with the principle of specificity of training, however, athletes training to increase movement speed or develop muscle power need to exercise with quick, ballistic type movements. To avoid injuries, it is important that these athletes develop an adequate strength base prior to engaging in exercises that are more challenging to the musculoskeletal system.

One popular and relatively inexpensive form of resistance training involves the use of free weights. Proponents of free weights point to the fact that the user must control the motion of the weight while at the same time maintaining balance. A disadvantage of free weights, however, is that if the load is jerked at the beginning of the lift, the weight's momentum can carry it along its path of motion with little contribution from the working muscles. Proper technique when using free weights includes not arching the back and avoiding full knee flexion to prevent injury. It is also important to use a spotter when working with heavy weights.

A variety of resistance machines and devices is available. The spectrum ranges from large, heavy, expensive machines to portable or "fold-up" equipment designed for use in the home. The resistance can be provided by weights, hydraulic or air compression cylinders, springs, or elastic cables.

Although resistance for legitimate exercises can be provided by different means, beware of products advertised to provide exercise benefits with minimal effort on the part of the user. Research has shown that some popular exercise devices provide no benefit to the user (Ross et al. 1993).

Placing Biomechanics Concepts in the Curriculum

Learning takes place most effectively when the learner is ready to learn. Because biomechanics concepts span different levels of complexity, the table beginning on page 88 contains suggestions for the introduction of specific concepts by grade level. The benchmarks and emphases described for National Standard 2, "Applies movement concepts and principles to the learning and development of motor skills," as well as National Standard 1, "Demonstrates competency in many movement forms and proficiency in a few movement forms," were used as a guide for matching concepts with grade levels. Most of the concepts are repeated across two or more grade levels because of the value of repetition in the learning process. By the end of the twelfth grade students should be able to apply the biomechanics concepts presented in learning new motor skills.

Integrating Biomechanics into Instruction

This section suggests ways in which teachers can incorporate biomechanics concepts into instruction. The intention is that while the examples provided in the box can be incorporated into class instruction, they also can trigger ideas for other activities appropriate to particular grade levels, class sizes, and student backgrounds and skill levels. In all cases, reinforcement of these concepts through appropriate questioning of students following the activity will facilitate student understanding and retention of the concepts.

Integrating Biomechanics into Instruction

Example 1: Early and Upper Elementary School

Concept: Off-center application of force to a ball causes the ball to spin.

Pair early elementary students, and have each pair bounce a ball back and forth between them. Ask students as a group if they can:

1. Toss the ball with no spin.
2. Toss the ball with forward (or top) spin.
3. Toss the ball with backward (or back) spin.
4. Toss the ball with spin to the right, and then to the left.

Question the group about how they tossed the ball under each condition, and about the effects of spin on the ball's path. Students should determine that applying force off-center causes spin in the direction of the force deviation from center, and that the ball tends to rebound in the direction of the spin.

A game can be made of this exercise for older students by setting up circular targets on the floor and having them toss balls at the targets using different spin conditions at the targets.

Example 2: High School Example

Concept: The difficulty of an exercise is affected by the moment arm as well as the magnitude of the resistance.

1. Have students hold a light dumbbell in their dominant hand with the arm horizontally extended to the point of fatigue while a partner times them with a stop watch.
2. Repeat the process with the same student holding the weight in the non-dominant hand, this time with the arm positioned horizontally and the elbow at a 90 degree angle.
3. Have the students switch roles and repeat.

This exercise is designed to illustrate the significance of the moment arm of a resistance. Even when using the non-dominant arm, students should be able to hold the weight longer when the elbow is at a 90 degree angle, because the distance between the weight and the center of rotation at the shoulder is much shorter than when the arm is fully extended. This exercise can also be repeated with several different weights to show that both moment arm and weight magnitude contribute to the difficulty of the exercise. Ask students what the implications of this exercise suggest for lifting and carrying a load. (The load should always be positioned as close to the trunk as possible to minimize the moment arm of the load with respect to the spine and thereby to minimize the work that must be performed by the low back muscles.)

Example 3: Upper Elementary and Middle School

Concept: The force generated by the moving body increases with the weight of the moving segments, movement range of motion, and number of involved body segments.

1. Have students experiment with kicking a ball from the ground for maximum distance under the following conditions:
• Knee and hip in slight flexion but motionless, kicking motion involves ankle dorsiflexion only.
• Ankle and hip stationary, kicking motion involves knee extension only.
• Hip and thigh are stable, kicking motion involves knee extension and ankle dorsiflexion.
• Knee and ankle are stable and leg is straight, kicking motion involves hip flexion only.

2. This exercise also can be performed by having students experiment with throwing a ball for maximum distance under some of the following conditions:
• Using wrist motion only.
• Using wrist and elbow motion, but with the upper arm remaining stationary.
• Using wrist, elbow, and shoulder motions, but with the trunk remaining stationary.
• Using all arm segments, and with trunk rotation encouraged.
Students should determine that an increase in swinging leg segment mass and in movement range of motion increases the distance the ball is kicked, and that generally, using more joint actions increases kick distance. Students also can try kicking a ball with no preparatory step, one preparatory step, two preparatory steps, and a run-up.

Example 4: Upper Elementary and Middle School
Concept: The weight, angular velocity, and length of the radius of rotation of a striking implement should be matched with the force requirements of the activity.
Students should work in pairs. Have one partner toss easy softball pitches for the other partner to bat. Have the students experiment hitting the ball under the following conditions:
1. Using bats of different sizes (weights).
2. Swinging a given bat at different angular speeds.
3. Choking up on the bat.
Students should determine that if other relevant factors are equal, they can hit a ball farther with a heavier bat, a faster bat swing, and a larger radius of rotation. For some students, however, there may be a trade-off between bat weight and the angular speed at which the student can swing the bat. Students should determine that a bat that is too heavy places them at a disadvantage, since it may make it more difficult to make contact with pitched balls.

Example 5: Upper Elementary and Middle School
Concept: Streamlining the body reduces drag and increases movement speed.
Have students on bicycles change quickly from a traditional crouched seating position for cycling to a fully upright seated position and then back again while going down a hill at a relatively fast speed.
Make sure that this experiment is carried out under safe conditions. There should be no vehicular traffic, and cyclists should be spread out. Students will experience dramatic changes in speed, with drag slowing them down in the upright position. This activity can also be done with students on roller skates, roller blades, ice skates, or skis.

Example 6: Middle School and High School
Concept: To maximize stability, lower the center of gravity and lean opposite the applied force.
Divide students into pairs of approximately equal size and strength. Have students practice non-swimming rescues using a pole, with no particular instructions. Then have students repeat the rescues under the following conditions:
• The rescuer must remain in an upright position and may not lean backward.
• The rescuer lies on his or her stomach on the pool deck and reaches with the pole to the person in the water.

After the activity, question the students as to what variables contribute to success in a reaching rescue in swimming. They should identify lowering the center of gravity and leaning opposite the applied force.

Example 7: High School
Concept: Skillful coordination of ballistic motions involves a sequential progression of segment motions, beginning with the more proximal segments and ending with the more distal segments. Have students experiment with a badminton clear for maximum distance under some of the following conditions:
• Using shoulder motion only, with the elbow and wrist remaining firm.
• Using shoulder and elbow motion, with the wrist remaining firm.
• Using shoulder, elbow, and wrist motions, but with the trunk remaining stationary.
• Using all arm segments, and with trunk rotation encouraged.
From this activity, students should determine that badminton clear distance is maximized by motion at all upper extremity joints. Ask students to identify the order in which these joints are called into action when a clear is executed skillfully. It may be helpful for one or more skilled students or the instructor to demonstrate several skillful clears.

Assessing Student Learning

Students should be able to use biomechanics concepts in class to improve their own performance and out of class to refine their motor skills. Many of the techniques teachers can use to assess learning are described in detail in *Moving into the Future: National Standards for Physical Education* (NASPE, 1995) under Standard 2, and more generally in Chapter 1 of this book

Checking for Understanding

Thirty-Second Wonders. Student understanding of biomechanics concepts is perhaps best assessed on a lesson-by-lesson basis through thoughtful questioning. Once students can describe the characteristics of a skillful performance, an effective follow-up question for the teacher to ask is, "Why?" For example: "Why do batters choke up on the bat in order to bunt a ball?" and, "Why do skilled gymnasts tend to be short?"

Written Tests. Periodic written examinations also can be constructed to more formally assess student understanding. Sample questions include: "Why does holding air in the lungs make it easier to float?" "Why are muscles stronger when the body is in some positions as compared to other positions?" and, "What is the optimal angle of release for throwing a softball for maximum distance?"

Peer Observation/Self-Assessment. Students can conduct qualitative observations of other students and of themselves on videotape. Once students have achieved some level of familiarity with a new motor skill, and common errors have been discussed, performance may benefit from careful qualitative observations followed by appropriate peer feedback. Students can work in pairs, with one student practicing the skill while the other carefully observes for errors. Following are some hints for maximizing the effectiveness of peer observations:

Table 1. Critical Student Concepts, K–6

Kindergarten	Second Grade	Fourth Grade	Sixth Grade
Biomechanics Concept I: What is force?	*Biomechanics Concept I: What is force?*	*Biomechanics Concept I: What is force?*	*Biomechanics Concept I: What is force?*
A force is a push or pull.	A force is a push or pull.	Force can cause both motion and change in shape of the body acted upon.	Force can cause both motion and change in shape of the body acted upon.
	More force must be applied to move heavy objects than light objects.	To produce spin on a ball, apply force away from the center of the ball.	Spin occurs when a force is applied anywhere on the object except through the center of gravity.
		For every action there is an equal and opposite reaction.	When opposite forces act on a body, movement occurs in the direction of the larger force.
		A body's balance point is called its center of gravity.	
Biomechanics Concept II: How is force effectively generated?	*Biomechanics Concept II: How is force effectively generated?*	*Biomechanics Concept II: How is force effectively generated?*	*Biomechanics Concept II: How is force effectively generated?*
Our muscles move our bodies.	Muscles move our bodies by producing force.	Large muscles like those in the legs can produce larger forces than the smaller muscles in the hands.	Large muscles like those in the legs can produce larger forces than the smaller muscles in the hands.
	Muscles act by pulling on the bones to which they are attached.	It is possible to tense a muscle without body motion occurring.	Muscles are arranged in functional pairs that can move our body segments in opposite directions.

Table 1. Critical Student Concepts, K–6

Biomechanics Concept III: How is force effectively matched to motor skill requirements?	*Biomechanics Concept III: How is force effectively matched to motor skill requirements?*	*Biomechanics Concept III: How is force effectively matched to motor skill requirements?*
Fast movements tend to produce more force than slow movements.	Larger body segments tend to produce more force than smaller body segments.	When we tense both muscles in a functional pair equally, no body motion occurs.
Lowering the body's center of gravity (bending the knees) increases ability to maintain balance (stability).	Increasing the size, number, or speed of moving body segments tends to increase the force generated.	Increasing the range of motion through which body segments are rotated tends to increase the force generated.
		Movement speed and the number of moving body segments should be adjusted in accordance with the force requirements of the activity.
		Longer or heavier bats and clubs tend to produce more force than shorter or lighter ones.

Table 1. Critical Student Concepts, K–6

Biomechanics Concept IV: How is force effectively applied to projectiles?	*Biomechanics Concept IV: How is force effectively applied to projectiles?*	*Biomechanics Concept IV: How is force effectively applied to projectiles?*	*Biomechanics Concept IV: How is force effectively applied to projectiles?*
The faster a ball is thrown or kicked, the farther it tends to go.	The faster a ball is thrown or kicked, the farther it tends to go.	The speed and angle at which a ball is thrown or kicked both help determine its flight path.	Neglecting air resistance, the initial speed, angle, and height of projection determine a projectile's trajectory.
	The greater the angle at which a ball is thrown or kicked, the greater the projectile's angles of ascent and descent during its trajectory.	A jumper's take-off speed and angle help determine the jumper's path in the air.	The greater the height from which something is projected, the longer it tends to remain in the air.
Biomechanics Concept V: What external forces influence motion?	*Biomechanics Concept V: What external forces influence motion?*	*Biomechanics Concept V: What external forces influence motion?*	*Biomechanics Concept V: What external forces influence motion?*
It is easier to float in water while holding a big breath.	It is easier to float in water while holding a big breath.	Increases in weight or the roughness of the surfaces in contact increase the friction between a moving body and the surface underneath it.	Increases in contact force or the roughness of the surfaces in contact produce more friction between the two objects in contact.
	It is harder to push heavier objects than lighter objects across a table or floor surface.	Gravity is the force that causes objects to fall to the earth.	Gravity causes objects dropped from the same height to fall at the same speed (neglecting air resistance).
			Streamlined shapes and smooth surfaces reduce air and water resistance on a moving body.

Table 1. Critical Student Concepts, K–6

Biomechanics Concept VI: What biomechanical concepts are important for safe participation in everyday physical activities?	*Biomechanics Concept VI: What biomechanical concepts are important for safe participation in everyday physical activities?*	*Biomechanics Concept VI: What biomechanical concepts are important for safe participation in everyday physical activities?*	*Biomechanics Concept VI: What biomechanical concepts are important for safe participation in everyday physical activities?*
When lifting or carrying something, it is important to hold it close to your body.	When lifting or carrying something, it is important to hold it close to your body.	When lifting or carrying something, it is important to hold it close to your body.	When lifting or carrying something, it is important to hold it close to your body.
	When lifting something, it is important to bend your knees.	When lifting something, it is important to bend your knees and not let your back slump.	When lifting something, it is important to bend your knees and not let your back slump.
		Always do sit-up exercises with knees bent.	Always face the object you are lifting so you do not have to twist or bend to the side.
			Always do sit-up exercises with knees bent and elevate your trunk only about 30 degrees.
			It is usually best to perform lifts and exercises in a slow and controlled fashion.

Table 1. Critical Student Concepts, 8–12

Eighth Grade	Tenth Grade	Twelfth Grade
Biomechanics Concept I: What is force?	*Biomechanics Concept I: What is force?*	*Biomechanics Concept I: What is force?*
When more than one force acts on a body, the effect on the body is the result of the sum of the sizes and directions of the forces.	The vector sum of all forces acting on a body is called the net force, and the vector sum of all torque acting on a body is called the net torque.	A body's state of motion is determined by the net forces and torques acting upon it.
Rotational force is called torque.	Motion of a body along a line is produced by the action of a net force, and rotational motion of a body is produced by a net torque.	A force's magnitude and moment arm contribute equally to the torque generated by the force at the body's center of rotation.
Both the size of the force and the distance of the force from the center of rotation contribute to torque.	When a body is stationary no net force or torque is acting upon it.	A body in equilibrium can be either stationary or moving at a constant speed in a given direction.
Equilibrium is a state of balanced forces and torque.	The shortest distance between a force's line of action and a body's center of rotation is called the moment arm of the force.	
	A body in equilibrium can be either stationary or moving at a constant speed in a given direction.	

Table 1. Critical Student Concepts, 8–12

Biomechanics Concept II: How is force effectively generated?	*Biomechanics Concept II: How is force effectively generated?*	*Biomechanics Concept II: How is force effectively generated?*
The terms used to describe a decrease, increase, and no change in the length of a tensed muscle are concentric, eccentric, and isometric.	Joint torque is the product of a force's magnitude and the force's moment arm with respect to the center of rotation at the joint.	Body movements occur in response to net joint torque.
Muscles with larger cross-sectional area can produce more force than smaller muscles.	Both muscle forces and resistance forces produce joint torque.	A change in the moment arms of the involved muscles or the resistance forces can increase or decrease the relative difficulty of an exercise.
	Body movements occur in response to net joint torque.	Forcefully stretching a muscle just prior to concentric contraction promotes the subsequent force of the contraction.
	A change in the moment arms of the involved muscles or the resistance forces can increase or decrease the relative difficulty of an exercise.	
Biomechanics Concept III: How is force effectively matched to motor skill requirements?	*Biomechanics Concept III: How is force effectively matched to motor skill requirements?*	*Biomechanics Concept III: How is force effectively matched to motor skill requirements?*
Movement speed, range of motion, and the number of moving body segments should be adjusted in accordance with the force requirements of the activity.	Movement speed, range of motion, and the number of moving body segments should be adjusted in accordance with the force requirements of the activity.	Movement speed, range of motion, joint extension, and the number of moving body segments should be adjusted in accordance with the force requirements of the activity.

Table 1. Critical Student Concepts, 8–12

The longer the distance between a bat, club, or racket's center of rotation and contact point with a ball (radius of rotation), the greater the amount of force that tends to be delivered to the ball.

Heavier people tend to be better at activities involving stability.

Lighter people tend to be better at activities involving quick motions or rotations.

Biomechanics Concept IV: How is force effectively applied to projectiles?

Neglecting air resistance, the initial speed, angle, and height of projection determine a projectile's trajectory.

Extension of the joints of moving body segments increases the radius of rotation for throwing or striking motions.

The radius of rotation for a bat or club striking a ball should be adjusted in accordance with the force requirements of the activity.

Positioning moving body segments close to the major joint center of rotation facilitates faster movement.

Heavier people tend to be better at activities involving stability and shorter people tend to be better at activities involving body rotation.

Biomechanics Concept IV: How is force effectively applied to projectiles?

Projection speed is usually more important than projection angle and relative projection height when projecting for maximum horizontal distance.

Bats, clubs, and rackets should be selected by both weight and length to match the anthropometric characteristics of the user.

Positioning moving body segments close to the major joint center of rotation facilitates fast movement by reducing moment of inertia.

Body anthropometry can make skillful performance of some motor skills easier or harder.

Biomechanics Concept IV: How is force effectively applied to projectiles?

Projection speed is usually more important than projection angle and relative projection height when projecting for maximum horizontal distance.

Table 1. Critical Student Concepts, 8–12

The greater the height from which something is projected, the longer it tends to remain in the air.	The shape of a projectile's trajectory is symmetrical in the absence of air resistance.	When projection and landing heights are equal, a projectile's landing speed is the same as its projection speed.
The optimum projection angle for maximum projection distance is 45 degrees when projection and landing heights are the same, but less than 45 degrees when projection height is greater than landing height.	Increasing relative projection height or projection angle tends to increase flight time.	There are tradeoffs among optimum projection speed, angle, and height when projecting for maximum horizontal distance when the human body is either applying force to a projectile or serving as the projectile.

Biomechanics Concept V: What external forces influence motion?	*Biomechanics Concept V: What external forces influence motion?*	*Biomechanics Concept V: What external forces influence motion?*
Buoyancy increases with the volume of the submerged body.	Whether a body sinks or floats depends on whether the buoyant force produced by submerged body volume is greater or less than body weight.	Individuals with high body density (and low body fat) have difficulty floating.
Gravity causes objects dropped from the same height to fall at the same speed (neglecting air resistance).	Friction is reduced when a layer of fluid is present between two surfaces in contact.	In sport and daily living activities it is desirable to optimize the amount of acting friction.
Streamlined shapes and smooth surfaces reduce air and water resistance on a moving body.		The effect of spin on a projected ball is constant throughout the ball's trajectory.

Table 1. Critical Student Concepts, 8–12

A ball with top spin rebounds on a lower trajectory and a ball with back spin rebounds on a higher trajectory than the same ball without spin.

Drag is a resistance force that slows the motion of a body traveling through air or water.

Lift is a force produced by a foil shape or spin that alters the path of a body moving through air or water.

Fluid forces increase with the density and viscosity of the fluid.

Biomechanics Concept VI: What biomechanical concepts are important for safe participation in everyday physical activities?

When lifting or carrying something, it is important to hold it close to your body.

When lifting something, it is important to bend your knees and not let your back slump.

Always face the object you are lifting so you do not have to twist or bend to the side.

Biomechanics Concept VI: What biomechanical concepts are important for safe participation in everyday physical activities?

When lifting or carrying something, it is important to hold it close to your body.

When lifting something, it is important to bend your knees and maintain normal spinal posture.

Always face the object you are lifting so you do not have to twist or bend to the side.

Biomechanics Concept VI: What biomechanical concepts are important for safe participation in everyday physical activities?

To minimize the load on the spine and back muscles during lifting, avoid bending or twisting, keep the trunk erect with normal spinal posture, and position the load close to your body.

Always do sit-up exercises with knees bent and elevate your trunk only about 30 degrees.

Table 1. Critical Student Concepts, 8–12

Always do sit-up exercises with knees bent and elevate your trunk only about 30 degrees.	Always do sit-up exercises with knees bent and elevate your trunk only about 30 degrees.	Perform exercises in a slow and controlled fashion unless training for muscular power development.
	It is usually best to perform lifts and exercises in a slow and controlled fashion.	Always use a spotter when exercising with heavy free weights.
	Always use a spotter when exercising with heavy free weights.	

1. If possible, select a setting that is well-lit and free of distractions.
2. Choose a viewing angle and distance that will provide an optimal perspective.
3. Observe several executions of a skill before formulating a diagnosis.
4. Pay attention to auditory as well as visual information.
5. Try to focus on performance execution as well as performance outcome.
6. Provide feedback to the performer that is specific, factual, and nonjudgmental.
7. Avoid offering too much feedback at once.

Group Projects. Students can work in small groups to analyze their videotaped performances. Use of videotape has several advantages: the performer can view and analyze the performance along with others, and a taped performance can be frozen at critical points, played in slow motion, or replayed repeatedly.

Concluding Comments

Biomechanical concepts provide a basis for understanding the ways in which human movements in exercise, sport, dance, and daily living activities can be executed safely and skillfully. An understanding of biomechanical concepts and their applications is an important part of the cognitive foundation for a physically educated person. Understanding why human movement mechanics differ from person to person and from performance to performance can enhance the experience of acquiring or maintaining a physically active lifestyle and facilitate lifelong learning.

How Can I Learn More?

A growing number of resources related to biomechanics are available on the World Wide Web. They can be accessed by searching the key word "biomechanics." Selected textbooks and other books related to biomechanics are listed below.

Chaffin, D. B., & Andersson, G. B. J. (1991). *Occupational biomechanics* (2nd ed.). New York: John Wiley & Sons.

Grabiner, M. D. (Ed.). (1993). *Current issues in biomechanics.* Champaign, IL: Human Kinetics.

Hall, S. J. (1995). *Basic biomechanics* (2nd ed.). St. Louis, MO: Mosby.

Hay, J. G. (1993). *The biomechanics of sports techniques* (4th ed.). Englewood Cliffs, NJ: Prentice Hall.

Hudson, J. L. (1995). Core concepts of kinesiology. *Journal of Physical Education, Recreation, and Dance,* May-June, 54-60.

Schrier, E. W., & Allman, W. F. (Eds.). (1984). *Newton at the bat.* New York: Macmillan-Charles Scribner's Sons.

References

Brand, R. A. (1979). Joint lubrication. In J. A. Albright & R. A. Brand (Eds.), *The scientific basis of orthopedics.* New York: Appleton-Century-Crofts.

Chaffin, D. B., & Andersson, G. B. J. (1991). *Occupational biomechanics* (2nd ed.). New York: John Wiley & Sons.

Drury, C. G., et al. (1989). Symmetric and asymmetric manual materials handling, part 2: Biomechanics. *Ergonomics, 32,* 565-583.

Hall, S. J. (1985). Effect of attempted lifting speed on forces and torque exerted on the lumbar spine, *Medicine and Science in Sports and Exercise, 17,* 440-444.

Hay, J. G. (1986). The biomechanics of the long jump. *Exercise and Sport Science Reviews, 14,* 401–446.

Liemohn, W. (1993). Exercise considerations for the back. In J. L. Durstein, A. C. King, P. L. Painter,

J. L. Roitman, L. D. Zwiren, & W. L. Kenney (Eds.). *ACSM's resource manual for guidelines for exercise testing and prescription* (2nd ed.), pp. 48-58.

McGill, S. M. (1992). A myoelectrically based dynamic three-dimensional model to predict loads on lumbar spine tissues during lateral bending, *Journal of Biomechanics, 25*, 395-414.

McGill, S. M., & Norman, R. W. (1993). Low back biomechanics in industry: the prevention of injury through safer lifting. In M. D. Grabiner (Ed.), *Current issues in biomechanics.* Champaign, IL: Human Kinetics.

Mital, A., & Kromodihardjo, S. (1986). Kinetic analysis of manual lifting activities: Part II: Biomechanical analysis of task variables, International *Journal of Industrial Ergonomics, 1*, 91–.

Ross, M., Hall, S. J., Breit, N., & Britten, S. (1993). Effect of a lumbar support device on muscle activity during abdominal exercise. *Journal of Strength and Conditioning Research, 7*, (4), 219-223.

Schleihauf, R. E. (1979). A hydrodynamic analysis of swimming propulsion. In J. Terauds & E. Bedingfield (Eds.), *Swimming III.* Baltimore, MD: University Park Press.

Glossary

Biomechanics: study of biological organisms using concepts from mechanics.

Center of gravity: a unique point around which a body's weight is balanced at a given time.

Concentric: involving shortening of a tensed muscle.

Drag: a force that acts to slow the motion of a body moving through a fluid.

Eccentric: involving lengthening of a tensed muscle.

Equilibrium: a state involving a balance of all acting forces and torque; net force and net torque are zero.

Force: a push or a pull in a linear direction.

Friction: force acting at the interface of bodies in contact that opposes the direction of motion.

Gravity: a force accelerating all bodies vertically toward the surface of the earth at about 9.8 m/s2.

Inertia: resistance to change in state of motion.

Isometric: involving no change in the length of a tensed muscle.

Lift: a fluid force directed perpendicular to the relative fluid flow.

Magnus effect: fluid force that causes a regularly shaped curve in the trajectory of a spinning object.

Moment arm: shortest distance between a force's line of action and the center of rotation of the body acted upon.

Moment of inertia: resistance to rotational motion.

Net force: the single force resulting from the vector addition of all forces acting on a body at a given time

Projectile: a body in free-fall subject only to the forces of gravity and air resistance.

Radius of rotation: distance from the center of rotation to a point of interest on the rotating body.

Reaction force: force generated by a body in response to a force acting upon it, equal in size and opposite in direction to the original force.

Tension: a pulling force.

Torque: rotary force.

Chapter 5

Exercise Physiology

By Judith B. Alter

The most vital term to associate with physiology is "dynamic." Movement is basic to life; it is the key to everything human beings do—from breathing and thinking to running and skiing. The study of exercise physiology provides an understanding of how the cardiorespiratory, digestive, and muscle/neural systems function in the moving body. The activities in which students engage during physical education class and leisure activities such as cycling, playing soccer, and dancing characteristically utilize the entire body. They require muscles to be strong and flexible, bodies to be aerobically fit and energetic, and minds to be mentally alert.

What Is Exercise Physiology?

The study of exercise physiology focuses on what happens inside the bodies of human beings when they exercise. Exercise physiology, a subdiscipline of physiology, incorporates information from other disciplines such as chemistry, physics, and anatomy. Exercise physiologists combine what they learn from looking under the microscope in their laboratories (*in vitro*) with actual experiences of thousands of people they have studied (*in vivo*). Information from exercise physiology includes the structure and chemical activity of human cells, tissues, and systems, and—most important—how the components in these systems interact in the human body.

Exercise physiologists have demonstrated the relationship between the kind of daily vigorous activity in which people engage and their mental and physical health. They studied the activities people do during their work and non-work time and what people eat and do not eat, and they learned how diet and exercise levels influence life expectancy and lifetime well being.

Why Is Exercise Physiology Important?

For many years, exercise physiologists have correlated regular physical activity with health, well being, and longevity. The vital importance of physical activity is emphasized in the 1996 Surgeon General's Report, *Physical Activity and Health*. The authors of that report decry the fact that "Nearly half of American youth 12 to 21 years of age are not vigorously active on a regular basis. Moreover, physical activity declines dramatically during adolescence" (p.10). Physical educators have watched this decline for several decades. This report simply verifies the necessity for implementing regular physical fitness programs in schools and convincing youth to participate in these life enhancing activities.

Judith B. Alter is associate professor of dance, Department of World Arts and Cultures, University of California at Los Angeles.

Knowledge about how the cells and tissues of the moving body work enables people to prepare correctly for any physical exercise: to warm up properly, to identify possible problems such as excessive fatigue, and to find solutions when problems arise. These solutions range from physical ones (such as undertaking an aerobic training program), to nutritional ones (such as eating more complex carbohydrates and less sugar). This kind of knowledge has helped athletes improve their performance to the extent that they have set new records.

Interval training (IT) helped runners break the four-minute mile record. Improved equipment, such as the cushioning in the soles and heels of running shoes, has helped reduce the number of serious injuries that occur. In addition, this knowledge about exercise physiology has enabled men and women to participate in physical activities during their entire lives, not just during their teens and twenties. Learning about how the cardiorespiratory, muscular, and digestive systems work in the moving body gives students real power in many ways.

Linking Exercise Physiology to the National Standards

Exercise physiology is central to two of the seven National Standards for what students need to know and be able to do in physical education:

- National Standard 3. Exhibits a physically active lifestyle.
- National Standard 4. Achieves and maintains a health-enhancing level of physical fitness.

These standards aim at countering the increasingly inactive lifestyle of many Americans. They align with the information and national guidelines experts have advocated for more than 30 years, going back to the advent of the Presidential Physical Fitness Programs. The authors of the 1996 Surgeon General's report, which aligns with the March 1997 report compiled by experts at the National Centers for Disease Control and Prevention, reiterate that regular physical activity prolongs life and diminishes the threat of serious and even life threatening diseases such as cardiovascular disease, colon cancer, non-insulin dependent diabetes mellitus, osteoarthritis, osteoporosis, and diseases related to obesity.

Regular physical activity has positive effects on mental health, is an established means of reducing stress, and may reduce or prevent serious depression. A fit life is fun. And it is free, give or take the cost of a good pair of shoes or a comfortable swimsuit.

Selected Exercise Physiology Concepts

The information from the field of exercise physiology that most directly applies to physical education relates to the main components of fitness: cardiorespiratory capacity, the strength, endurance, and flexibility of muscles, and body composition. Information about anatomical structures and physiological functions clarifies how the fitness components contribute to health and well being. It also demonstrates why preventing injuries and taking safety precautions are crucial to maintaining lifelong fitness. These ideas are organized around four major themes:

1. What factors contribute to an appropriate cardiorespiratory fitness program?
2. How does the structure and function of human anatomy contribute to and restrict the development of lifetime fitness?
3. What characterizes a safe and appropriate muscular stretching and strengthening program?
4. How do body composition and nutrition interrelate to develop and maintain lifetime fitness?

Each of these themes is described in this section. Critical student concepts relating to each theme are listed later in this chapter, in Table 1.

What Factors Contribute to an Appropriate Cardiorespiratory Fitness Program?

Most people who live in the western world have some understanding of what it takes to develop and maintain cardiorespiratory health. "Cardio" means heart, and "respiration" is the function of the lungs in breathing. When people build and maintain the fitness capacity of their heart and lungs, they gain endurance—the ability to continue a vigorous activity, like running, for longer and longer periods of time without undue fatigue. This kind of endurance is also called cardiovascular or aerobic. The term "cardiorespiratory" emphasizes the cooperation between the heart and lungs, the term "cardiovascular" emphasizes the heart function, and "aerobic" describes the kind of physical activity that builds cardiorespiratory or cardiovascular fitness.

Warm-up. Before engaging in any exercise, be it aerobic, strength training, or stretching, warm-up is necessary. Warm-up has two purposes: It is required to prepare the muscles for the activity—stretching and strengthening the muscles to be used in the activity—and to prepare the heart for the activity. Except on one point, experts disagree about the definition of warm-up. All agree that it must raise the body's core temperature above its resting state. (The resting state is when a person first wakes up from sleeping.)

Most students have been awake for some time when they come to their physical education classes, so, by this definition, they are warmed up. But that is only partially correct. A look at the various guidelines for warm-up and their respective problems can be instructive. Some experts insist that people must begin to sweat before warm-up is complete. However, some people sweat easily and some don't. Other experts insist that joint fluid must be warm. But joint fluid can be warm while muscles remain in their contracted state. Warm, lubricated joints won't change the state of the muscles. Dancers do not feel warmed-up until doing 30 to 40 minutes of a dance class, because so much of their activity requires sustained use of all the major muscle groups. In some sports—such as tennis or bicycling—even the professionals generally don't stretch their muscles as part of their warm-up.

The preparatory warm-up must be tailored specifically to the activity. The most important guideline to follow is to stretch the muscles that will be contracted and strengthen the ones that will be stretched. For example, if the activity includes running and jumping, then the leg and gluteal muscles should be stretched and the abdominal muscles strengthened.

Ways of warming up for vigorous physical activity differ according to experience and habits, and the activity itself. Pushing hard against a wall for 10 to 15 seconds can actively use all the major muscle groups, and this action raises the core temperature. Running in place for 30 to 60 seconds while shaking the arms and hands can provide an adequate warm-up for vigorous physical activity because it increases the heart rate.

Since physical education classes are generally 30 to 50 minutes long, an effective but short warm-up is essential. After a few minutes of stretching and strengthening exercises, running in place while wiggling the entire body for 30 to 60 seconds will begin to increase the heart rate. Then begin the activity slowly, and gradually build speed and intensity.

Principles of Fitness. The basic principles of fitness include overload (going beyond what is comfortable), individual differences (adapting the program to fit each starting level), specificity (adapting the exercise regimen to the activity in which the person is engaged), progression (gradually increasing time and intensity), and regularity (engaging in activity on a routine schedule). These principles are summarized in an acronym: FITT–frequency, intensity, type(mode), and time (duration).

Principles of Fitness (FITT)

Frequency
Intensity
Type (mode)
Time (duration)

Cool-Down. The cool-down is as important as the warm-up because it provides protection from injury. Most students in physical education classes are accustomed to ending their activity with a moderate to slow jog around the field or gym to prevent the pooling of lactic acid in their muscles. However, most students are not in the habit of stretching the major muscle groups they have used.

Keep in mind that muscle, tendon, and ligament tissue are gelatinous. When these tissues are warm they become pliable, and when they are cool they become firm. A few extra minutes of stretching will prevent students from feeling stiff later. And, they will be more comfortable the next time they stretch because their muscles will have cooled in their lengthened state.

Aerobic Activity. Jogging has received much publicity since the early 1970s when Dr. Kenneth Cooper, an air force physician, publicized the worrisome facts about the large numbers of 18-year-old inductees in the armed services. These young men had inadequate endurance; they were unable to run for long distances or engage in heavy training exercises. And because their diets were high in saturated fat, their arteries resembled those of much older adults. Dr. Cooper devised an effective training regime that has become known as "aerobic exercise."

This term literally means "with oxygen," and it applies to exercise that introduces sufficient oxygen into the body—pumped by the heart and processed by the lungs—to develop and then maintain an identified level of endurance. Jogging at a steady, comfortable, yet challenging pace for 20 to 30 minutes four times a week, or engaging in other activities such as walking, bicycling, swimming, tennis, or handball for a longer period will increase and then maintain aerobic fitness.

Some forms of exercise are anaerobic, or literally "without oxygen." The high intensity of these activities does not utilize oxygen for energy. Anaerobic exercise is carried out for short periods of time, such as two or three minutes. This kind of exercise puts more stress on the heart and lungs than aerobic exercise does. Though anaerobic activities such as a 100 meter dash build the body's capacity for speed and strength, they do not exercise the heart and lungs in the way that aerobic exercises do. Anaerobic exercises do improve muscle strength, however, which in turn enables people to more easily increase and maintain their cardiorespiratory capacity.

Kinds of Aerobic Exercise. One way to engage in aerobic exercise is to do an exercise continuously for a set amount of time, such as 15 to 20 minutes a session. Another way to carry out aerobic exercise is by interrupting the time by walking, then jogging, and then running fast. The interrupted form, known as Interval Training (IT), has helped athletes train to break running records. The demand on the heart and lungs in continuous aerobic activity is steady, whereas IT requires that the heart and lungs to be able to adapt rapidly to the change of exercise intensity. This adaptability enables people in good condition to maintain and increase their training level.

Although low impact aerobic dance is not intense enough to reach and maintain training level heart rate, this kind of exercise works the major muscle groups and increases tone and flexibility. Many kinds of exercise—such as weight training with light weights—can enhance a person's ability to engage in aerobic activity by increasing the power of the muscles used. Circuit training, where participants move through a series of varied anaerobic and aerobic exercises, increases fitness and provides variety. Each kind of exercise supplements the other.

Benefits of Aerobic Exercise. Dr. Cooper and members of his fitness institute discovered other important facts about the value of fitness. For instance, people in automobile accidents often suffer heart attacks caused by that sudden shock to their system. In this extremely stressful circumstance, the automatic fight or flight emergency reaction of the body floods the bloodstream with adrenaline. If the heart is strong and can circulate this emergency chemical quickly, the high level of adrenaline can help the body handle the trauma (Cooper Institute 1994). If the heart is not in good condition and circulation is poor, this large amount of adrenaline in the heart can cause a heart attack. Researchers also discovered that when people undertake and maintain a regular aerobic training program, they are able to recover from several hypokinetic diseases such adult-onset diabetes, asthma, high blood pressure, obesity, and even nervous tension.

An added benefit of engaging in regular aerobic programs is that a person generally feels better psychologically after the workout. Thus, proponents of aerobic activity recommend it as a major tool to reduce stress. Increased aerobic activity releases neurotransmitters called endorphins. Endorphins act like tranquilizers that the brain releases naturally, the same way it does when people smile and give and receive hugs.

Structure and Functions of Cardiorespiratory System. The heart and lungs work together to supply oxygen-rich blood to the muscles and the tissues of the internal organs in the body. Blood flows through the right half of the heart by means of the pulmonary arteries, and into the lungs, where it receives fresh oxygen. The oxygen-rich blood exits the pulmonary veins into the left

Common Forms of Aerobic and Anaerobic Exercise

Aerobic*	*Anaerobic***
walking	downhill skiing
running	tennis
jogging	handball
bicycling	racquetball
rowing	weight lifting
cross-country skiing	calisthenics
aerobic dancing	golf
jumping rope	circuit training
roller or ice skating	figure skating
stair climbing	sprinting
swimming	volleyball

* Activities that use support for the body such as the water in swimming or a bicycle in bicycling require more time for aerobic training to occur than activities in which the sole support of the body is the legs.
** Some anaerobic activities require aerobic fitness such as basketball and soccer, but because they are stop-and-start activities they are usually classified as anaerobic.

half of the heart, which circulates it throughout the rest of the body by means of the systemic arteries. The oxygen-poor blood returns to the heart through the systemic veins. Cooper realized that the heart and lungs work like muscles; the more they are exercised—contracted and released—the better their shape.

Regular exercise makes the heart and lungs work hard; it conditions them. The primary goal of aerobic activity is to raise the heart rate to the training level appropriate for the age group and to maintain it at that level or better.

Cardiorespiratory Training. What does training level mean? Why is it important? The heart and lungs together must be challenged—overloaded—to increase their capacity and their strength. Researchers have determined how hard these muscles must work to increase their capacity. Exercise physiologists at the Cooper Institute for Aerobics Research have published *The Prudential Fitnessgram*, a guide for developing and measuring endurance of school children.

Authors of the *Fitnessgram* apply the FITT guidelines: frequency (how often a person exercises), intensity (how hard a person exercises), time (how long in minutes a person exercises), and type of exercise. As a way to evaluate the fitness level at which students start, the authors suggest using a one mile run/walk. Students keep track of the time. As their endurance increases, their time decreases. The one mile distance is ideal for physical education classes, and can serve as an excellent evaluation tool.

Another way to determine aerobic fitness is to measure the rate of exercise to insure that it is high enough to challenge the heart and lungs. To determine the appropriate level, students first learn how to take their non-exercise pulse rate, preferably at the wrist, by counting the number of beats in 10 seconds and then multiplying that number by six. Do not teach students to take the pulse at the carotid artery of the neck, because if they press too hard, they can cause dizziness and even fainting. After they have run for a pre-established time, they can count their pulse again. They can then calculate if they have reached the appropriate training level for their age to develop and then maintain the fitness of their hearts and lungs.

In *Teaching Strategies for Improving Youth Fitness*, (Corbin and Pangrazi 1994) provide the following guidelines for elementary school children and beginners:
- If the resting heart rate (rhr) is 60 or less, then the training heart rate (thr) should be 150.
- If rhr is 60-64, then thr should be 151.
- If rhr is 65-69, then thr should be 153.
- If rhr is 70-74, then thr should be 155.
- If rhr is 75-79, then thr should be 157.
- If rhr is 80-84, then thr should be 159.
- If rhr is 85-89, then thr should be 161.
- If rhr is 90+, then thr should be 163.

While this calculation gives specific information about the student's level of aerobic work, emphasis should be on the activity, its pleasure, and its purpose, and not on the numbers.

The training heart rate is not an absolute target but can be considered a zone toward which to aim. Students can reach their training level by working approximately 10 beats below or 10 beats above the calculated rate. As fitness improves and the resting heart rate decreases, the training level can be increased.

Applying the FITT principles then, the frequency of aerobic training can increase from three days a week to four, and the intensity of the training can increase. Students can safely run a little faster but still within their target heart rate range, and they can extend their training time from 20 to 30 minutes. And the students might vary the type of aerobic exercise they do. For example, they might change from running to swimming or bicycling. The variation in exercises will challenge their muscles and introduce variety into the training regimen while the students continue to develop cardiorespiratory endurance

The bottom line is that *any* exercise is better than *no* exercise. Researchers have found that when people simply walk for a half hour during lunch time, they increase their endurance and metabolism, and may even reduce their body fat. Because of their passive life styles, many young people today are unusually unfit.

Moorhouse and Gross (1975) suggest several easy ways for people to increase their endurance if they have too little time to schedule regular aerobic activity:
• Walk or bicycle to work or school.
• Climb the stairs instead of taking an elevator or escalator.
• Jog or walk quickly down the halls or stairs of buildings when they are not too crowded to be hazardous.
• Park the car a block from the destination and walk.

These minor lifestyle changes increase muscle use, challenge the lungs and heart to do a little more work than usual, and help people keep their bodies in better condition.

Over Exercising. Can young aerobic exercisers get too much of a good thing? Yes. Moderation is vital when engaging in aerobic exercise. The acute injuries that can result from too much exercise range from muscle, ligament, and tendon sprains and strains to contusions. More serious are the chronic injuries where articular cartilage and epiphyseal and apophyseal growth plates in the leg joints of these young athletes are damaged.

How Do the Structure and Function of Human Anatomy Contribute to and Restrict The Development of Lifetime Fitness?

A brief anatomical picture of the human body will provide the context for understanding the importance of muscle strengthening and stretching. There are approximately 206 bones in the human skeleton. Ligaments hold most of these bones together. Tendons attach most muscles to bones, and muscles move the bones at their joints. Bones, ligaments, tendons, and muscles are interdependent; they make up a system that enables the whole body or parts of the body to move. Metabolized food provides the energy for the body's movements. The heart pumps blood and circulates food energy and oxygen processed by the lungs throughout the system. And the brain and the autonomic nervous system direct the entire process. All these processes working together enable the body to move.

Skeletal System. Bones are the framework of the body. They not only support the body, but some—such as the skull for the brain or the rib cage for the heart, lungs, and other internal organs—provide protection. The marrow of bones serves as a central factory for producing red blood cells.

The skeleton, made up of bones bound together by ligaments, cannot stand by itself. The muscles move the body, and their structure, size, function, and location enable the body to stand upright. That is why the largest and strongest muscles are located in the back of the lower half of the skeleton: the gluteal muscles (gluteus maximus, medius, and minimus) are at the back of

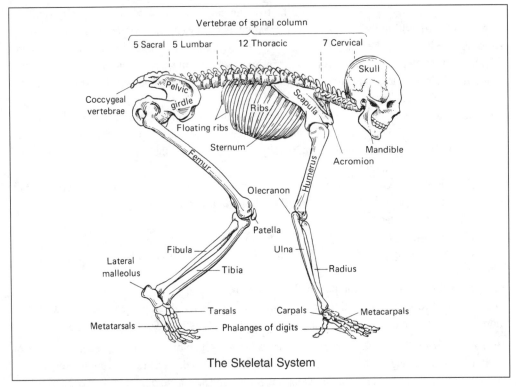

The Skeletal System

the pelvis; the hamstrings (biceps femoris, semitendinosus, and semimembranosus) are at the back of the thigh bone or femur; and the calf muscles (gastrocnemius and soleus) are at the back of the lower leg bones—the tibia and fibula.

Joints. Places where different bones meet are called articulations or joints. Fibrous joints hold together immovable joints (i.e., where the bones of the skull meet). Cartilaginous joints hold together slightly movable bones such as those in between the spinal vertebrae. Synovial joints, which hold together most of the other bones of the body, are found where bones move freely such as in the knee, elbow, hip, and shoulder. This type of joint is surrounded by a capsule that encases it and is lined with a synovial membrane that secretes fluid to lubricate the joint. The bony surfaces of the joint are covered by a thin layer of articular cartilage that lessens friction and provides cushioning. Inside many of these joints are little sacs of fluid, called bursa, which act like air bags in a car's steering wheel; they inflate on severe impact, limiting mobility and potential damage.

Ligaments act like hinges where free moving bones join. The names of these synovial joints describe their function or appearance. Nonaxial joints do not move, but simply meet—or in the case of vertebral joints—glide. Joints that move in one axis (uniaxial) can be hinge joints such as the elbow, or pivot joints such as the axis and atlas joint at the top of the neck, just below where the skull and spine join. Biaxial joints allow movement in two planes (e.g., the radio-carpal joint at the wrist, called condyloid, and the saddle joint of the thumb). Triaxial joints, those which allow movement in three planes, facilitate the widest range of movement. These ball and socket joints are found at the shoulder and the hip.

The similarities in the range of movement of many of these joints makes understanding

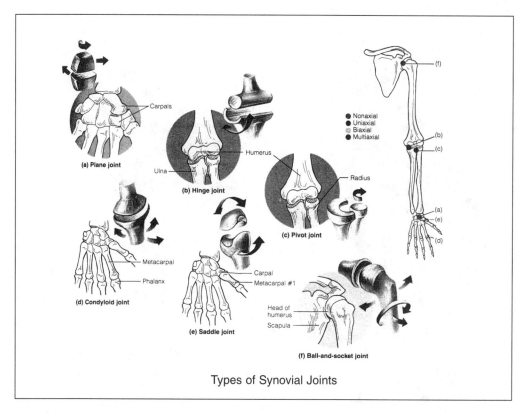

Types of Synovial Joints

them fairly simple. Feet and hands have similar joint structures because they have a similar way of moving and can function in similar ways, except that the big toe cannot move as freely as the thumb. Elbow and knee hinge joints only bend and straighten, but the entire arm and leg can rotate in almost complete circles because of the ball and socket joints at the hip and shoulder. The trunk moves forward and back and side to side, and turns to both sides, rotating around its vertical axis, much like the head.

Muscles. The muscles work in groups to move the bones in the directions for which their joints are designed. Like the names of joints, the names of muscles often describe their function and the location on the bone to which they are attached. Some names of muscles on the upper and lower areas of the body are similar because they attach to and move limbs which have similar functions.

In addition to having similar names and functions, muscles have another property in common: they only contract. To relax, extend, or repeat a movement, the muscles on the opposite side of the limb or body part must contract and thereby cause the other set of muscles to extend. The following example will help clarify this idea.

> Bend your head forward and down to look at your waistline. The muscles in the front of your neck contract while the muscles in back relax to lower your head into that position. To return your head to its upright position, the muscles on the back of your neck contract. If you are to look up at the ceiling, those same muscles must contract even further, pulling the muscles on the front of your neck into a stretched position.

Neurons. In the above example, as with all movements, the body parts respond to the many com-

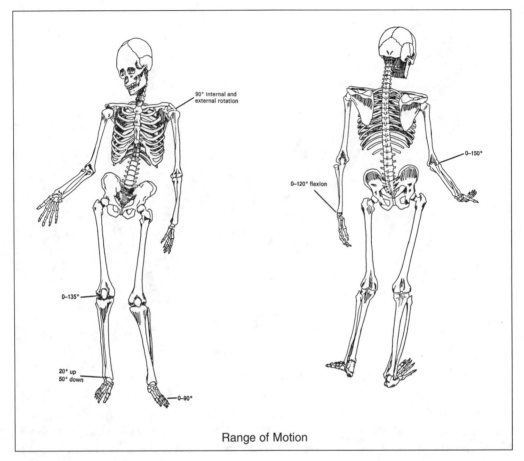

90° Internal and
external rotation

0–150°

0–120° flexion

0–135°

20° up
50° down

0–90°

Range of Motion

mands they receive. The chemical reactions of potassium and sodium in cells called neurons enable the brain to give and receive signals to and from the vital internal organs and muscles. Calcium facilitates these signal transmissions. Neurons typically have dendrites, which receive the messages, called nerve impulses; cell bodies that contain all the standard parts of a cell, which can also receive messages; and axons, which conduct nerve impulses.

Three kinds of nerves enable all the body's systems to function: sensory neurons to the sense receptors; somatic motor neurons to the skeletal muscles, skin, and fascia; and autonomic motor neurons to the organs. These neurons have three modes of functioning: conducting messages from the periphery of the body to the central nervous system (afferent neurons), conducting messages from the central nervous system to the periphery of the body (efferent neurons), and a combination of these which form a network of interconnecting neurons (interneurons). Interneurons enable the transfer of efferent and afferent messages. Nerves send all the movement messages of the body to and from the brain, from the largest jump to the smallest fleeting thought.

What Characterizes a Safe and Appropriate Muscular Stretching and Strengthening Program?

Proper stretching and strengthening can ready the body for activity and lessen the possibility of stress and strain injury. For muscles to do their job, they must be strong. They also must be stretched so they can facilitate range of motion.

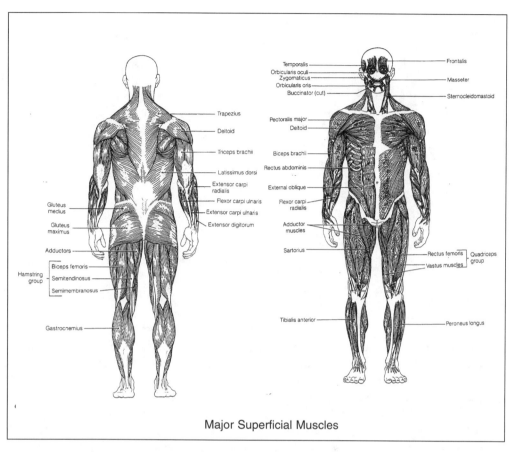

Major Superficial Muscles

Three Types of Muscular Strength. Muscles need three kinds of strength: basic strength, power strength, and aerobic strength (endurance). Basic strength underlies the other two kinds of strength, and all training for any activity requires basic strength. Power strength allows muscles to hold, shift directions, and lift and control significant amounts of weight. Aerobic strength enables muscles to continue moving for long periods of time without excess or overwhelming fatigue, such as climbing several flights of stairs while carrying a bag of groceries.

Power and aerobic strength training are usually task specific, whereas basic strength training for all major muscles groups is general and transfers to power and aerobic strength training. All three kinds of strength are necessary for normal daily activity as well as for vigorous physical activity. According to Corbin and Lindsay (1997), the power gained by sensible strength training is vital to physical fitness and to health.

Types of Muscular Strength Training. Power strength (the ability of a muscle group to lift and hold weight), and aerobic strength or muscular endurance (the ability for muscles to endure long periods of activity), are best developed in the context of the activity for which they are needed, such as repeatedly dribbling the ball with the feet as in soccer, or sprinting for short distances and stopping quickly to change direction for any number of other games.

The three types of muscular strength training are isotonic, isometric, and isokinetic. Dynamic (isotonic) strengthening activity builds basic strength: Slowly move the muscles of the

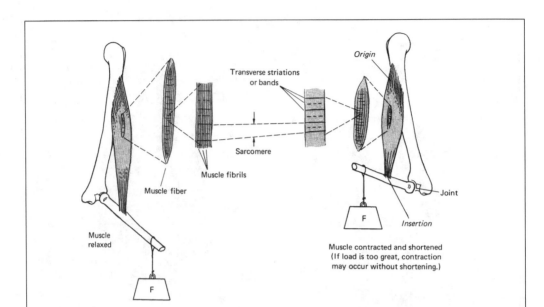

Muscle Contraction

limb or body part up and down, or down and up against gravity along the line of pull (the direction of the muscle as it is attached to the bone) of that muscle group until it is tired and then once more, carefully move the limb up and down to achieve an overload.

Overload describes the effect on the muscles when they become fatigued and reach their usual strength capacity. Going beyond this point, or overloading the muscles, increases their capacity to lift and control weight. This type of strengthening increases capacity along the entire length of the muscle, and can be done with or without free weights or special equipment. Slow movement is necessary to prevent momentum from taking over the work the muscles need to do to become functionally strong. The following basic strengthening exercise is often prescribed by physical therapists for people who are recuperating from knee injuries.

> Sit in a chair with your back firmly supported. With both legs bent at right angles, place your feet on floor. Slowly, to the count of eight, straighten, (extend) one leg so the lower leg is now parallel to the floor. Do not lock your knee. Now slowly, to a count of eight, lower your lower leg (flexing it) and return it to the beginning position. Repeat this sequence four to eight times, or until your thigh muscle group on the front of your thigh (the quadriceps), is tired. Then, carefully, do the exercise one more time for the overload effect. Repeat this sequence using the other leg. After a two minute rest, repeat this sequence.

The slow speed prevents momentum from doing the majority of the lifting and lowering. This exercise uses two kinds of contraction: concentric (coming together or shortening), and eccentric (moving apart or lengthening).

Strength (isokinetic) training utilizes special equipment with variable resistance. Hoeger and Hoeger (1992) explain that, "the speed of the muscle contraction is kept constant because the machine provides a resistance to match the user's force through the range of motion" (p.66). The guideline for slow speed and the principle of overload described for isotonic training applies for isokinetic training when beginning this kind of exercise session. However, the equipment allows the exerciser to gradually increase the speed.

Isometric strengthening uses a static contraction. This means tightening the muscle without moving any part of your body (e.g., pushing against a wall), or not changing the position of parts of the body (e.g., holding in the abdominal muscles). Isometric strengthening is not as effective as dynamic (isotonic) strengthening except when specific static strength is required, such as for some positions in gymnastics or in a caste.

Training Guidelines. Coaches in many sports as well as directors of dance companies have added weight lifting to their regular training regimens with positive results. FITT specifications for individualized weight training programs are now readily available and these programs are applicable to many activities. The guidelines usually help students pretest their muscle strength and then specify the number of times each exercise should be repeated (sets), how long the rest period between sets should be, how many sets should be done during the first training period, and how many should be done thereafter as strength increases (progression). (See Fitnessgram for specifications.)

The specific muscular strength protocol (mode, resistance, sets, and frequency of training) depends on the individual's age, the activity for which the training is undertaken, and current muscular strength. Lifting very heavy weights one or two times a session (power lifting) does not develop aerobic strength in muscles; thus, for most sports except perhaps weight lifting itself, the use only of power training is not recommended. In fact, it may even be counterproductive. (See Chapters 9, 10, and 11 in Corbin & Lindsey 1997.)

A major criterion by which to judge the safety as well as the value of the many available weight training guidelines centers on how they follow the principles of sound training. Guidelines must recommend that each program be tailored to the individual and to the specific sport or activity in question. They must be carefully calibrated to increase gradually how much weight is lifted, how many repetitions and how many sets of repetitions are done, and how much weight is added when the amount of overload is increased.

Muscle Stretching. The term "flexibility" can be used in two ways that are often confused. Flexibility can refer to the result people achieve after they do some stretching exercises. It also can be used in reference to people with loose joints. The popular term for these people is "double jointed." These people have excessively flexible joints; that is, their ligaments are extra long or lax. In medical terms, having lax ligaments is considered a disability, because these people have a 75 percent higher injury rate than people with normal joints. In athletic and dance activities, these people have a hard time stretching adequately. Their muscles are often excessively tight, and therefore they have less control over their limbs than people who have normal joints. Joint flexibility is a disadvantage, whereas muscle flexibility is an advantage. This section is entitled muscle *stretching* and not muscle *flexibility* to avoid any confusion.

Strengthening is only half of the preparation that muscles require. They also need to be stretched properly. Since muscles do not stretch on their own—they only contract—they often remain in a semi-contracted state after people finish their physical activities. Proper stretching should be done before and after each weight training session, game, or practice. In general, stretch positions should be held from 30 seconds to one minute or longer if necessary, depending on how tight the muscles in the group are. The feeling of the stretching should be a gradual softening or diminishing of the tight sensation compared to when the stretch is begun. The pattern to follow is: one leg, then the other, one arm, then the other, one side then the other, because stretching both limbs or sides at once is too strong a stretch, and the sides of the body are unevenly strong. As an example, right handed people are usually stronger and tighter on that side. The stretch positions should be held longer on the tight side. The sensation of stretch should be felt in the long surface of the muscles, but never in the joints.

Three kinds of stretching techniques are commonly used to help lengthen muscles and enable them to contract effectively. Static stretching is where the body part is placed in a position where the weight of the body, with the assistance of gravity, lengthens the muscles. The position is held for a period of time. Ballistic stretch is commonly known as bouncing or pulsing. It requires the muscles to contract and release in rapid succession. This kind of stretching is not recommended because it causes soreness. Proprioceptive neuromuscular facilitation (PNF) combines a three-second contraction of the muscle to be stretched with a stretch. This is often done with a partner, but can also be done alone. PNF uses the "stretch reflex" which enables body parts to respond to an emergency. When a rapid contraction is needed, the opposite muscle group automatically relaxes to facilitate this emergency response.

The most effective form of stretch is a combination of static stretching with modified PNF. Before stretching a muscle group, first contract it with an isotonic strengthening exercise. Then put the body part in the position where gravity can help to lengthen the muscle and actively and gently pull the body part for 30 to 60 seconds. Consider the following example.

> Hold the arms out to the sides at shoulder height. Make four circles about 10 inches around, taking 10 to 12 slow counts for each circle. Afterward, grasp the hands behind the back and lift them up. Bend over at the waist and rotate one shoulder down toward the floor so that the stretching sensation is felt on the shoulder that is toward the ceiling. Hold that stretch for 30 to 60 seconds and then continue gradually to lift the arms up. Take care not to lock the elbows and not to let the shoulders roll forward. Rotate the stretched shoulder down toward the floor and the other one up and repeat the active stretching. When both shoulders have been stretched separately, lift them both at the same time.

The principles of FITT must be modified when applied to proper stretching techniques. A stretching exercise should be repeated once before the activity and once after the activity, and held until the tight sensation in the muscle group softens or lessens significantly. When training for general sport or physical activity, stretching sessions should be done at least three times a week, and more often if there is time. In any program that includes strength training, the muscles to be strengthened should be stretched before and after the sets are completed.

Injury Prevention. When exercising, stretching, or strengthening, special care should be given to the knees and the lower back. No sensation should be felt in the knee when stretching. The knee is the most vulnerable and most frequently injured joint in all sports and dance activities. It only bends one way, but it can wiggle sideways a little when it is bent at a right angle. That is the time it is most vulnerable to injury, and the position in which most injuries to the knee occur.

If, during activity, students use their toe muscles fully by pressing the toes down firmly (not gripping or squeezing), they can keep the knee aligned over the foot and protect the knee joint. Students can further protect their knees by keeping the muscles above (quadriceps and hamstrings) and below (calf muscles) adequately stretched. Leg muscles are constantly in use, but they are rarely stretched properly. If these muscles are safely and adequately stretched, the knee joint can safely serve its primary function.

The lower back is the most frequently injured area of the body among adults in the western world. Eight out of 10 adults at some time in their lives will experience severe back pain or

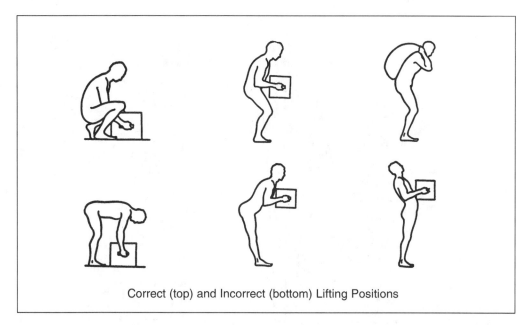

Correct (top) and Incorrect (bottom) Lifting Positions

injury. The main reasons for the back's vulnerability are: poor structure (ideally the lumbar spine should be one or two vertebrae shorter), weak or improperly used abdominal muscles, hyper-extended knees with associated tight calf and hamstrings, and the lack of pain-sensitive nerve endings in the case of the intervertebral discs where the injuries tend to occur. Without pain there is no warning when the lower back is being overstressed and injured. Even people with very strong abdominal muscles can injure their backs.

Like the knee, the muscles around the spinal column need to have a balance of flexibility and strength. While the abdominal muscles require regular strengthening because the act of breathing and daily activity causes them to stretch, the muscles above the spine in the neck and shoulders and below the spine in the buttocks and leg need stretching because they remain in a contracted state in order to help keep the body in its vertical position. Balance is the key here: Stretch the muscles that will be strengthened in the activity, and strengthen the ones that will be stretched.

Three areas of the body need never be deliberately stretched: the abdominal muscles, the front of the neck, and the back top of the shoulders. Since breathing is a constant requirement of all activity and the abdominal muscles expand and relax during respiration, abdominal muscles require strengthening before or after activity. Because people reach or slump their heads forward frequently during normal daily activity, the weight of the head pulls the top of the shoulder area into a rounded position and the muscles in the front of the neck relax. Finally, when people feel fatigue they allow their shoulders to roll forward, their heads to sink forward and down, and their abdominal muscles to relax. These areas require constant monitoring of posture as well as daily strengthening.

Guidelines for safe strengthening and stretching exercises can be simply stated in seven "don'ts" (Alter 1983, 1990): don't bounce, don't swing, don't do stretching or strengthening fast, don't lock (hyperextend), don't overbend, don't arch the lumbar and cervical spine in any situation or exercise, and don't click (or pop) your joints. The reasons for these cautions follow:

• Bouncing, or even pulsing—called ballistic stretching—initiates the stretch reflex and thus causes a contraction. Bouncing is the main cause of soreness in muscles. Some people con-

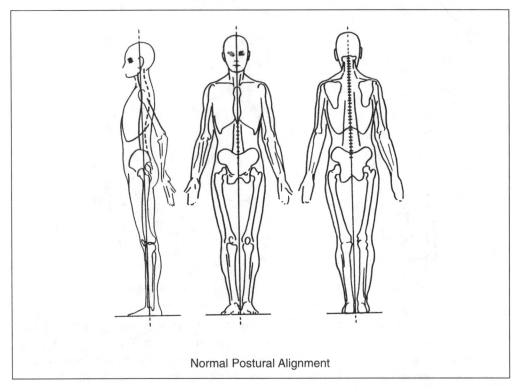

Normal Postural Alignment

tinue to bounce to stretch their muscles, even when information about more efficient and less harmful ways to stretch have been disseminated for more than 30 years. Because the action of a bounce is a combination of one brief second of stretch followed by a brief second of contraction, the strengthening cancels out the stretch. At the same time, the microscopically fine cross fibers that hold each of the longitudinal muscle fibers to one another tear because of the percussive mini-trauma that bouncing causes. The body secretes protein laden fluid to heal these tears, and the increase of fluid in the tissues which causes the soreness.

- Swinging to warm up the muscles and joints depends mainly on momentum, not muscle power. Swinging can cause injury, especially when the swinging limbs go back and forth from one side of the body to the other, as in waist twists.
- Fast stretching is bouncing, and it uses momentum. Stretches should be held for 30 to 60 seconds, and strengthening requires slow movement, down and up against gravity.
- Locking a joint severely strains the ligaments and cartilage in the joints that have them, and can misalign the bones.
- Overbending is the opposite of locking. This action stretches ligaments, and they do not unstretch. Just like locking, overbending progressively weakens the bindings of the joint. Deep knee bends usually overbend the knee joint. When push-ups are done too quickly, the elbow can be overbent if the exerciser goes down too low.
- Arching is what people do when they do a backbend or drop their heads back so far that they can no longer talk. Muscles in the front of the neck or the abdominal muscles in the front of the lumbar spine can no longer hold (stabilize) the spine, and the discs can be permanently injured.

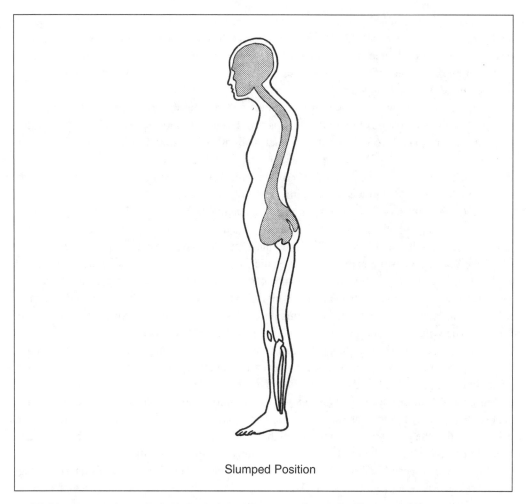

Slumped Position

- Clicking or popping sounds occur in joints such as the ankle, hip socket, and neck. The sounds are caused by ligaments or tendons rolling over each other, and/or bones suddenly sliding back into place after a slight misalignment. Although the sudden corrected alignment feels better, the action can be done slowly with only muscles doing the realigning to prevent the sound and rubbing from occurring. In time, this rubbing can cause wear and tear and arthritis-like symptoms.

Harmful Exercises. Modified versions of stretching and strengthening exercises should be substituted for the following commonly used warm-up exercises, which can be harmful or inefficient. The causes of harm, as described above, are built into these traditional exercises. Many students do not like doing exercises that hurt when they do them, and—in most cases—the students are correct to respond to the pain signal. The most important guideline, therefore, is: Stop if it hurts!

Head Circles. Arch the neck, risking damage to the intervertebral discs; use momentum and actually contract the neck muscles, achieving the opposite goal to stretching and relaxing these tight muscles. When done fast they cause sore muscles. To correct, gently pull down on the top of the head, keeping the neck vertebrae aligned and never letting the chin touch the chest. Hold for 30 to 60 seconds. Then, pull and hold the aligned head, sideways, over each shoulder, in turn.

Arm Swings or Circles. These use momentum, are mostly passive, and do not adequately stretch or strengthen any muscles. If any sensation is felt, it is in the shoulder joint and this can be a sign of joint irritation leading to injury. To correct, slow down the circles, take 12 to 16 slow counts to make one circle, and then reverse the direction of the circle. Repeat 6 to 8 times or until fatigued. (See example on page 114.)

Waist Twists. The swing action uses momentum and also puts intervertebral discs of the lumbar spine in a vulnerable position (when that part of the spine rotates, it also slides slightly sideways and when it bends to the side it also rotates slightly). To correct, with knees relaxed and arms extended overhead, pull up as much as possible, and then more. Hold to feel the tight muscles in the upper back and rib cage release. In the same position, pull to the high right and then left diagonal where the wall meets the ceiling and hold as before.

Side Bends. Stretch the side abdominal muscles, making the waist line wider; can cause similar harm to the lumbar discs as waist twists. They often are done with a bouncing action causing the soreness which can result from bouncing. Side abdominal muscles need strengthening, not stretching.

Back Bends. This is the name of the acrobatic stunt that uses lumbar back arching. (See the explanation of arch, above, for the severe and often permanent harm these can cause.) There is no correct way to arch the lumbar spine. In a high chest arch with the lumbar spine held in a vertical position by strongly contracted abdominal muscles, the ribcage can tip back, sideways, and forward. These positions and movements require great strength and control.

Prone Arch or Trunk Lift. The purpose of this exercise is to strengthen the upper back muscles; in the position of lying on the floor, however, the lumbar spine is severely arching whether or not both the upper back and legs are lifted. This can cause the same injury to the intervertebral discs of the lumbar spine as backbends. A small pillow can be placed under the abdominal area to help protect the lumbar spine, but another position—such as standing with knees bent enough to align the pelvis over the thighs and then slowly lifting and lowering the ribcage, neck, head, and arms—also can be used when strengthening the upper back muscles.

Fast, Straight-Legged Sit-Ups. Use momentum, strengthen the hip flexors (usually already strong and tight); can hurt the lumbar spine because often people do them by pushing out their abdominal muscles. Curl-downs are the most effective dynamic abdominal muscle exercise.

Crunches. This way of strengthening the abdominal muscles is a substitute for fast straight-legged sit-ups and double leg lifts. Although crunches may lessen the risk of back injury somewhat, the exercise is often done fast, using momentum. It uses the arm muscles to do most of the work, only mildly strengthens the upper third of the rectus abdominus muscle while the other two thirds are stabilizing the trunk (isometrically), and does not lift and lower weight along the entire length of the abdominal muscles. Also, even when a twist of the ribcage is incorporated, the exercise does not challenge the side abdominal muscles. To correct this, begin in the curled up position of crunches with the ribcage lifted up but most of the pelvis on the floor, keep the rectus abdominus held in firmly and arms crossed on the chest, slowly lower the ribcage for 3 to 4 counts, and then come up 3 to 4 counts, to the original curled position. Tip the entire body sideways to an angle where one buttock is off the floor and then uncurl down 3 to 4 counts toward the floor and curl up in that same side-tipped position 3 to 4 counts. Repeat to the other side, and then repeat the entire sequence center, side, side, two more times. To add overload, increase the counts to 6 to 8 going down and 6 to 8 coming up. Then, add a fourth set. This curl-down is a very challenging strengthening exercise.

Double Leg Lifts. This exercise causes the same harm as fast straight-legged sit-ups, with the additional serious risk to the lumbar spine and potential separation of the abdominal muscle attachments from the linia alba, the long cartilage that reaches from the pubic bone at one end and to the bottom of the sternum at the other. It uses the abdominal muscles to stabilize the upper body and primarily strengthens the hip flexors, a group of muscles that usually are very strong and tight already. To correct, use curl-downs instead.

Deep Knee Bends and Squat Thrusts. These overbend the knee joint, require momentum percussively to push the body up from the deepest dropped position. They can cause torn cartilages and ruptured ligaments; if they do not actually cause such severe damage, they can seriously weaken the joint. To correct, simply lower the body slowly to the point above where the body drops below the control of the muscles. Come up slowly, 4 to 6 counts in each direction.

Hurdler's Stretch. This position is used to bounce in a hamstring stretch. It can hyperextend the knee, put severe stress on the lumbar spine, and cause sore hamstring muscles, if the student actually can stretch them into this position. It also can jeopardize the bent knee if it is placed on the floor at a right angle. There are several very effective alternative ways to stretch the hamstrings. (See below.)

Straight-Legged Toe Touch. These are also often bounced (potentially causing sore muscles), and the knee joints are often locked back and hyperextended (weakening the knee joint). The lumbar spine is forcefully rounded, often the abdominal muscles are passive, and thus the lumbar spine is vulnerable to injury. To correct, bend the knees and fold the entire upper body down so the pelvis and ribcage are touching the thighs. Drop the head and arms, placing the hands on the ground. Gradually unbend one leg at a time while keeping the upper body touching the thighs. Feel the stretch sensation in the back of the thigh only. Hold for 8 to 10 counts. Bend the first leg and repeat with the other. Repeat this sequence 4 to 6 times, or hold the stretched position longer each time.

The commonly used exercises described above do not effectively accomplish the goal for which they are intended, and they severely stress the vulnerable joints they are meant to protect. As noted, most of these exercises can be modified, or safe and effective alternative exercises can be substituted. Alter (1983, 1990; 1986, 1990) provides more details about these corrections.

Other Safety Factors. Even with proper stretching, strengthening, and cardiorespiratory fitness training, accidents can occur. Accidental injuries most frequently occur at the beginning of the school term when participants are out of shape, and at the end of the term when they are excessively fatigued. This knowledge can help everyone concerned take extra precautions during these times and arrange practice and playing schedules accordingly.

Poorly cared-for or slippery playing surfaces, severe weather conditions, and inadequate or worn-out playing equipment also can contribute to accidents. Careful surveillance and repair of playing surfaces and equipment can help diminish the risks of accidents.

Clothing and shoes also can affect health and safety. The manufacturers of sports clothing and shoes may appear to have the players' interests at heart, but since their goal is to make a profit, sensible, non-market-driven guidelines should be considered. Natural fabrics made of cotton or wool allow the skin to breath and they absorb sweat more effectively than do artificial fabrics, even mesh. If artificial fabrics fit too snugly, the problem of proper air circulation for the skin increases. Though young people are very style conscious, not all styles are sensible for the sports and activities for which they are designed.

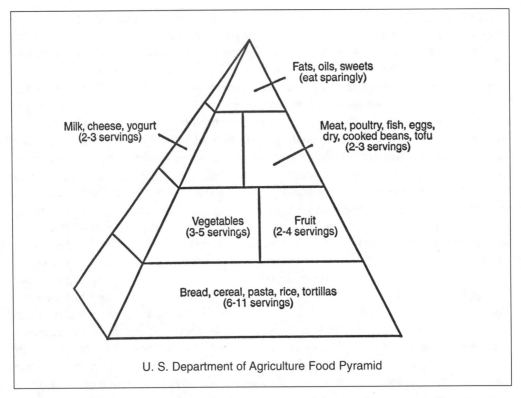

U. S. Department of Agriculture Food Pyramid

An example of poor design in sportswear is the high-top plastic or leather basketball shoe. The high top is so inflexible that most teenagers wear them untied because when tied, the back of the high top puts too much pressure on the top of their Achilles tendon. The cloth high-top "gym shoe" that students wore in the 1940s, 1950s, and 1960s has returned to shoe stores and again is in style. The fabric is flexible enough for the ankle to bend when laced up, but the soles of these shoes are insufficiently cushioned compared to the more recently designed running shoes.

How Do Body Composition and Nutrition Interrelate to Develop and Maintain Lifetime Fitness?

Food provides the body with sufficient nutrients to maintain energy, repair the body, and support the immune system. In most circumstances, any informed person can eat a balanced diet. Proper nutritional guidelines in relation to body composition follow the discussion of metabolism.

Metabolism. Think of the body as a machine, with the bones as the supports, the joints as the hinges, the nerves as the electrical wiring, and the muscles as the movers of the bones. The only thing missing here is the energy to fuel this living machine. This energy, of course, comes from the processes of digestion and metabolism that transform food into usable energy. Digestion is the mechanical and chemical breaking down of food in the digestive track. Metabolism occurs in the cells where food molecules are further broken down into chemical compounds that can be absorbed into the bloodstream and distributed to the muscles, the brain, and the organs. If this energy is not used for the body's essential functions, it is released as heat, or stored in the liver or in fat cells for use at a later time.

The chemical compound adenosine triphosphate, known at ATP, is the major molecule in which living cells store energy. The main source of ATP is glucose, which comes from the food groups: carbohydrate (grains, vegetables, fruits), proteins (animal products such as meat, fish and eggs, and vegetable sources such as beans and seeds), and fats (from animal and plant sources). Although most food supplies the body with glucose, it comes most directly from carbohydrates. Glucose, a simple sugar, is the main source of energy for the brain and heart. After food is digested in the small intestine and broken down into three simple sugars, the sugars are transported into the liver where they are converted into glucose. The liver not only converts the final digested states of foods into the components the body parts require, it distributes (releases) them when and where they are needed.

Carbohydrates are the main component of starches such as bread, rice, and potatoes. They supply about half of western society's dietary needs. Fruits and vegetables also contain carbohydrates, but they contain much more water than starches. Fruits and vegetables also supply the body with essential vitamins, minerals (different from the ones supplied by starches), and natural complex unrefined sugars.

The U.S. Department of Agriculture food pyramid recommends the following number of daily servings of these food groups: 6 to 11 servings of starches such as bread, cereal, rice, and pasta; 3 to 5 servings of vegetables; 2 to 4 servings of fruit; 2 to 3 servings of 4 to 6 ounce portions of protein; and fats, oils, and sweets to be eaten sparingly.

The starches that are so popular among young people—such as french fried potatoes, pasta, white bread, donuts, pretzels, and white rice—do not supply the necessary trace minerals to maintain the body in its optimal state of readiness for physical activity. Magnesium, for instance, which is so necessary for the synthesis and use of energy-rich compounds and in the maintenance of membrane properties of cells, is present in high quantities in the skin of the potato, the bran of whole grain wheat, and the bran of brown rice. Thus, the starches in the common diet do not supply enough magnesium, especially if the diet does not contain dark green leafy vegetables.

Proteins are found in nuts, animal products, and vegetables such as beans and seeds. Although they also supply the body with glucose, fats, and energy, their primary function is to supply the body with the necessary amino acids that it does not manufacture itself. Amino acids maintain, build, and repair cellular tissue and bodily structures that enable the body to function effectively. The liver plays a major role in combining and separating amino acids and proteins for its own use, as well as for the rest of the body. Twelve to 15 percent of the daily diet should be protein, preferably of the low fat and vegetable or fish variety.

Here again, the proteins popular with young people, such as hamburgers and fried chicken, tend to be high in animal fat. Even when students choose to follow a vegetarian diet, they often eat large amounts of saturated fat from cheese, ice cream, and eggs, and they fill up on starches made of refined wheat flour. Because eating a vegetarian diet without careful guidance and detailed knowledge is difficult, young vegetarians often become deficient in iron. Eating foods that are high in iron will not correct this deficiency. For the iron to be absorbed, high-iron foods such as oats must be eaten in combination with other foods containing minerals such as magnesium. Teachers should clarify what eating a balanced regular or vegetarian diet means: eating a wide variety of fruits, vegetables, grains, and low fat proteins.

In spite of the bad press that fats have received in the past 20 or 30 years, they are necessary. They supply and store fuel, and they furnish insulation. This insulation provides both warmth and electrical conduction, and is part of the structure of cell membranes. Fats also enable oil-soluble vitamins, such as vitamin E, to be absorbed. Fats have received bad press for two major reasons: their contribution to arteriosclerosis—the hardening of the arteries which contributes to hypokinetic diseases such as heart disease—and obesity. Obesity is defined as weighing more than 30 percent more than the recommended weight of "normal" people. Normal weight depends on, and is calculated in relation to, one's height, age, and gender. No more than 10 to 20 percent of the daily food intake should contain fat, especially animal fat.

The serious problem connected with fat is its association with cholesterol, the fatty substance found only in animal tissues. Human bodies need cholesterol, and they utilize it in essential ways: in fat digestion, in some hormone building, in the skin, in nerve tissues, and in cell membranes. Recently, researchers have questioned the causal relationship of dietary intake of high cholesterol foods in arteriosclerosis; the issue may relate more to how the liver breaks down, transports, and distributes the cholesterol in the body than to fat intake, per se. Researchers do agree that people should choose more polyunsaturated fats than saturated ones, because saturated fat interferes with the regulation of the cholesterol level in the blood. Polyunsaturated fatty acids, the technical way of describing these fats, are found in the liquid form of vegetable oils. These do not interfere with the liver's ability to regulate the cholesterol level.

Crisp, salty snack foods such as potato chips are popular with young people. These snacks have two disadvantages: They have little food value (essential vitamins and minerals) and add extra fat and calories to the diet, and, when people eat something salty, they are often stimulated to eat something sweet afterward. Young people often reach for refined, sugar-filled carbonated drinks or candy bars to fill this need. These have little food value and add empty calories to the diet.

Empty calories contain few essential vitamins. They only add energy, often at the expense of balanced metabolism. Refined sugar enters the bloodstream without much processing by the digestive system. When this extra sugar suddenly floods the system, the balance of glucose released into the bloodstream, which the liver maintains, is thrown off. To correct this imbalance, the liver stores the glucose it is processing. In the meantime, the person who just ate the candy or drank the soda experiences a rush of energy. Then, about a half hour later, a feeling of fatigue occurs because it takes time before the liver resumes its function of glucose distribution. To satisfy their yen for something sweet, students can reach for a banana, or dates, or raisins, which are sweet but whose sugars are digested as part of the carbohydrate metabolism, and then the liver can maintain the even flow of glucose.

The habit young people have of eating frequent snacks may be physiologically driven. In our society, people are expected to eat three meals a day, although advertisers offer many choices for snacks and suggestions for when to eat them. Some researchers now recommend that people eat six small balanced meals during the day rather than the traditional three large ones. The eating habits of teenagers, then, may be more sensible than would seem. They do need to modify their snacking habits, however, and reach for low-fat proteins such as yogurt, and low-fat carbohydrates such as whole grain bagels, or fresh fruits such as bananas, apples, or grapes.

Body Composition. Body composition refers to the relative amounts of muscle, fat, bone, and other tissues. Teachers can help young people monitor and keep track of their body fat by using the skin fold measure under the center of the triceps muscle of the arm and the inside (medial) of the widest part of the calf. The sum of these two measurements indicates the level of body fat

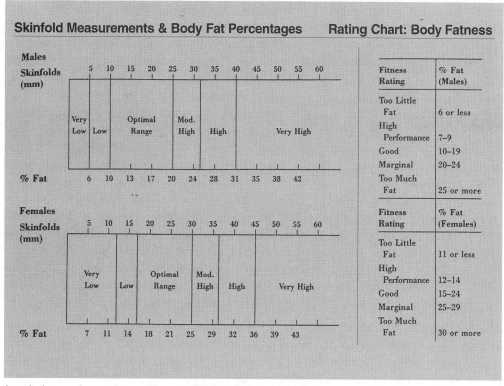

Skinfold Measurements & Body Fat Percentages

Males

Skinfolds (mm)	5	10	15	20	25	30	35	40	45	50	55	60
	Very Low	Low	Optimal Range		Mod. High	High			Very High			
% Fat	6	10	13	17	20	24	28	31	35	38	42	

Females

Skinfolds (mm)	5	10	15	20	25	30	35	40	45	50	55	60
	Very Low		Low	Optimal Range		Mod. High	High		Very High			
% Fat	7	11	14	18	21	25	29	32	36	39	43	

Rating Chart: Body Fatness

Fitness Rating	% Fat (Males)
Too Little Fat	6 or less
High Performance	7–9
Good	10–19
Marginal	20–24
Too Much Fat	25 or more

Fitness Rating	% Fat (Females)
Too Little Fat	11 or less
High Performance	12–14
Good	15–24
Marginal	25–29
Too Much Fat	30 or more

in relation to the total percentage of body fat. Tables of the relationships between this skin fold test sum and total body fat can be found a number of books.

According to Corbin and Lindsay (1993), the optimal range for boys is a total skin fold sum of 10 to 25 millimeters (mm), which indicates the total percentage of body fat is between 10 and 20 percent. The optimal range for girls is between 17 and 30 mm for total skin fold, which indicates between 16 and 25 percent total body fat. If students have body fat beyond that range, they should increase their physical activity by using FITT principles and reduce their consumption of fat, sugar, and alcohol (if applicable). These are the main sources of empty calories.

Teachers must de-emphasize weight reduction diets and focus on lifetime eating habits. Because fat cells store potential energy for the body, dieting can disrupt the normal functioning of fat cells. An automatic feast or famine response takes over when a person is dieting. When that person completes the weight reduction diet, the cells will automatically replenish their stores of energy. The common and frustrating result of dieting, then, is that the dieter regains the weight. The cells continue to store fat rather than resume their normal function, especially if the person is not physically active on a regular basis.

In today's society, the abundant messages about body composition are double-edged, loaded, and contradictory. The challenge for teachers is to inform students about real body composition facts and to help them understand that one size does not fit all. The next challenge is to help students recognize the potentially harmful messages conveyed in snack food and beverage advertisements. The diet industry and the accompanying media messages provide an important tool to use in teaching students how much inaccurate, ill-advised, and deceptive information is available today.

Inherited, familial, and cultural factors influence the size and shape of young people's bodies. Not everyone can be tall, thin, and blonde, although advertisers would have us believe otherwise. That fact is difficult for many young people to accept. It is also difficult for them to accept that not all body features are under their control. While exceptions occur, familial tendencies operate automatically as young people grow toward their adult shape and size. If, beginning in the elementary grades, teachers help young people to understand the difference between internal and external beauty, while they study the infinite variety of human features, sizes, and preferences that exist in the world, then perhaps they will enter adolescence with a greater sense of self-acceptance.

On the other hand, when young women train excessively for any kind of activity, be it running, gymnastics, or dancing, and they do not maintain 15 to 18 percent body fat, their bodies cannot naturally progress into puberty. As a result, their reproductive organs may sustain permanent damage. Some young women—and a few young men who are unnecessarily concerned with excess or apparent excess body fat—use inordinate amounts of aerobic exercise, three to four hours a day, to lose fat.

They may be suffering from the disease known as anorexia nervosa. These unfortunate young people engage in excessive amounts of aerobic exercise while consuming as little food as possible. Their physical state can become so weakened that hospitalization and constant supervision are necessary to prevent them from starving. These young people are overly susceptible to the contemporary emphasis on slimness that pervades the media.

Nutrition and Health. How do the physiological components of nutrition affect safety and health? To answer this question, it is helpful to return to the image of the body as a machine. When proper fuel is used in the machine, it remains in good working condition. And when it is in good running condition, it can do almost anything and go almost anywhere. However, human beings are not machines. They need more than just proper fuel to keep their bodies in good condition. Sufficient rest and water and a balanced variety of activities with supportive people are basic needs of growing young people. Psychological well being and the resulting positive sense of self that physical health produces can enable youngsters to cope with the many difficult and unpredictable events they will encounter during the transition from adolescence to adulthood.

One of the most dangerous and difficult choices young people face today is whether or not to experiment with or use drugs, alcohol, cigarettes, or even nutritional ergogenics such as caffeine, extra amino acids, or large doses of vitamin B12. Researchers such as Melvin H. Williams, Director of the Human Performance Laboratory at Old Dominion University in Norfolk, Virginia, have studied the effect of drugs, nutrients, chemicals, and so-called "performance enhancers" and report that most have no effect on athletic performance. Some drugs, such as steroids, are forbidden for use in the Olympic games and by professional and college sports teams. Although they do enhance performance, they also can cause serious and even permanent harm, and possibly death, to those who use them.

People of all ages have an strong drive to find ways to achieve a state of euphoria, and some people will take extreme risks to achieve it. In studies of elite athletes, sports psychologists have identified the characteristics of what has been called peak performance. Psychologist Mihaly Csikszentmihalyi (1990) has studied this state, which he calls "flow," in people all over the world. Flow is the euphoric state of unselfconscious concentration in an activity where time seems irrelevant, where ease seems to substitute for effort, and where work feels like play. Flow gives people such a high level of enjoyment that they will engage in the activity over and over again for its own sake. Mountain climbers, dancers, musicians, marathon runners, and young people playing basketball all describe this state.

Flow is what young people seek in their recreational and social activities, and because they do not realize that skilled concentration is necessary to create this sensation naturally, they turn to artificial means such as drugs and alcohol. Physiologically, flow activities all stimulate brain-secreted endorphins, the built-in tranquilizers to which all humans have access. A major goal of educators is to help young people turn to positive flow activities.

Unfortunately, many young people do not make wise decisions about food, sleep, clothing, recreational activities, and so forth. The reasons for this are developmental, and they are difficult to counteract. Young people have little understanding of the future and they believe that, in some magical way, they will be fine no matter what happens. When adults suggest they exercise caution, the message has little meaning. Unfortunately, it takes a serious incident before some young people will begin to make wiser decisions.

Placing Exercise Physiology Concepts in the Curriculum

Decisions must be made about where to place exercise physiology concepts in the physical education program. Table 1, beginning on page 128, organizes the concepts according to the four basic questions presented in the previous section. These concepts include short-term and long-term programs, and are listed for every other grade level. If students in the earlier grades have not previously had age-appropriate activities and have not learned the necessary information, then teachers might consider giving assignments listed for younger students to the older ones before moving on to more advanced study and experiences. The pedagogical goal is to help students form healthy and life serving habits. To create these positive habits, it is important that the learning be sequential.

Integrating Exercise Physiology Concepts into Instruction

Exercise physiology is an integrated area made up of many sources of knowledge, from the laboratory to the playing field. Teachers can integrate exercise physiology concepts into their programs on a daily basis. And, they can model a few of these concepts by teaching safety in their daily warm-up exercises. They can provide grade-level learning experiences in which students can understand and apply these concepts directly. The box provides some examples.

Integrating Exercise Physiology into Instruction

Elementary School Example: Grade 2
Concept: Activities that make the heart beat faster also make the heart stronger.
From a group discussion, teachers can compile a list of daily physical activities in which their students participate. They can label them as easy, moderate, and vigorous. Young students can keep a list of daily activities and the time they spend in each area—physical activity, school activity, recreational activity, and sleep—for several days. This record will show them how they use their time and how much time they spend engaged in vigorous physical activity.

Elementary School Example: Grade 4
Concept: Carbohydrates, proteins, and fats should be eaten every day.
From a group discussion, teachers can compile a list of foods their students eat and label

them as carbohydrates, starches, proteins, and fats. Young students can use the list to record the foods they eat for several days. This will show students how their diet contributes to their nutritional needs and how they might modify their intake beneficially. In a similar manner, young students can keep track of their liquid intake for several days. Older students can keep their personal intake logs for a week or two. Students also can observe and record family members' eating and physical activity patterns.

Middle School Example: Grade 6
Concept: Inherited, familial, and cultural factors influence the size and shape of people's bodies.
When students study body composition they can focus on describing their own body type and those of family members. Students can interview family members about their childhood patterns of eating, recreation, and physical activity, and inquire about inherited anatomical and structural characteristics such as height, bone structure, and body composition.

Middle School Example: Grade 6
Concept: Family, school, and community attitudes toward proper nutrition influence an individual's commitment to a physical fitness program.
Have students interview a schoolmate whose family has recently moved to the U.S. from another country. Ask about eating, recreation, and activity patterns in that country. This activity will help students appreciate the diversity of attitudes and practices in their own community. To understand the diversity of attitudes, practices, and nutritional and physical needs of older people, have students interview an adult who regularly works out at a gym or does aerobic activity. Students can ask about motivation, rewards, drawbacks, and changes in metabolism and nutritional needs that occur with long-term physical training.

High School Example: Grade 10
Concept: Body composition and nutritional needs interact and change.
As students grow older they can keep a record of and calculate the caloric value of each of the food groups they eat and analyze their diet for empty calories. This will make the academic study of nutrition a personal learning experience and perhaps stimulate a change in eating habits.

High School Example: Grade 10
Concept: Maintaining a regular physical fitness program requires dedication and updated information.
When students are in middle school and high school, they may consider devoting a large portion of their time to a challenging physical activity. To understand what time, energy, and social sacrifices this commitment may require, young people can interview a friend who participates regularly in dance, ice skating, competitive gymnastics, or on a varsity sports team to learn about commitment, sacrifices, and rewards. In the interview, students can ask about what drives, inspires, and discourages the person, and how he or she handles homework and friends. Students can read a biography or autobiography of a sport or dance figure to understand his or her motivations, hardships, goals, and social relationships.

High School Example: Grade 12
Concept: A proper strength training program fits the individual's body composition, current strength, and the specific needs of the physical activity for which it is undertaken.
In the light of their academic study of the physiology of strength and anaerobic exercise, students can analyze their own physical strength. They also will benefit from looking at the common sports injuries their classmates have experienced, and learning how they can be prevented and treated. They can identify an exercise sequence and analyze it for its proper application of stretching and strengthening principles.

Assessing Student Learning

Teachers can use a variety of assessment techniques to determine student progress in the applications of exercise physiology. Many of these are described in detail in *Moving into the Future: National Standards for Physical Education* (NASPE 1995) under Standards 3 and 4, and more generally in the reference section of that book.

Student Journals and Logs. Because fitness programs are student centered and do not involve competition, the process of self-study is inherent in them. Students in all grades should keep an ongoing record of their progress in sports, games, and activities that they enjoy. This record will provide them with a history of their fitness development and clues to potential lifelong involvement in some activities. It also serves as a central assessment tool.

Observation. Teacher observation of students participating in vigorous physical activity is the primary way to assess achievement in Standards 3 and 4 for having a physically active lifestyle and maintaining a life-enhancing level of physical fitness. The National Standards recommend using the Cooper Institute *Fitnessgram* (mentioned earlier) beginning in the fourth grade, because it provides for an ongoing record of students' progress in body composition (percent of body fat), aerobic capacity, muscle strength, endurance (for the abdominal, upper arm, and upper back muscles) and flexibility. The *Fitnessgram* is especially useful for helping students set goals, keep track of their fitness status, and see the results of their commitment for themselves. In assessing student progress in this area, the role of the teacher serves as monitor and supporter, not as judge or critic.

Student Projects. Students can create and implement a fitness plan that includes cardiorespiratory, muscular strength, endurance, and stretching exercises as well as dietary goals. This program serves as an authentic assessment tool for determining student understanding and ability to apply the concepts related to exercise physiology. The detail of this plan can become more specific and challenging as the student advances from one grade level to the next.

Concluding Comments

The central concepts of exercise physiology center around how the internal systems in the human body function and how they can function in an optimal way. The study of the heart and lungs, nutrition, metabolism, and body composition, and muscles—their strength, endurance, and flexibility—can inform students about how best to care for their own bodies.

Table 1. Critical Student Concepts, K–6

Kindergarten	Second Grade	Fourth Grade	Sixth Grade
Exercise Physiology Concept I: What factors contribute to an appropriate cardiorespiratory fitness program?	*Exercise Physiology Concept I: What factors contribute to an appropriate cardiorespiratory fitness program?*	*Exercise Physiology Concept I: What factors contribute to an appropriate cardiorespiratory fitness program?*	*Exercise Physiology Concept I: What factors contribute to an appropriate cardiorespiratory fitness program?*
Vigorous physical activity contributes to a healthy body.	The heart and lungs (the cardiorespiratory system) respond differently to different kinds of daily and vigorous physical activities.	Cardiorespiratory endurance, muscular strength, endurance, flexibility, and body composition are the major components of health-related fitness	The principles of body composition and nutrition, muscle strength, endurance, and flexibility must be considered in developing a weekly physical fitness program.
Exercise makes the heart beat faster and the lungs work harder.	Aerobic exercise provides people with many benefits— both physical and mental.	Heart and lungs work together to supply oxygen-rich blood to the muscles and organs.	The principles of cardiorespiratory fitness program include frequency, intensity, type, and time (FITT).
	Activities that make the heart beat faster also make the heart stronger.	Personal preferences, skills, and talents influence students' choices, successes, and pleasure when engaging in vigorous physical activity.	Undertaking an ongoing physical fitness program requires adequate information, preparation, and dedication.
			Regular monitoring of progress of cardiorespiratory endurance, muscular strength, endurance, flexibility, and body composition demonstrates the benefits of engaging in a fitness program.

Table 1. Critical Student Concepts, K–6

Exercise Physiology Concept II: How do the structure and function of the human anatomy contribute to and restrict the development of lifetime fitness?	*Exercise Physiology Concept II: How do the structure and function of the human anatomy contribute to and restrict the development of lifetime fitness?*	*Exercise Physiology Concept II: How do the structure and function of the human anatomy contribute to and restrict the development of lifetime fitness?*	*Exercise Physiology Concept II: How do the structure and function of the human anatomy contribute to and restrict the development of lifetime fitness?*
Every activity in life requires movement.	The body is made up of a coordinated system of bones, joints, and muscles.	Ligaments hold bones together.	The largest and strongest muscles of the body—the gluteal, hamstring group, and calf muscles—are located in the back lower half of the skeleton to help hold it up.
Muscles move bones.	Muscles move bones by pulling them.	Tendons attach muscles to bones.	
		Bones meet at joints.	Ligament, tendon, and bone structure are inherited.
Exercise Physiology Concept III: What characterizes a safe and appropriate muscular stretching and strengthening program?	*Exercise Physiology Concept III: What characterizes a safe and appropriate muscular stretching and strengthening program?*	*Exercise Physiology Concept III: What characterizes a safe and appropriate muscular stretching and strengthening program?*	*Exercise Physiology Concept III. What characterizes a safe and appropriate muscular stretching and strengthening program?*
Exercising muscles makes them stronger.	Exercising muscles makes them stronger.	Proper warm-up and stretching and strengthening exercises prepare muscles for vigorous physical activity.	Regular monitoring of progress of muscular strength, endurance, and flexibility demonstrates the benefits of engaging in a fitness program.
	Muscles need safe stretching to be ready to exercise.	Proper stretching and strengthening exercises serve to cool down muscles after vigorous physical activity.	Stretching exercises for the major muscles groups should be held for 30 to 60 seconds or longer, to

Table 1. Critical Student Concepts, K–6

Exercise Physiology Concept IV: How do body composition and nutrition interact to develop and maintain lifetime fitness?	*Exercise Physiology Concept IV: How do body composition and nutrition interact to develop and maintain lifetime fitness?*	the point of a strong pull that diminishes as the muscle stretches during the hold.
Food provides the body with energy for daily life and vigorous physical activity.	Whole grain breads, crackers, and muffins are better sources of energy than those made with only white flour and lots of sugar.	The principles of muscle strength, endurance, and flexibility include overload, individual differences, progression, and regularity.
	Dynamic strengthening exercises help develop muscular strength, which contributes to overall body endurance.	*Exercise Physiology Concept IV: How do body composition and nutrition interact to develop and maintain lifetime fitness?*
	Muscles function by contracting to move or stabilize bones; they do not stretch on their own.	Body composition and nutritional needs interact and change.
	Muscles require regular stretching to maintain their contracting function.	Regular monitoring of changes in body composition demonstrates the benefits of engaging in a fitness program.
	Exercise Physiology Concept IV: How do body composition and nutrition interact to develop and maintain lifetime fitness?	Inherited, familial, and cultural factors influence the size and shape of peoples' bodies.
	Carbohydrates, proteins, and fats should be eaten every day.	
	Body composition refers to lean and fat components of the human body, and both affect and are affected by vigorous physical activity.	

Table 1. Critical Student Concepts, 8–12

Eighth Grade	Tenth Grade	Twelfth Grade
Exercise Physiology Concept I: What factors contribute to an appropriate cardiorespiratory fitness program?	*Exercise Physiology Concept I: What factors contribute to an appropriate cardiorespiratory fitness program?*	*Exercise Physiology Concept I: What factors contribute to an appropriate cardiorespiratory fitness program?*
The principles of cardiorespiratory fitness program include frequency, intensity, type, and time (FITT).	Maintaining a regular physical fitness program and it benefits requires dedication and updated information.	Vigorous physical activity positively influences health and well being during the various stages of life.
The FITT guidelines for a cardiorespiratory fitness program include exercising a minimum of 20 to 30 minutes three days per week to a maximum of 50 to 60 minutes every other day, within one's target heart rate range.		Regular aerobic activity releases endorphins, which enable people to enjoy and sustain commitment to their fitness programs.
Regular vigorous physical activity and proper nutrition contribute to physical and mental health.		
Physical, emotional, and social growth influence individual needs and the results of a regular physical fitness program.		
Family, school, and community attitudes toward vigorous physical activity and proper nutrition influ-		

Table 1. Critical Student Concepts, 8–12

ence an individual's commitment to a physical fitness program.

Exercise Physiology Concept II: How do the structure and function of the human anatomy contribute to and restrict the development of lifetime fitness?

Muscles contract, which is why they are typically found in functional pairs.

Flexion, extension, abduction, adduction, and rotation of muscles at their joints provide the body parts with their specific and wide range of motion.

Different types of joints—nonaxial, uniaxial, pivot, biaxial, and tri-axial—serve different purposes.

Exercise Physiology Concept II: How do the structure and function of the human anatomy contribute to and restrict the development of lifetime fitness?

The design of different types of synovial joints facilitate the range of movement found in the body.

The muscles, joints, and range of motion of the arms and legs are similar.

Exercise Physiology Concept II: How do the structure and function of human anatomy contribute to and restrict the development of lifetime fitness?

Fitness activity needs to be adjusted to each stage of human development as people mature and age.

Neurons enable the brain to send and receive signals to and from the muscles and organs.

Table 1. Critical Student Concepts, 8–12

Exercise Physiology Concept III: What characterizes a safe and appropriate muscular stretching and strengthening program?

The principles of muscle strength, endurance, and flexibility include overload, individual differences, progression, and regularity.

Stretching exercises for the major muscles groups should be held for 30 to 60 seconds or longer, to the point of a strong pull that diminishes as the muscle stretches during the hold.

Dynamic, isometric, and isokinetic methods of weight training each contribute to various physical activities.

Bouncing, swinging, stretching, strengthening fast, locking, over-bending, arching, and clicking the joints are harmful aspects of some exercises.

Exercise Physiology Concept III: What characterizes a safe and appropriate muscular stretching and strengthening program?

The FITT principles of strength training include frequency of training (F), intensity—amount of weight (I), type of exercise—using body weight, free weights, or weight machines (T), and time—sets of repetitions (T).

Muscular strength is improved by performing isotonic, isometric, or isokinetic exercises every other day.

Specific exercises such as neck circles, hurdler's stretch, deep knee bends, back arching, and double leg lifts are harmful to the body and should be avoided.

Exercise Physiology Concept III: What characterizes a safe and appropriate muscular stretching and strengthening program?

A proper strength training program fits the individual's body composition, current strength, and the specific needs of the physical activity for which it is undertaken.

Goal setting and recording progress in a stretching and strengthening program enable students to overcome barriers to continued participation.

Table 1. Critical Student Concepts, 8–12

Most common sports and work-related injuries can be prevented and successfully treated.	*Exercise Physiology Concept IV: How do body composition and nutrition interact to develop and maintain lifetime fitness?*	*Exercise Physiology Concept IV: How do body composition and nutrition interact to develop and maintain lifetime fitness?*
Exercise Physiology Concept IV: How do body composition and nutrition interact to develop and maintain lifetime fitness?	Body composition and nutritional needs interact and change as students grow, engage in different physical activities, and increase their fitness levels.	Proper nutrition and vigorous physical activity positively influence health and well being during the various stages of life.
Body composition and nutritional needs interact and change as students grow, engage in different physical activities, and increase their fitness levels.	Excess sugar, starch, fat, alcohol, caffeine, and food supplements impede performance of physical activities.	Nutritional and exercise needs change with and must be adapted to various stages of life.
Proper nutrition contributes to physical and mental health.		Excess sugar, starch, fat, alcohol, caffeine, and food supplements impede performance of physical activities.
Family, school, and community attitudes toward proper nutrition influence an individual's commitment to a physical fitness program.		Eating disorders such as anorexia nervosa and bulimia can be life threatening, but they are treatable.
Excess sugar, starch, fat, alcohol, caffeine, and food supplements impede performance of physical activities.		

How Can I Learn More?

Alter, J. (1986). *Stretch and strengthen.* Boston, MA: Houghton Mifflin.

_____. (1990). *Stretch and strengthen.* Boston, MA: Houghton Mifflin.

_____. (1983). *Surviving exercise.* Boston, MA: Houghton Mifflin.

_____. (1990). *Surviving exercise.* Boston, MA: Houghton Mifflin.

Bailey, C. (1994). *Smart exercise: Burning fat, getting fit.* Boston, MA: Houghton Mifflin.

Cooper, K. H. (1982). *The aerobics program for total well-being: Exercise, diet, emotional balance.* New York: Bantam Books.

Corbin, C. B., & Lindsay, R. (1993). *Fitness for life.* Glenview, IL: Scott, Foresman and Company.

Corbin, C., and Pangrazi, R. P. (1994). *Teaching strategies for improving youth fitness.* Reston, VA: AAHPERD.

Greenberg, J. S. , & Pargman, D. (1989). *Physical fitness: A wellness approach* (2nd ed.). Englewood Cliffs, NJ: Prentice Hall.

Hoeger, W. K., & Hoeger, S. A. (1992). *Lifetime physical fitness and wellness: A personalized program* (3rd ed.). Englewood, CO: Morton.

References

Clarkson, P. M. (1995, February). *Micro-nutrients and exercise: Antioxidants and minerals.* Paper given at the International Scientific Consensus Conference on Nutrition in Athletics, Monaco.

Cooper, K. H. (1982). *The aerobics program for total well-being: Exercise, diet, emotional balance.* New York: Bantam Books.

Corbin, C. B., & Lindsay, R. (1997). *Concepts of fitness and wellness with laboratories.* Madison, WI: Brown and Benchmark.

Csikszentmihalyi, M. (1990). Flow: *The psychology of optimal experience.* New York: Harper Collins.

Falk, B., & Tennenbaum, G. (1996). The effectiveness of resistance training in children. *Journal of Sports Medicine, 20* (3) 176-186.

Friede, A. (Ed.). (1997).*CDC prevention guidelines: A guide for action.* Baltimore, MD: Wilkins & Williams.

Jones, B., Cowan, D. N., & Knapic, J. J. Exercise, training and injuries. *Journal of Sports Medicine, 18* (3) 202-214.

Kapit, W., Macey, R. I., & Meisami, E. (1987). *The physiology coloring book.* Cambridge: Harper Collins.

Kapit, W., & Elson, L. M. (1977). *The anatomy coloring book.* New York: Harper and Row.

Moorhouse, L. E., & Gross, L. (1975). *Total fitness in 30 minutes a week.* New York: Pocket Books.

_____. (1995). *Moving into the future: National standards for physical education, A guide to content and assessment.* St. Louis MO: Mosby.

Rowland, T. (1994). Effect of prolonged inactivity on aerobic fitness of children. *Journal of Sports Medicine and Physical Fitness, 34* (2) 147-155..

Watkins, J., & Peabody, P. (1996). Sports injuries in children and adolescents treated at a sports injury clinic. *Journal of Sports Medicine and Physical Fitness, 36*, 43-48.

Williams, C. (1995, February). *Macro-nutrients and performance.* Paper presented at the International Scientific Consensus Conference on Nutrition in Athletics, Monaco.

Williams, M. H. (1995, February). *Nutritional ergogenics in athletics.* Paper presented at the International Scientific Consensus Conference on Nutrition in Athletics, Monaco.

_____. (1994). *The Prudential fitnessgram test administration manual.* Dallas TX: The Cooper Institute for Aerobics Research.

_____. (1996). *Physical activity and health: A report of the surgeon general.* Rockville, MD: U. S. Department of Health and Human Services.

Glossary

Adenosine triphosphate (ATP): major molecule in which living cells store energy.

Aerobic: exercise that requires oxygen to produce energy.

Aerobic strength: enables muscles to continue moving for long periods of time without fatigue.

Anaerobic: high intensity, short-term activities that do not utilize oxygen for energy.

Calorie: a unit to measure heat energy derived from food.

Cardio: heart.

Concentric: coming together or shortening (in a description of a muscle contraction).

Eccentric: moving apart or lengthening (in a description of a muscle contraction).

Flexibility: description of ligament structure such as lax or tight; often confused with muscle flexibility, as in flexibility exercises instead of stretching exercises.

Frequency: how often a person exercises (sessions per week).

Glucose: blood sugar, the main source of energy for the human body.

Individual differences: adapting a program to fit an individual's starting and developmental levels.

Intensity: how hard a person exercises (i.e., overload for strength, speed of aerobic activity).

Joint: where two bones meet.

Ligaments: tissues that hold bones together

Mode: different kinds of exercise for training, such as running, walking, bicycling.

Overload: going beyond what is comfortable in strengthening and aerobic exercise; increasing demand.

Power strength: enables muscles to lift and hold a very heavy weight.

Progression: graduated increases in time (duration) and intensity of exercise.

Regularity: engaging in activity on a routine schedule.

Resistance: the amount of weight that is lifted in strength training.

Respiratory: function of the lungs in breathing.

Sets: number of groups of repetitions in which a resistance exercise is done.

Specificity: the mode of exercise that enables a person to increase and maintain fitness and adequately fulfill the needs of the person and the activity.

Tendons: tissues that attach muscles to bones.

Time: how long in minutes a person exercises.

Type: ways of achieving the same goal, such as isotonic or isokinetic strengthening exercise.

Chapter 6
Historical Perspectives

By Jan Patterson

Physical education and activity have a tremendous history, beginning with movement for survival and daily living, to training and exercise for war, to understanding the role of play in human development, the origin of sports and their relationship with society, and the evolution of the modern-day Olympics. From the ancient Chinese, who were involved with understanding human body movement and developing exercises to enhance that movement, to the games of the ancient Romans, to the influence of war on fitness and physical education programs, to the medical aspects of physical education, to modern day concepts of recreation and play, the history of movement and physical education is multifaceted. By studying the past we learn to appreciate the present and plan for a healthy and active lifestyle in the future.

What Is Historical Perspective?

History is the study of change or lack of same over time. The study of history, in general, provides a perspective on what has occurred in the past, what can be learned from the past, and what the past can predict about the future. By studying this chronicle of events we can develop an understanding of how mankind has reached a particular moment in time and what we can hope for or speculate about the future. In physical education, historical perspective provides teachers and students alike with a deeper appreciation of a field that has evolved from such diverse roots as medicine and war.

Why Is Historical Perspective Important?

We must learn from the past in order to appreciate the present and plan for the future. Historical perspective is a process by which we can learn and improve ourselves, lest history repeat itself. Through the study of history, students of physical education will learn why present practices occur and will be able to predict future best practices.

Linking Historical Perspectives to the National Standards

The National Standard that most fits this subdiscipline is Standard 6: "Demonstrates understanding and respect for differences among people in physical activity settings." The study of historical perspectives in physical education highlights the influences of many cultures and many people. It explains the origin of sport, exercise, and recreation. It also is a study of personal history. For example, the knowledge we can gain from understanding an aging muscular-skeletal system and its genetic predisposition will allow us to develop and maintain a healthy, active lifestyle.

Jan Patterson is a sixth grade teacher at La Costa Heights, California, Elementary School.

While the National Standards do not state that the subdiscipline of history should be part of the instruction, they do indicate that historical knowledge enhances the appreciation of individual movement and multicultural activities and the understanding of sport and activity.

Selected Historical Perspectives Concepts

This subdiscipline of historical perspectives revolves around four themes:
1. The history of the modern day Olympics.
2. The history of exercise and training.
3. The history of physical activity and sport.
4. The history of physical education.

The History of the Modern Day Olympics

The Olympic Games is an international sports festival that began in ancient Greece. The ancient games were held for several hundred years, until they were abolished during the early Christian era. The purpose of the ancient Olympics was to honor the gods. In addition to athletic events, they included competition in music and oratory and theatrical performances. The purpose of the modern Olympics is to acknowledge the athletic abilities of participants from around the world.

Ancient Times. It is believed that the ancient Olympic Festival was born sometime around the year 1200 B.C. The first Olympic games had only one event, the stade, which was a race of about 200 yards. No records were kept of competitors' actual scores, only of the events that occurred. It was not until almost 700 B.C. that the first champion was recorded—a cook by the name of Coroibus of Elis.

The Olympic Festival was a time of truce between warring factions. For several weeks prior to the events, athletes would train before game officials who could disqualify individuals who lacked sufficient physical ability.

Events were added in ensuing years. First came longer running races, then wrestling, a pentathlon (running, jumping, spear-javelin throwing, discus throwing, and wrestling), boxing, and chariot racing. One of the most unusual events was the pankration, which was a combined effort of upright wrestling and kicking.

By 632 B.C., the games had been extended to include five days of competition. The Olympic Festival occurred once every four years until 349 A.D. At that time, Emperor Theodosius I declared the event unchristian. Despite this setback, there is some speculation that the games may have continued into the 5th century.

Medieval and Renaissance Times. There has been much speculation that, in the Middle Ages, people resumed a similar type of athletic tournament. This allowed the knights to maintain a level of physical fitness. The longbow contest was probably one of the most familiar events of these tournaments. The crossbow was very popular, and it was used extensively during the Hundred Years War. Jousting and javelin throwing also were common events during this era.

In later years, festivals, tournaments, and other such games and activities were forgotten. During the Renaissance, the focus turned to exercise and training. There was a resurgence of interest in educating the whole human being. Vittorino da Feltre, an Italian educator, echoed the teaching of Plato: "A sound mind in a sound body." Da Feltre believed that through physical exercise an individual could develop a personalized physical style, something he saw as important in the total education of the person.

The 17th and 18th Centuries. In the eighteenth century, the impact of the German culture on the resurgence of the modern Olympics began with the opening of a school for gymnastics. Johann Christoph Friedrich Guts-Muths developed a training program in which athletes could work on strength, agility, and fitness skills. His athletes combined locomotion and nonlocomotion skills with posture and balance to prepare for both war and competition. At the same time, scholars and trainers in Sweden and Denmark began to develop training programs and schools for gymnastics, fencing, and other similar sports. These programs were a manifestation of the resurgence of nationalism, and the desire of many countries to develop strong men to fight wars.

The 19th and 20th Centuries. However, a Frenchman by the name of Pierre de Coubertin had a different vision. He wanted to develop a forum that would foster peace as well as national pride. His vision was to resurrect the Olympic Games. In 1896, de Coubertin succeeded. Representatives of 13 countries met to compete in nine events: cycling, fencing, gymnastics, lawn tennis, shooting, swimming, track and field, weight lifting, and wrestling. Women first competed in the Olympics in 1900, and in 1924 the first winter games were held in Chamonix, France.

Since 1896, numerous world events have had an impact on the Olympic Games. In 1916, 1940, and 1944, the games were suspended due to war. In the 1936 Olympics in Berlin, Adolph Hitler tried to ban black athletes. However, Jesse Owens, through his remarkable performance, sent his own message to the world refuting Hitler's political and social propaganda regarding minorities.

In Mexico City in 1968, African American medal winners Tommie Smith and John Carlos garnered worldwide attention with their award ceremony protest of racial discrimination in the United States. In Munich in 1972, terrorism struck the Olympics, and 11 Israeli athletes were killed by Palestinian guerrillas.

Political boycotts also have had their impact on the Olympics. In 1956, Iraq, Egypt, and Lebanon boycotted the Melbourne Games to protest the Anglo-French seizure of the Suez Canal; and the Netherlands, Switzerland, and Spain boycotted to protest the Soviet invasion of Hungary. In 1976, in Montreal, 33 African nations boycotted the Games to protest apartheid in South. The 1980 boycott by the United States was followed by a Soviet boycott in 1984. Most recently, at the 1996 Games in Atlanta, the concern about possible terrorist attacks resulted in the highest degree of security ever for an Olympic Village.

The History of Exercise and Training

Throughout history, people have believed in the healing power of exercise and the physical protection provided by a strong body. As early as 2700 B.C., the Chinese devised a method of exercise founded on massage, pressure points, friction, vibration, and other passive exercise movements. The early literature often refers to these exercises as dances. What appears to have survived through the centuries are some physical therapy practices for rehabilitation as well as the discipline of Yoga.

Ancient Times. The Greeks spent most of their time performing repetitions of skills and running. Their primary concern was in being able to win contests at various games and festivals rather than exercising for health or fitness. The ancient Romans believed in a vigorous exercise program. This program was reported to be so rigorous that anyone found unfit was excluded from the ranks of the gladiators or soldiers. From this dedication to fitness came the phrase mens sana en corpore sano (a strong mind in a healthy body). This phrase is used frequently today to emphasize the connection between fitness and wellness.

Medieval and Renaissance Times. During the Renaissance, Leonardo Da Vinci furthered the study of the human body by identifying and illustrating specific muscle groups. Through his anatomical studies, Da Vinci was able to shed light on the structure of muscle groups and how they worked. During this period, individuals were more interested in going to heaven than in becoming physically fit.

The 17th and 18th Centuries. During the seventeenth and eighteenth centuries, various countries established schools or training places for men. Their common function was to train individuals in strength, agility, and physical fitness. In Germany, Sweden, and France, these schools were meant to train soldiers to be better fighters. The premise was to keep the military strong at all times.

As society entered the Age of Enlightenment (18th century), Jean Jacques Rousseau, a philosopher, revolutionized education when he placed health at the forefront of the fully developed citizen. In his treatise on education, entitled "Emile," Rousseau wrote about the need for children to mature in harmony with nature. Rousseau believed that the body was strengthened through exercise guided by nature, and that in order to learn, individuals must exercise the body, senses, and organs.

His philosophy dictated that a strong mind was developed through a strengthened body. This was the first time a link had been made between health and wellness. Many of these same ideas and beliefs were restated in the writings of Rene Descartes, John Locke, and John Dewey.

The 19th and 20th Centuries. In the years between the early 1800s and the onset of World War I, a theory suggesting that the mind controls the body emerged. This was espoused by philosophers Georg Hegel and Karl Marx. These men felt that an individual needed to become physically strong through exercise in order to be a contributing member of a political society. They believed that logic based upon scientific information, rather than emotion, caused an individual to select a particular physical activity.

They believed that a person's "state of being" (mental attitude) could guide the selection of a physical activity and the subsequent determination of how hard to perform it. Hegel concluded that the mind controlled the body, and therefore operated separately; that is, an intellectual rationale could be made for participation in physical activity. This type of thinking, according to Hegel's philosophy, lead to a "higher order human being."

With the advent of World War I and the high level of war-related injuries came an increase in the need for physical rehabilitation programs. Thus, the medical strand of physical education was reborn into physical therapy. And, we had come full circle, recognizing the early Chinese belief that through exercise, the body could be to some degree, restored.

With a new emphasis on fitness and exercise, researchers in the late 1800s began to study the effects of strength training and how to measure increased fitness. They also began to study the various types of fitness testing. These studies set the stage for future fitness testing for military and educational purposes.

During the 1940s, the Roger's Strength Index and Physical Fitness Index testing programs were used in many schools. A general motor fitness test during this time included balance, flexibility, agility, strength, power, and endurance items. Fitness testing was an initial part of the physical education curriculum at the college level. Wartime training tests included jogging, aquatics, survival swimming, steeplechase, and combat games.

As a result of low fitness scores during the 1950s, colleges and universities began to hold sport fitness days. During this time, the Kraus-Weber Test analyzed the fitness levels of children in America and in Europe. The low scores of the American children led to a national conference on fitness, which led—during the Kennedy administration—to the establishment of the President's Council of Physical Fitness. One of the activities of the Council was to recognize individuals who met a rigorous criteria in agility, endurance, strength, and flexibility.

During the last 50 years, the body of knowledge related to exercise has changed and improved exponentially. From the early 1940s until the 1970s, ballistic stretching was the preferred warm-up method. Hyperextension of neck, back, and knees also was considered standard stretching practice. The level of sophistication that currently exists related to exercise includes not only how to stretch and exercise, but why one stretches and exercises, as well as how to do so safely.

Rapid changes in technology are having a tremendous impact on the fitness industry. Exercise devices such as treadmills, rowers, climbers, and cross country skiers are equipped with heart monitoring devices. Some of these devices not only provide the participant with immediate feedback about heart rate during the exercise period, they also store the data, analyze it, and at the end of the workout provide the participant with information related to the next workout period. One can only speculate about the advances that will occur in exercise equipment and monitoring systems in the next 10 to 20 years!

The History of Physical Activity and Sport

Many of today's physical activities and sports had their beginnings in ritual and religious activities, and there are several schools of thought related to their historical implications. Piaget (1966) for example, tends to deal more with the physical activity aspect of human involvement, whereas Guttmann (1978) subscribes to a multifaceted rationale for sport.

Guttmann says six characteristics of physical activity have transformed sports from ritualistic, religious activities to what they are today:

1. Guttmann says sports began as adult behavior that was ceremonial in nature and pleasing to the gods. He suggests that the ancient Olympic Festival, as well as some Native American games, were performed strictly for the purpose of evoking positive favor from the gods.

2. The second characteristic to emerge was "equality." The philosophy of physical activity was that everyone should participate and that the competition among the contestants should be fair. Guttmann espouses that modern sport has its roots in the concept of equality.

3. "Specialization" is the third characteristic in this theory of sport evolution. Specialization describes full-time training in a sport, unencumbered by job or financial concerns. Guttmann's examples span from the days of the ancient Greeks who would train for the Olympic Festival to modern day athletes who earn scholarships for athletic prowess.

4. "Rationalization" is the fourth characteristic. In other words, the rules of competition are an integral part of any sport. Guttmann cites the rules for competition from the Ancient Olympics to modern times as an example of this characteristic.

5. The fifth hallmark in sports evolution is "quantification." This is the apparent need to quantify success or failure related to sport. For example, the Polynesians kept score in their dart games, the Romans measured distance and time, and today we measure batting averages and earned run averages.

6. Seventh in Guttmann's theory theory is "records." Along with the need to quantify sports, there is also the need to record those statistics for future reference.

Piaget described physical activity in the developing child as the fulfillment of the need to play. He outlined a developmental hierarchy of skill building from play as enjoyment, to play as a sense of accomplishment and control, to play as a socially interactive activity. In his treatise on interpreting play, Piaget alludes to the notion that physical activity and play are essential in the lives of humans. He cautions that how one interacts in that social environment can determine how well one makes the transition from child's play to adult play.

Piaget's belief that physical activity and play are an integral part of life provides an explanation of why so many different physical activities exist. In understanding play, physical activity, and sport across the world, it becomes readily apparent that almost every culture has contributed to the mix.

Ancient Times. Early childhood activities included spinning tops and swinging in swings. Early adults spent much of their time participating in sports such as throwing a discus or javelin, boxing, and wrestling. The Greeks were especially fond of contests such as chariot racing, foot racing, and other individual events.

The Romans participated in ball games that required throwing and catching skills. It is believed that this is where handball originated. The Romans also performed rigorous exercises that included the use of weights. Like the Greeks, they competed in chariot races and gladiator events. The Romans introduced the skill of kicking a ball, and the Chinese developed the skills necessary to fly kites.

Medieval and Renaissance Times. During Medieval times, jesters participated in juggling, stilt walking, and an activity called loop and stick, where they used a stick to rotate a circular object on its side. The squires participated in what we would today call basic tumbling and self-defense moves, including hand to hand combat. The knights participated in "melee" (hand-to-hand sword fighting), jousting, and "long bow" (archery). Such activities prepared them for war. During the Middle Ages, there also was a continued interest in ball games such as "boule," which may have been the origin of modern day soccer, and "rounders," a form of baseball.

Recreational activities during this time period included hunting, hawking, handball, tennis, billiards, and shuffleboard. Despite the seeming abundance of physical activity, however, physical activity actually decreased during this era. In fact, only music, games, and dancing were considered acceptable upper class pursuits. The common people of this era participated in more violent games, such as foot fighting and wrestling.

The 17th and 18th Centuries. During these 200 years, games evolved from many different cultures. Native Americans (Huron Indians) played a game that involved tossing a bladder type ball that was caught in a net like object. This game was played over great distances. It often involved more than 100 players and lasted for several days. This game eventually developed into modern day lacrosse.

The Puritans wanted physical activity be more "Christian," without the violence or competition exhibited by many games. Therefore, activities such as fishing, hunting, and walking were encouraged in their communities. They believed that play was actually a poor use of time. It was only useful in assisting individuals to recover from or to prepare for work. From this philosophy came the term recreation (re-creation). The Quakers enjoyed golf, tennis, bowling, and cricket. Like the Puritans, they preferred to be involved in physical activities that were less competitive in nature.

The 19th and 20th Centuries. During the Industrial Revolution, the populations of cities increased, and playgrounds and other recreational facilities were developed. These facilities resulted from the growing concern about the poor health of children and the lack of space in which they could play. The assembly-line production of sporting goods and increased leisure time made it possible, even in during the 1800s, for more people to be involved in sports and activities.

During the late 1800s, there was an upsurge of new team sports in America. Basketball was born in 1891, at a school for Christian Workers in Springfield, Massachusetts. (It later became a YMCA.) Sensing the need for something that could be played indoors during cold weather, James Naismith developed a game that involved bouncing a ball and tossing it into a peach basket. Although basketball proved to be very popular, many businessmen complained that it was too demanding for a lunch break activity. So, in 1895, William Morgan invented volleyball for members of a businessmen's class at the YMCA. The original game involved striking the bladder of a basketball back and forth over a tennis net.

The influence of other countries is apparent in many of the games that were developed during the 19th century. For example, the British game of "rounders" may be the forerunner of baseball. Rounders, in turn, was an offshoot of older games that may date back to the Egyptians. Football is another game whose history goes back many centuries; many related games involved kicking a ball, but the shape of the ball and the rules of the game varied.

As participation in sports continued to increase, so did spectatorship. After the Civil War, professional teams began to appear. For example, in 1871, the National Baseball League was organized. With this League came written rules, specialized roles, statistics, public information, and national competitions.

In the United States today, baseball, basketball, and football are the most popular spectator and participation sports. Popular recreational activities include boating, fishing, bowling, bicycle riding, jogging dance, tennis, and golf.

However, ours is a country of immigrants who bring their cultural preferences with them, and these preferences eventually affect recreation. For example, with the increase in the number of Latin Americans and Western Europeans in this country, we have seen an increase in the popularity of soccer. Knowing about the popular recreational activities in other countries can increase our understanding of these people and their cultures.

In Canada, ice hockey is the most popular sport to play and watch. Canadians also enjoy skiing, tobogganing, swimming, fishing, tennis, and golf. In Eastern Europe, sports are serious business. Children are required to participate, and the most promising athletes are groomed for events such as the Olympics. Eastern Europeans also enjoy many cultural activities, such as the ballet and concerts. Western Europeans enjoy skiing and ice hockey, as well as soccer.

Latin Americans enjoy jai-alai and soccer. Indian dances are an integral part of many religious ceremonies, and from these traditions have evolved many popular dances and music, such as reggae and the samba. Northern Africans enjoy soccer, hunting, and fishing. The unique sport of camel racing also is one of their favorites. Southern Africans, with their predominantly agricultural economy, have very little leisure time compared to the rest of the world. However, there is time for dancing and for sport festivals.

The people of the South Pacific prefer swimming, boating, and fishing. They also enjoy soccer, cricket, and rugby–which they learned from British settlers. In South Asia, dance and music are extremely popular. Dance is used to tell stories and to explain religious beliefs. Some individuals also participate in table tennis, sumo wrestling, and the martial arts. In Southeast Asia, dancing and kick boxing are the favorite activities. Fire dances abound, along with other religious and traditional dances. There also are dances that depict events such as battles between witches and dragons.

In this country in recent years, both professional sports and community recreational programs have experienced tremendous growth. There are women's teams, men's teams, and coed teams for sports, including softball, volleyball, field hockey, basketball, and tennis. Along with the interest in sporting activities, there also has been a growing popularity in workout facilities. These range from private gyms to programs run through the YMCA and YWCA. Activities include aerobic workouts, racquetball, tennis, weight lifting, and swimming.

Finally, while it is beyond the scope of this chapter, each community has its own history related to physical activities and sports, and it is important for students to learn about that history in physical education classes.

The History of Physical Education

In the western world, the study of physical education as a discipline can be traced back to the days of Plato and the concept of a sound mind in a sound body. Plato espoused the importance of maintaining physical health and conditioning in order to improve one's intellect. While Plato was concerned with training military individuals rather than health-conscious people, the principles are similar. Plato suggested that a balance between intellectual and physical education results in character training and renders an individual healthy in both body and soul.

Ancient Times. Perhaps the earliest accounts of physical education can be found in the training of the Spartans. Spartan youth were instructed in swimming, running, fighting, wrestling, boxing, ball games, horsemanship, archery, discus and javelin throwing, field marches, and pancratium (a combination of boxing and wrestling). These activities were designed to prepare them for military careers.

In Ancient Athens, music (meaning academics) and gymnastics were the two curricular focuses. Students began their education around the age of seven with physical conditioning. Gymnastics (or physical education) in Athens included boxing, wrestling, jumping, ball games, games with hoops, military skills, running, wrestling, dancing, javelin and discus throwing, and the pancratium. Wealthy families in Athens hired a paidotribe (a physical education teacher who owned his own palestra, or wrestling center) to educate their children. This seems to be very similar to today's personal trainer or private health club. The women in Athens did not receive physical education instruction, although Spartan women participated in gymnastic exercise.

The training of youths in Rome had one purpose: to develop disciplined, obedient, and able warriors. They were taught jumping, running, swimming, horsemanship, wrestling, boxing, archery and fencing.

Medieval and Renaissance Times. During this era, sporting activities and physical education seemed to disappear, except for purely military activities. This may have been due, in part, to people's primary interest in going to church and getting into heaven.

During the Age of Science, physical education and sport again became accepted. Philosophers approved of the notion that creating a well rounded individual through physical education was a prudent goal. Students studied swimming, dancing, wrestling, running, leaping, fencing, climbing, walking, riding, hunting, playing ball, and shooting. There was a renewed interest in hygiene, along with swimming and water safety. These areas were then included in physical education instruction for all students, but primarily for boys.

The 17th and 18th Centuries. In Colonial America, education in general was left to the parents. Health and physical education were not valued, and therefore were not taught. This attitude probably stemmed from the lifestyle of the time, which was geared toward basic survival. Farming was a common occupation, and children were expected to assist.

However, in 1790, Noah Webster voiced his views on physical education. He reviewed the statements of ancient philosophers about the value of a sound mind and body. Webster's ideas provided a stimulus for a renewed interested in the worthiness of physical education.

The 19th and 20th Centuries. In the early 1800s, education varied with the area in which children lived. For example, in California, many families lived on ranches. Therefore, tutors came to the home. Physical education consisted of instruction in horseback riding.

Between 1830 and 1860, there were three major influences in physical education programs in U.S. schools. These were Swedish calisthenics, which emphasized participation in a series of exercises performed on command; German gymnastics, which included vaulting, high jumping, wrestling, and pole vaulting; and English sports and games. Not until 1850 did public schools begin to emphasize physical education instruction. After the Civil War, the emphasis shifted to physical exercise as a way to improve and maintain a healthy body. During this period, many states passed laws governing physical education instruction in public schools.

In the mid 1800s, the field of medicine broke into specialty groups, and physical education was one of them. George Barker Windship (1834-1876) was a key figure in this movement. While his name is not commonly known, he had a tremendous impact on the field of exercise physiology. Windship was particularly interested in developing personal strength because of his own slight stature. His focus was gymnastics. Windship entered Harvard Medical School, where he studied physiology and anatomy. He was so intrigued with this area that upon graduation, he prescribed mostly exercise to cure the ills of his patients. As result of Windship's influence, programs in physical education began to incorporate medical aspects.

Teacher training and preparation for physical education began with the normal schools. These quasi-institutes focused solely on the preparation of teachers. Individuals interested in physical education attended a normal school and then enrolled in summer school courses that dealt with physical training, or they attended one of the few four-year universities. During the beginning stages of professional preparation programs, the study revolved around calisthenics, remedial exercise, and health. Medical professionals were generally the instructors and the decision makers about the course of study in physical education.

Dudley Allen Sargent (1849-1924), another physician who greatly influenced the discipline of physical education, created one of the first teacher training colleges for physical educators, and specifically for women physical educators. As a youth, Sargent was prone to physical activity. As a man, he espoused the strong connection between strengthened muscles and strengthened morals. During Sargent's college career, he became extremely interested in the connection between health and medicine, and more specifically in the connection between physical training and the study of physiology and anatomy.

Sargent eventually founded a private school for women at Harvard University. Fortunately, the President of Harvard was an advocate of preventive medicine and Sargent's beliefs, and he allowed Sargent to establish professional credentials for physical educators. Sargent then opened a gymnasium (a type of teacher-training facility) in Cambridge. Students were prepared to become "wholesome and efficient" as they entered the discipline of physical education instruction. Sargent's program developed the profound connection to medicine and physical education that exists today. By 1914, 24 colleges offered teacher training in physical education, including baccalaureate degrees in the discipline (Davenport 1984).

While the early physical educators were debating the virtues of the Swedish and German gymnastics, the English sport model was sweeping the country. Many physical education classes focused on recreational activities including golf, tennis, track and field, and basketball. By 1921, physical education was required in 28 states.

In the late 1930s, an educator by the name of Jesse Firing Williams suggested that the benefits of physical education included not only improvements in muscular strength and endurance, but also in social enlightenment and personal enjoyment. He encouraged participation in physical education purely for pleasure and happiness. Williams went on to discuss the benefits of participation in socially-appropriate physical education, including the development of leadership skills. He felt that the activities should be sporting in nature, rather than calisthenics. Williams further believed that physical education would eventually establish the basis for maintaining a healthy lifestyle. Many physical educators consider Jesse Firing Williams to be the father of modern day physical education.

Since World War II, physical education has gone through a number of cycles, from an emphasis on physical fitness to an emphasis on movement education, lifetime activities, health-related fitness, and social skills. Currently, there seems to be an emphasis on the conceptual understanding of physical education through a variety of activities (e.g., dance, team sports, gymnastics, aquatics, outdoor education, individual and dual sports, self defense). In addition, there seems to be a return to the idea of everyone being successful and working together for a common goal.

This shift in philosophy includes a move away from an emphasis on competition and winning to activities where everyone has a chance to be successful, where individuals can appreciate diversity, and where students are taught to be in charge of their own learning. One catalyst for this change occurred in 1977, with Public Law 94-142, which mandated physical education instruction for all individuals, even those with special needs. Today, many physically and mentally challenged individuals participate in physical education instruction alongside their non-challenged peers.

The research of Cain and Cain (1994) on the relationship between physical activity and learning provides yet another important reason for including physical education in schools. In today's colleges and universities, physical education trends are reflected in teacher training programs that include the study of human body systems as well as teaching methodology, curriculum development, and much more.

Placing Historical Perspectives in the Curriculum

How historical concepts are integrated into the physical education curriculum is a professional decision that must be made by the individual teacher. However, it is recommended that the physical education teacher work closely with the history/social science teacher in order to align the study of history with the study of movement. The physical education teacher also must be able to coordinate instruction and instructional units with grade-level standards and benchmarks.

The key concepts shown in Table 1 match those of the national benchmarks and support National Standard 6: "Demonstrates understanding and respect for differences among people in physical activity settings." In addition, the outline is aligned with the following history/social science curriculum:

- Kindergarten: Study of oneself in time and space.
- Grade 2: Study of one's local community.
- Grade 4: Study of one's state.
- Grade 6: Study of ancient and medieval times.
- Grade 8: Study of the United States through the nineteenth century.
- Grade 10: Study of the United States in the twentieth century.
- Grade 12: Study of current world history.

Integrating Historical Perspective Concepts into Instruction

Teachers must determine the best method for integrating historical concepts into their instructional program. This decision should be based on the individual needs of the school, grade level teaching approach, individual teaching style, and the learning needs of the students. Much research has been conducted on connecting new information with previous learning. Most certainly, teaching the historical perspectives of physical education as a separate entity would be dull at best, and would lack the impact that a more integrated, thematic instructional design would provide. It is probably most logical to begin this quest by looking at the history/social science curriculum, and then to align the study of the history of movement. The box beginning on page 155 contains several examples.

Assessing Student Learning

When students can use historical concepts in class to explain the importance of a physical activity to its country of origin or analyze the role of physical education and sport in American history, the curriculum has been effective in teaching historical concepts. It is important for teachers to use assessment techniques throughout the instructional process to assess student learning. Many of these assessment techniques are described more generally in Chapter 1 of this book.

Checking for Understanding. This assessment tool provides the teacher with a quick method of determining how well students are understanding the information being presented. Students may be asked to describe the history of an activity, the type of exercises people performed during a particular period of time, or particular events that have affected the modern Olympics.

Written Tests. The written test is an efficient way to assess student understanding, especially in highly cognitive areas such as historical perspectives. Test questions can parallel the questions included in the checking for understanding section, as well as higher level questions, such as "Why were many team sports created at the end of the 1800s?"

Student Projects. Student projects are another useful assessment technique in higher cognitive areas of physical education. Students can create a pictorial story of what they do during a lesson in physical education. They can do a "broadcast" or write an anthology related to how physical education experiences have changed during the past 100 years in America. They can create a study guide or game that teaches the origin of a specific sport or physical activity. They can develop an "Ancient Sports Digest," complete with pictures, interviews with ancient Olympians, or stories about things

Table 1. Critical Student Concepts, K–6

Kindergarten	Second Grade	Fourth Grade	Sixth Grade
Historical Perspectives Concept I: What is the history of the modern day Olympics?	*Historical Perspectives Concept I: What is the history of the modern day Olympics?*	*Historical Perspectives Concept I: What is the history of the modern day Olympics?*	*Historical Perspectives Concept I: What is the history of the modern day Olympics?*
The Olympic Games began a long time ago.	The Olympic Games began a long time ago.	Countries that have hosted the Olympics have had an impact on the events of the Olympics.	The Ancient Olympics began around 1200 BC and concluded around 349 AD.
Summer Olympics are now held every four years.	Summer Olympics are now held every four years.	There are specific areas (e.g., gymnasiums, fields, mountains) where Olympic events and other contests are held. Some of them may be in your state.	The stade was the only event in the first Olympics.
Winter Olympics are now held every four years.	Winter Olympics are now held every four years.	There are successful Olympic athletes on and off the field, some of whom may be in your state.	Each year new events were added to the ancient Olympics, such as the pentathlon, wrestling, chariot races, and boxing.
	There are successful Olympic athletes on and off the field, some of whom may live in the local community.		The ancient Olympics were considered to be both a sport and a religious festival.
Historical Perspectives Concept II: What is the history of exercise and training?	*Historical Perspectives Concept II: What is the history of exercise and training?*	*Historical Perspectives Concept II: What is the history of exercise and training?*	*Historical Perspectives Concept II: What is the history of exercise and training?*
Many people exercise to have strong bodies.	Throughout history, there have been many purposes for exercise.	Research has changed the way we exercise for the better.	Exercise was valued in ancient times.
Over time, people learn more about how to exercise better.	People throughout the ages have exercised to stay healthy.	Before today's research, people used to exercise in ways that could cause injuries.	In Ancient Greece, running was a popular activity.

Table 1. Critical Student Concepts, K–6

Historical Perspectives Concept III: What is the history of physical activity in general and sport specifically?	*Historical Perspectives Concept III: What is the history of physical activity in general and sport specifically?*	*Historical Perspectives Concept III: What is the history of physical activity in general and sport specifically?*	*Historical Perspectives Concept III: What is the history of physical activity in general and sports specifically?*
Games that are played at school in modern times may have looked different long ago.	There are reasons why games change.	Geography influences the kinds of physical activity in which people participate.	The purpose of games, dance, and sport in the ancient world was to maintain the culture, train for combat, perform religious ceremonies, and to respond to a need for physical activity.
	People living within the community make a difference in society through physical activity.	Various cultures have had an impact on sports and leisure-time recreational activities throughout the local area.	The early Romans enjoyed ball games, lifting weights, and chariot racing.
	There are many games to play.	Changes in games throughout the ages have been influenced by multicultural factors (beliefs and practices).	Early Greeks enjoyed chariot racing, foot racing, and other individual activities.
			During Medieval times, jesters, squires, and knights participated in different activities.
			Spartan training was rigorous and mostly for military training.
			In Ancient Rome, bathhouses served as places to participate in strenuous exercise.

Table 1. Critical Student Concepts, K–6

Historical Perspectives Concept IV: What is the history of physical education?	*Historical Perspectives Concept IV: What is the history of physical education?*	*Historical Perspectives Concept IV: What is the history of physical education?*	*Historical Perspectives Concept IV: What Is the history of physical education?*
Physical education may have looked different long ago.	Physical education may have looked different long ago.	Physical education has changed during the last 100 years.	The young children of Sparta were given physical education instruction in activities such as swimming, running, and wrestling.
Physical education is good for people, and that is why it is taught in school.	Physical education is good for people, and that is why it is taught in school.	Many states have laws governing physical education instruction in both elementary and high school.	In Ancient Athens the only two curricular areas were music (academics) and gymnastics (physical education).
	There is a difference between someone who pursues a single sport (athlete) and someone who wants to stay healthy through physical activity, but physical education is for everyone.		Physical education in Athens included boxing, jumping, ball games, dancing, throwing, wrestling, running, and the pancratium.
			Athenian women did not receive physical education instruction; however Spartan women were allowed to participate in gymnastics.
			In the Medieval times, religious convictions led to a decline in physical activity.
			There was a renewed interest in games and physical activity during the seventeenth and eighteenth centuries.

Table 1. Critical Student Concepts, K–6

The Romans used physical education to prepare for war.

There was a decline in physical education during Medieval times.

During the Renaissance period there was renewed interest in physical education.

Table 1. Critical Student Concepts, 8–12

Eighth Grade	Tenth Grade	Twelfth Grade
Historical Perspectives Concept I: What is the history of the modern day Olympics?	*Historical Perspectives Concept I: What is the history of the modern day Olympics?*	*Historical Perspectives Concept I: What is the history of the modern day Olympics?*
In 1896, the Olympic Games were revived in Athens, Greece, by Pierre de Coubertin. He wanted to further the cause of world peace, and to highlight athletes from different parts of the world.	There have been many political events in world history that have affected the Olympics.	There have been many political events in world history that have affected the Olympics.
Thirteen countries participated in the first modern Olympic Games, which had nine events.	In 1916, 1940, and 1944, the Olympics weren't held due to war.	In 1916, 1940, and 1944, the Olympics weren't held due to war.
Each year new events are added to the modern Olympics. The most recent are baseball and softball.	Racial conflicts affected the 1936 and 1968 Olympics.	Boycotts affected the Olympics in 1956, 1976, 1980, and 1984.
The modern Olympics also had its roots in preparing individuals for war.	Terrorism struck the United States when a bomb went off in Atlanta, Georgia, during the 1996 Olympics.	Terrorism continues to be a concern in the modern Olympics as a result of the 1972 killing of Israeli athletes.
	The host country may choose one demonstration sport for inclusion in the Olympics.	The host country may choose one demonstration sport for inclusion in the Olympics.

Table 1. Critical Student Concepts, 8–12

Women first competed in the Olympics in 1900.

Historical Perspectives Concept II: What is the history of exercise and training?

Rehabilitation became the focus of exercise during the war years.

Throughout history, exercise has been used for military training.

In the late 1800s, researchers began studying a variety of fitness tests.

Historical Perspectives Concept II: What is the history of exercise and training?

Fitness tests are currently conducted, some by state mandate, and are changed from year to year based on research findings.

The results of early fitness tests such as the Kraus-Weber indicated a need to focus on the fitness of American youth.

There is currently an emphasis on health-related fitness rather than performance-based fitness.

Research has focused attention on fitness changes in individuals who participate in preconditioning programs as opposed to inservice or specialized athletic training programs.

Historical Perspectives Concept II: What is the history of exercise and training?

Research has improved the way people exercise.

Research has improved exercise equipment.

Rousseau emphasized the importance of health and wellness.

Table 1. Critical Student Concepts, 8–12

Historical Perspectives Concept III: What is the history of physical activity in general and sports specifically?	*Historical Perspectives Concept III: What is the history of physical activity in general and sports specifically?*	*Historical Perspectives Concept III: What is the history of physical activity in general and sports specifically?*
As leisure time increased for the American population, so did the interest in sports (especially team sports) for both participation and spectator purposes.	Every game and sport we play has a history.	Every game and sport we play has a history.
The Industrial Revolution was a catalyst for the development of playground and recreational facilities.	Understanding the purpose and history of physical education and sports helps people to make informed decisions regarding education and recreation.	Philosophers such as Piaget and Guttmann have different beliefs as to why people play.
Many American sports and games have their roots in other countries.		Different sports are popular in different countries.
Professional sports emerged after the Civil War.		Understanding the purpose and history of physical education and sport around the world helps people to better understand different cultures and appreciate the contributions of different groups of people.
Sports rules are influenced by societal events.		
Historical Perspectives Concept IV: What is the history of physical education?	*Historical Perspectives Concept IV: What is the history of physical education?*	*Historical Perspectives Concept IV: What is the history of physical education?*
During the nineteenth century, three major programs (English sports and games, German gymnastics, and	Before the 1920s, physical education instruction consisted mostly of marching and calisthenics.	Plato believed in a sound mind in a sound body.

Table 1. Critical Student Concepts, 8–12

Swedish calisthenics) influenced American physical education.

Public schools begin to include physical education programs in the 1850s.

Medicine had a tremendous influence on physical education.

Colleges and universities were the first settings for physical education programs.

In the late 1800s, colleges and universities began training individuals to be instructors of physical education.

In 1921, 28 states had mandatory physical education instruction in their public schools.

In the 1920s, recreational activities were the primary focus for physical education. These activities included tennis, swimming, golf, and basketball.

During the World War years, the emphasis in physical education programs returned primarily to fitness.

Physical education has emphasized different areas (e.g., fitness, movement, lifetime sports, social activities) during the last 50 years.

In 1977, Public Law 94-142 stated that all children from ages 3 to 21 with a handicapping condition had the right to receive specialized physical education instruction.

There are programs and careers that are related to the physical activities and the sports in the United States and around the world.

Integrating Historical Concepts into Instruction

Theme I: The history of the modern day Olympics
Secondary Example (Grade 12)
Concept: The host country may choose one demonstration sport for inclusion in the Olympics.
Students research the demonstration sports that have appeared in the Olympics over the last 20 years. They work in groups of four, and do in-depth research on one demonstration sport from another country. The groups then present their findings to the rest of the class. During the presentation, each group should discuss the origin and social importance of the sport, and then compare it to something that may be similar in the United States. In order to perform this task, students may be required to read nonfiction novels, essays, and journals related to the sport or country of origin. At the conclusion of all the reports, the class discusses how accepting cultural differences has changed the history of the Olympics.

Theme II: The history of exercise and training
Elementary School Example (Grade 4)
Concept: Research has changed the way we exercise for the better.
Students interview adults about the way they exercised in elementary or high school. They then research six ways to exercise safely. Finally, they explain why the new exercise forms are safer than those used by their interview subjects.

Secondary School Example (Grade 10)
Concept: Rehabilitation became the focus of exercise during the war years.
This concept is addressed through an interdisciplinary approach to learning. In physical education, students learn about safe stretching and exercises, and they research rehabilitation techniques throughout the war years. Through peer coaching, students teach one another the safe ways to exercise and stretch while explaining how these methods have changed over time. In history/social science, they learn about the second World War, the types of injuries that soldiers sustained, and the need to assist these soldiers in returning to the work force. In science, the students learn about the human body and the history of medical treatment during war. At the conclusion of this interdisciplinary unit, students write an essay explaining the relationship between safe exercise and rehabilitation. The assignment is assessed for quality of writing by the language arts teacher.

Theme 3: The history of physical activity and sport
Middle School Example (Grade 6)
Concept: During Medieval Times, jesters, squires, and knights participated in different activities.
This is an interdisciplinary learning experience held in conjunction with the Medieval unit offered by the history/social science teacher. At the beginning of this unit, the students are taught the activities of the jesters—including juggling, stilt walking, and loop and stick. During the middle part of the unit, the students are taught the activities of the squires—including basic tumbling and self defense. Finally, toward the end of the unit, the students are taught the activities of the knights—including melee, jousting, and long bow. This unit concludes with a

Medieval Festival, where some of the students are jesters, some are squires, and some are knights participating in tournaments. Other Festival activities will depend on what is taught by the history/social science teacher. Students research Medieval activities and create a "newspaper" article about them.

Middle School Example (Grade 8)
Concept: As leisure time increased for the American population, so did the interest in sports (especially team sports), both as participants and spectators.
Students work in groups of six to research the origin of team sports in America during the late 1800s. Each group is assigned one sport (e.g., volleyball, basketball, football, baseball) to examine. Students investigate the origin of the sport, the social importance of the sport, and the original rules and strategies of the sport. They explore the reasons why the sport was invented during this particular time period. The groups then present their sport to the rest of the class. During the presentation, the group teaches the original version of the game and provides an opportunity for the class to play.

Theme 4: The history of physical education
Elementary School Example (Kindergarten)
Concept: Physical education may have looked different long ago.
Students draw pictures depicting the activities they perform during physical education class. They take their pictures home to share with parents. The students interview their parents to learn about the activities they performed during physical education when they were in Kindergarten.

that occurred during the Olympics. Students can create an historical brochure that outlines physical activity during different eras. The purpose of the brochure is to acquaint other students with physical activity opportunities in the past. Finally, after analyzing why a particular activity may have present day popularity, student can create a "sales pitch" to promote that activity.

Closing Comments

It is remarkable that the study of physical education dates back to at least 2700 B.C. The ancient Chinese, the ancient Greeks and Romans, and people from the Middle Ages into the 19th and 20th centuries all have had an impact on physical education as we know it today. The appreciation of this diversity and the uniqueness of world cultures as they participate in movement helps students to develop an historical perspective of physical education.

As Piaget wrote, play and physical activity are a part of the human personality. If that is true, then a piece of all aspects of the world is in each of us when we play, dance, select a leisure activity, or perform any physical activity.

Sir Isaac Newton acknowledged his ancestors and their historic contributions to his life when he said, "I saw what I saw because I stood on the shoulders of giants." As we study physical education, let the history of the discipline be the shoulders of the giants in the field, and let us use their wisdom to see the future of physical education.

How Can I Learn More?

Lucas, J. A. (1992). *Future of the Olympic Games.* Champaign, IL: Human Kinetics.

Mechikoff, R., & Estes, S. (1993). *A history and philosophy of sport and physical education.* Madison, WI: Brown and Benchmark Publishers.

Wiggins, D. K. (1995). *Sport in America.* Champaign, IL: Human Kinetics.

How Can Students Learn More?

Ashe, A. (1988). *A hard road to glory: A history of the African American athlete.* (Vols. 1–2). New York: Warner.

Bland, A. (1981). *The Royal Ballet.* New York: Doubleday.

Caerter, J. M. (1992). *Medieval games: Sports and recreation in feudal society.* New York: Greenwood Press.

Cook, J. J. (1978). *Famous firsts in tennis.* New York: G.P. Putnam's Sons.

Fisher, L. E. (1980). *Nineteenth century America: The sports.* New York: Holiday House.

Fradin, D. B. (1983). *A new true book: Olympics.* Chicago, IL: Children's Press.

Frommer, H. (1988). *A hundred and fiftieth anniversary album of baseball.* New York: Watts.

Gulbok, S., & Tamarin, A. (1976). *Olympic games in ancient Greece.* New York: Harper & Row.

Guttmann, A. (1992). *The Olympics: A history of the modern games.* Chicago, IL: University of Illinois Press.

Hackins, J. (1991). *Black dance in America.* New York: Watts.

Henry, B. (1981). *An approved history of the Olympic Games.* Los Angeles, CA: Color Graphics.

Johnson, K. (1990). *The concise encyclopedia of sports.* New York: Crowell.

Kent, Z. (1992). *U.S. Olympians.* Chicago, IL: Children's Press.

Lyttle, R. B. (1982). *The games they played–Sports in history.* New York: McClelland & Stewart.

Merriam Webster. (1976). *Webster sports dictionary.* New York: Author.

Moldea, D. E. (1989). *Interference: How organized crime influences professional football.* New York: Morrow.

Nash, B., & Zullo, A. (1993). *The greatest sports stories never told.* New York: Simon & Schuster.

Reidenbaugh, L. (1985). *The sporting news: First hundred years 1886-1986.* New York: Sporting News.

References

Caine, D., & Caine, R. (1994). *Making connections.* Alexandria, VA: Association for Supervision and Curriculum Development.

California Region 9. (1994). *California region 9 sample physical education curriculum.* San Diego, CA: San Diego County Office of Education.

Cottrell, D. M. (1984). The Sargent school for physical education. *JOHPERD, 65*(3), 32-37.

Davenport, J. (1984). The normal schools: Exploring our heritage. *JOHPERD, 65*(3), 26-28.

Guttmann, A. (1978). *From ritual to record.* New York: Columbia University Press.

Henry, B. (1981). *An approved history of the Olympic Games.* Los Angeles, CA: The Southern California Committee for the Olympic Games.

Melograno, V. J. (1994). Portfolio assessment: Documenting authentic student learning. *JOHPERD, 65*(8), 50-61.

Patterson, A., & Hallberg, E. C. (1966). *Background readings for physical education.* New York: Holt, Rinehart and Winston.

Paul, J. (1986). George Barker Windship. *JOHPERD, 57*(4), 29-31.

Glossary

Enlightenment: a period during the 1700s when individuals believed they became more aware of the infinite world and hence became more intelligent.

Jousting: an event in which two armored horseback riders charge each other.

Nationalism: a keen sense of pride in one's own country.

Pankration: an event in which a competitor used any means to force his opponent to give up, including boxing with bare hands, twisting an arm, and kicking in the stomach.

Pentathlon: a five-event contest in which the competitors participated in running, jumping, throwing the discus, spear throwing/javelin, and wrestling.

Stade: a foot race that measured the length of the stadium in which it was run; generally, the length was about 200 yards.

Chapter 7
Social Psychology

By Rita Mercier and Gayle Hutchinson

Today's student population is increasingly culturally and ethnically diverse. Students also differ greatly in physical, social and cognitive abilities, socioeconomic status, and basic values and beliefs, and these differences can have a profound effect on student learning needs. Unless careful and ongoing consideration is given to these learning needs when curriculum and instruction are planned, schools can be enigmatic and sometimes intimidating places for students. The complex human interactions that occur in schools provide daily challenges, as well as opportunities, for students to develop their personal and social capabilities.

Personal and social development is the primary focus of social psychology, and it is the focus of this chapter. As students explore selected concepts of social psychology, they will learn strategies for developing positive self-concept, self-esteem, coping skills, and prosocial behaviors. These concepts and understandings are addressed in the affective domain of teaching.

The affective domain is unique in conceptual understanding and student proficiency; in fact, the teacher's ability to understand and apply the concepts in daily interactions is critical to the learning and practice of affective concepts by students. For example, teachers do not have to model the kind of practice necessary to improve a motor skill in order to teach it to students. If, however, a teacher is teaching students to understand the concept of "courtesy" and does not demonstrate courtesy in his or her interactions with others, the concept's meaning will be distorted. Social psychological concepts are feeling/sensing in nature, making it difficult to separate the process of understanding them from actual practice.

Cognition does not occur without emotion. The brain uses emotion as a filter for cognition (Golden 1995). Every thought is attached to emotion. In the affective domain, thoughts, feelings, and actions are analogous. Arguably, a person can understand courtesy conceptually without practicing or demonstrating it. However, the knowledge of the concept of courtesy is embedded in the use of courtesy. For these reasons, this chapter will take a somewhat different approach to the teaching and learning of social psychological concepts. To be specific:

1. The presentation of social psychological concepts is based on the belief that knowledge and understanding of concepts in the affective domain is inextricably bound to the application of

Rita Mercier is a senior associate of the California School Leadership Academy and a former curriculum coordinator for the Riverside and San Bernardino County, California, Offices of Education. Gayle Hutchinson is associate professor, California State University, Chico.

those concepts. The concepts in this chapter will be illustrated and discussed, at times, in terms of demonstrated student behaviors.

2. Considerable attention will be focused on the teacher's role in influencing student understanding of social psychological concepts.

3. Social concepts and psychological concepts are not discrete and learned independently of one another, therefore some overlap will occur in the presentation.

What Are Sociology, Psychology, and Social Psychology?

Establishing a working definition of social psychology sets the stage for learning important social psychological concepts. Social psychology is understood best by defining sociology and psychology. Separate definitions will help students note the distinctions between these disciplines. Once the differences are evident, students will understand more clearly the working definition used for social psychology.

Sociology examines the characteristics of social groups and their relationships to other social groups. Sociologists are concerned with patterns of conduct among groups of people, such as students; or among larger groups, such as schools, states, or whole societies (Hewitt 1984). In physical education, sociology of sport is the subdiscipline that focuses specifically on sociological concepts in sport and physical activity. Sociology of sport operates on the premise that sport is an integral aspect of society, and it has a significant impact on the behaviors of individuals and groups.

Sport sociologists typically investigate social structure, social relations, and social problems as they relate to sport (McPherson, Curtis & Loy 1989). Using sociological concepts from both sociology and sociology of sport, students in physical education classes may consider how groups of students with ethnic cultures different from their own view the importance of physical activity to their health, or how individuals who speak English perceive and relate to individuals who speak English as a second language. Students might examine the ways that students in physical education classes participate or don't participate in activities. Ultimately, those who study sociological concepts are interested in how groups of people interact with other groups of people, or how social systems like schools or communities relate to other social systems.

Psychology tends to focus on the behaviors and mental processes of the individual. Psychologists are primarily interested in what the individual does and the kinds of things that may or may not influence his or her behavior. Sport psychology applies psychological principles to sport settings in order to improve or enhance motor performance (Cox 1994). Many sport psychologists investigate the emotional and personality profiles of athletes, examine the effects of stress on performance, and help athletes reach their highest level of motor performance.

Students exploring psychological perspectives in physical education may ponder questions like: "What is the best way for me to learn motor skills?" "How can I help myself remember fitness principles?" "Why do some people adhere to exercise programs while others do not?" "What attitudes do my friends have about physical activity?" and, "What affects my own attitude/participation in physical activity?

The definition of social psychology is a combination of the working definitions for sociology and psychology. The primary focus of social psychology, then, is the social nature of the individual. It examines the influence of other human beings on the thoughts, feelings, and behaviors of individuals. Succinctly stated, social psychology "is the field...that studies individuals' social interactions, relationships, perceptions, and attitudes" (Allen & Santrock 1993, p. 490).

Many sport sociologists, along with sport psychologists, spend a great deal of time examining the influence of sport and physical activity on human development. In fact, they are concerned with the "social psychological aspect of human enrichment" (Cox 1994, p. 5). Many social psychological concepts have been explored by sport sociologists and psychologists. Therefore, it is important to note that the concepts reviewed in this chapter have been drawn from the disciplines of sociology, psychology, social psychology, sociology of sport, and sport psychology.

Why Is Social Psychology Important?

Interest in social psychological concepts in physical education stems from our professional concern for the emotional and physical safety and well being of all students. Teachers are interested in helping students interact cooperatively and respectfully, solve conflicts in constructive and peaceful ways, and feel safe in class and in school. The nature of physical activity and sport presents abundant opportunities for students to develop social psychological knowledge and skills. Thoughtful consideration to affective elements, including the continuous enhancement of teacher knowledge and skills, produces a learning climate that is conducive to building student self-esteem. Social psychological concepts provide the foundation for the successful teaching of all other concepts.

As students understand selected social psychological concepts that influence and potentially enhance their sense of self and well being, they are more apt to engage in more meaningful practice of these concepts. Understanding coupled with meaningful practice may help students adopt these concepts and related skills to their daily lives.

Linking Social Psychology to the National Standards

The National Standards emphasize the importance of defining what a *physically educated person* should know and be able to do, not what an *athlete* should know and be able to do. To remain consistent with this definition, this chapter will de-emphasize sports psychology in favor of a generalist sociology and psychology perspective as applied to physical activity settings. Rather than try to fit strategies for developing social and psychological concepts and skills into already prescribed games and sports, this chapter reflect the belief that if the game/sport/instructional strategy is not developing the desired social and psychological concepts and skills, then it should be changed.

Three of the National Standards affirm the benefits of social and psychological development as an outcome of a physically educated person:

- Standard 5: Demonstrates responsible personal and social behavior in physical activity settings.
- Standard 6: Demonstrates understanding and respect for differences among people in physical activity settings.
- Standard 7: Understands that physical activity provides opportunities for enjoyment, challenge, self expression, and social interaction.

The concepts of "self as an individual" and "self in relation to others" are emphasized in Standards 5, 6, and 7. In Standard 5, the development of personal and social behaviors are emphasized through physical activity. Social responsibility and social interactions with people different from ourselves are the focus of Standard 6. The importance of aesthetics and enjoyment of physical activity for individuals as well as groups is highlighted in Standard 7. These standards guide teachers in their planning of appropriate personal and social development experiences for all students.

Selected Social Psychology Concepts

Establishing an environment conducive to learning, where students feel emotionally safe, is the first step in helping students to understand social and psychological concepts. Traditionally, physical education classes have been places where teachers have determined the curriculum, designed unit plans, and conducted lessons. Delivering information to students has been the primary responsibility of the teacher. Teachers explain and demonstrate motor skills, sport skills, and game rules. Students demonstrate basic sport skills and memorize what is known as surface knowledge (Caine & Caine 1995) for a variety of sports and games. Student learning is assessed through skills tests, knowledge tests, and fitness scores. This teacher-dominated approach requires students to learn on an inflexible schedule containing many time constraints. Such a traditional model rarely maximizes student learning and development of positive personal skills and appropriate social skills.

The alternative to such a traditional model is one where teachers shift from rote practice of skills and memorization of facts to more meaningful learning—described today as a student-centered physical education program. In such a setting, the teacher's role is to help students make meaning of new information. Teachers create opportunities for students to explore, discover, and practice what they learn. Together, teachers and students find experiential ways to link information and understanding. This kind of interactive setting is ideal for helping students understand and develop their self-concept, self-esteem, and self-confidence as well as the ability to interact positively with others.

Teachers may use a number of teaching strategies such as positive discipline, thematic instruction, cooperative learning, reciprocal teaching, and meaning-centered curriculum to establish a student-centered environment (Mosston & Ashworth 1994). As a result, students are involved, and not merely "busy, happy and good" (Placek 1983). Students are responsible for setting goals, assessing their progress, and monitoring their own learning. They feel more comfortable learning and taking safe risks. They grow personally and socially as they develop motor and cognitive skills. The lesson examples in this chapter illustrate a student-centered approach to structuring lessons.

Positive self-concept and positive socialization help a student feel good about him or herself when participating in physical activity. In this chapter, the social psychological concepts are organized around six concepts for student learning. Concepts I, II, and III pertain to the student as an individual:

- Concept I: How do people feel about themselves when participating in physical activity?
- Concept II: How can people improve their sense of self through physical activity?
- Concept III: How can people continue to develop toward their full potential through physical activity?

These first three concepts are closely related, yet subtly different. For instance, in Concept I self-concept and self-esteem are defined. Six principles (security, selfhood, affiliation/belongingness, purpose, competence, and virtue) that lead to positive self-concept and self-esteem are explained. People need to comprehend these core principles in order to understand their own feelings and to move forward to Concept II. Positive self-concept and self-esteem are directly related to one's achievements and beliefs about one's own potential. Self-talk, goal setting, and self-assessment are several concepts/skills discussed in Concept II that people use to succeed in areas like motor performance and social interactions. Understanding self-concept and self-esteem, along with self-talk, goal setting, and self-assessment set the foundation for Concept III, where individuals strive toward self-actualization.

Concepts IV, V, and VI address the individual as he or she interacts with others:
- Concept IV: How do people learn to understand and respond to individual and group diversity?
- Concept V: What kinds of social skills must people learn in order to perform successfully with others?
- Concept VI: How do people achieve the social skills needed to perform successfully with others?

How Do People Feel About Themselves When Participating in Physical Activity?

Participating in physical activity can be enjoyable and exciting. Physical activity provides many opportunities for people to explore their bodies and their abilities. It is an ideal way to develop positive self-concept and self-esteem. Self-concept can be defined as how a person sees his or her own abilities, behavior, and personality. It is often recognized by the attitudes a person holds about him or herself (Gallahue 1993). Self-esteem is the process used to assess oneself; it is influenced by how a person thinks other people perceive him or her. Together, self-concept and self-esteem create a complex foundation upon which people build their perceived sense of worthiness and competence.

Many researchers have found that physical activity significantly affects children's self-concept and self-esteem (Payne & Isaacs 1995). Developmentally appropriate and student-centered physical education programs, physical activity experiences, and other forms of guided play provide excellent opportunities for students to develop positive self-concepts and self-esteem. This is essential if students are to develop self-confidence and exhibit improved social behavior and school achievement (Borba 1989). Researchers have identified six factors that affect the development positive self-concept and esteem. They are: security, selfhood, affiliation/belongingness, purpose, competence, and virtue (Borba 1989, Hellison 1995, Gallahue 1993).

Security. Security is the feeling of comfort and safety within an environment. Individuals feel secure when they know what to expect from their surroundings. These feelings are enhanced when class rules and consequences are clear and consistent. The presence of reliable and dependable people (students and teachers) also enhances the sense of security. When people feel secure in their environment, they are more open to learning.

Selfhood. Selfhood is the development of one's sense of individualism. As individuals develop selfhood, they learn about their abilities and their limitations, enabling them to understand themselves better.

Affiliation/Belongingness. Affiliation and belongingness means that individuals feel accepted by others. Acceptance involves feelings of appreciation and respect.

Purpose. Purpose is having a reason for living; something to strive for. Individuals with purpose are motivated to set and pursue goals. Purpose leads to a greater sense of self-empowerment.

Competence. Competence relates directly to the achievement of goals and to success. According to Harter (1978), individuals are intrinsically motivated to be competent in all aspects of their lives. Individuals typically develop competency through mastery of skills. Mastery of skills improves self-concept and self-esteem, and this relates directly to one's confidence in his or her ability to participate in regular physical activity, find enjoyment in physical activity, and develop positive beliefs concerning the benefits of physical activity (Surgeon General's Report 1996).

Virtue. Virtue is the demonstration of behavior that is consistent with an established moral code. In physical education, the moral code may encompass acceptance of diversity, fair play, conflict resolution, mutual respect, honesty, etc.

How Can People Improve Their Sense of Self Through Physical Activity?

Self-concept and self-esteem are complex and multidimensional ideas. Although teachers can give students some tools for improving their sense of self, they cannot control all of the variables. Therefore, it is important to provide students with an understanding of how their sense of self is developed, and to enable them to change the variables in their lives that are not contributing to a positive sense of self.

There are many things that individuals can do to develop a healthy sense of self. These include self-talk, goal setting, and self-assessment.

Self-Talk. Self-talk is a cognitive process. Individuals make statements to themselves that serve to direct their attention, judge themselves or others, and critique their abilities to perform. Self-talk is a powerful tool that helps make perceptions and beliefs conscious and actions realized (Bunker, Williams & Zinsser 1993). Many elite athletes use positive self- talk during competition to heighten their focus, increase self-confidence, and reduce feelings of self-doubt (Williams & Leffingwell 1996). People can use self-talk to encourage continuing effort in physical activity if they find themselves discouraged. They can use it to improve skill performance, focus attention, and increase and maintain self-confidence.

When using self-talk to improve skill performance, a person must emphasize desired actions and behaviors. Self-talk may range from a short description to one word cues. For instance, students practicing dribbling in basketball may use cues such as, "Knees bent, eyes up, dribble ball with fingertips." People engaging in a team building activity may say, "Always spot my partner, safety first, everyone participates."

People may use words and cues to help focus their attention on a task or activity. They might say such things as: "Listen and be alert for encouragement." "Look at group member's faces and pay attention." "That's the way." Cues for attention can help students stay on task or regain their focus during class.

Self-talk can have a positive or negative influence on an individual's self-confidence. Negative self-talk, such as, "You're stupid, loser! You can't do that." is self-defeating. It replaces self-confidence with self-doubt.

Positive statements like, "You can do that. Go ahead, try it. Taking safe risks is fun." serve to increase self-confidence. People must become aware of the positive and negative statements they make. The paper clip exercise is one easy way to help develop student awareness: Have each student carry a handful of paper clips in a pocket. Each time a student makes a negative statement, he or she must transfer one paper clip to another pocket. During one class period, students will become aware of how often they make negative comments.

Encouragement is the ability to say positive things in order to support and stimulate self and others. Sometimes people find it difficult to encourage themselves; they may think of it as arrogance. It is important for youngsters to learn that self-encouragement is healthy. When teaching students how to give self-encouragement, begin small. Have them tell how they feel about doing physical activity. For instance, "When I threw the ball and hit the target, I felt happy and excited." Next, help students think of ways they can encourage themselves, such as looking at mistakes as possible learning experiences; or by engaging in positive and supportive self-talk. For instance, encourage them to say things like, "good effort," "I tried my best that time," and "I love trying new activities and sports."

Another good way to elicit self-praise is to have students answer this question: "What did I do well in this effort/performance?" Once students learn to encourage themselves, they will feel good, and they will be able to encourage others. (Encouraging others will be discussed further when we look at Concepts V and VI.)

Goal Setting. Achieving goals helps people identify their own levels of competency and degrees of success. There are two major goal perspectives: task orientation and ego orientation (Dweck & Elliott 1983, Nicholls 1984, Duda, Olson & Templin 1991). Task-oriented goals focus on personal improvement and mastery of skills. People with a task-oriented approach set self-referenced goals. They measure how much their performance on tasks and activities improves over past performances (criterion-referenced). People with an ego orientation are more concerned with how their abilities compare with others (norm-referenced).

Research has shown that individuals with task orientation tend to be persistent and unafraid of failure. They pursue mastery and choose moderately difficult challenges. Individuals operating from an ego orientation are not persistent. They are easily discouraged, withdraw from efforts when success is not ensured, and tend to choose tasks that are either too easy or too difficult.

There is a correlation between fair play and task orientation, and between unfair and violent play and ego orientation (Duda, Olson & Templin 1991). Individuals with a task orientation tend to be more cooperative and interested in playing by the rules, whereas their ego-oriented counterparts seem more interested in winning and defeating opponents.

To help students take responsibility for their own learning and to demonstrate prosocial behaviors like fair play, it is important to teach students the principles for setting short and long-term, task-oriented goals (O'Block & Evans 1984, Cox 1994):
1. Task-oriented goals focus on personal improvement and are more beneficial in helping people achieve success.
2. People must accept goals as worthwhile and achievable, and as their own.
3. Goals should be special and challenging.
4. Goals are more easily understood when they are described in behavioral terms.
5. Goals should be measurable so that progress can be determined.
6. Short-term goals set a natural progression toward realizing long-term goals.
7. It is important to determine specific strategies for attaining goals.
8. Goals should be monitored and assessed periodically in order to determine progress, success, and the need for any modifications.

Self-Assessment. Assessing personal progress toward short and long-term goals is another important aspect of developing a positive sense of self. Self-assessment allows individuals to reflect on or cognitively review their own progress. Consider the following points:
1. Self-assessment provides information about progress toward achieving goals.
2. Clearly stated goals that are measurable enable individuals to assess their behavior and motor performance accurately and consistently.

3. A number of strategies may be employed to help individuals collect information to use in assessing their own progress. These may include things such as task sheets, checklists, journals, and progress logs.

4. Open-ended questions such as, "What was my goal?" "How have I made progress toward my goal?" "What do I need to do to modify my goal?" "How do I need to change my practice in order to achieve my goal?" "What have I done well?" and, "What do I need to improve on?" can provide the structure for quick self-assessments.

5. Students can develop a positive sense of self through student-centered instructional strategies. As the students' sense of self develops, teachers may guide student thinking toward continuous improvement of their knowledge and performance. As a result, students can attribute their success to their own abilities and not to luck or the easiness of tasks.

As students learn to consistently and accurately evaluate their progress, they will also learn to recognize when goals have been achieved and when goals should be modified. Some individuals may find self-assessment a difficult thing to do initially, but as they learn to provide accurate self-talk and focus on authentic indicators of progress, they will enhance their ability to conduct self-assessments. Accurate self-assessment reinforces appropriate behaviors and aids in skill development. It is a powerful learning tool for encouraging individuals to look at mistakes and poor performances as opportunities for learning.

How Can People Continue To Develop Toward Their Full Potential Through Physical Activity?

Abraham Maslow (1954) introduced a hierarchy of needs that identified certain basic necessities—food, shelter, water, safety, belongingness, love and positive sense of self—that had to be realized before a higher need for self-actualization could be addressed. Teachers see examples of this daily: Students come to school hungry, thirsty, and tired. Some students are homeless or highly transient. In many areas, students fear physical violence at home, on the streets, and at school. When young people's fundamental needs are not met it is of little wonder that they have difficulty learning.

Self-actualization can be described as one's motivation to reach his or her fullest human potential. This is a lifelong process. Positive self-concept and self-esteem lend themselves to self-confidence. Creating conditions that stimulate and promote thinking skills increases student cognition, enabling them to recognize and internalize concepts, ideas, and understandings more readily. Increased cognitive ability contributes to student self-confidence, motivating them to set new goals and challenges, and to strive to reach their potential. When they have a positive, healthy, realistic sense of self, people intrinsically pursue opportunities to learn, explore, and create.

Teachers can motivate student desire by providing learning environments that promote risk taking, and by setting achievable challenges that stimulate personal growth and development. The following principles can be applied toward the achievement of self-actualization:

1. Basic needs such as food, shelter, water, safety, belongingness, love, and positive sense of self must be addressed before progress toward self-actualization can take place.

2. Safe learning environments increase motivation toward self-actualization by providing a positive and secure structure for meeting students' basic needs.

3. Positive self-talk, goal setting, and self-assessment help improve self-concept and self-esteem, making work toward self-actualization possible.

4. When learning is perceived as meaningful, students become more motivated to learn, thus engaging in the process of self-actualization.

5. Ethical decision making involves the ability to choose the appropriate action and adhere to an established moral code. It promotes personal integrity and self-actualization.

How Do People Learn To Understand and Respond to Individual and Group Diversity?

Diversity encompasses distinct characteristics and qualities of people such as culture, language, race, religion, ability, gender, family lifestyle, and beliefs. Diversity creates the foundation for a rich array of thoughts, ideas, and interests that embody the American culture. Along with the advantages of diversity, however, comes the challenge of living, playing, and working together with people who may have varied needs and wants. Having insufficient or inappropriate information regarding others can lead to fear and misunderstanding. This kind of stereotyping can prevent us from appreciating different individuals for who they are.

Learning to understand and respond to the diverse needs of others is a complex process that can be enhanced throughout a lifetime. Learning the skills needed to respond appropriately to individual differences usually requires a willingness to learn about others, as well as the ability to demonstrate empathy. A willingness to learn increases the likelihood that people will learn. Empathy involves identifying with and understanding another person's situation, feelings, and motives. Understanding the feelings of others forms the basis of many other social skills. Empathy is usually learned as we receive love and attention from parents, guardians, or primary care givers (Goleman 1995). The more people try to see, understand and feel someone else's point of view, the more empathetic they will become.

Although understanding others is influenced by experiences acquired from every aspect of life—including family, friends, community, and spiritual beliefs—physical education offers a powerful opportunity to enhance this skill in a way no other content area can. The interactive nature of physical activity lends itself to limitless opportunities for learning about the cultures of others; their abilities, thoughts, and feelings; their similarities and differences; their learning styles; their activity preferences; their communication skills; and their needs and wants. When students participate in physical education activities, they make active choices about the way they allow new knowledge and information to influence their interaction with others. The teaching and learning of social skills can greatly enhance the understanding of diversity.

Social skills are skills that help people build positive feelings with others and perform successfully with partners and in groups. Understanding social skills begins with the acceptance that everyone can learn these skills. Social skills can be thought of in much the same way as skills in other subjects. Some people are very knowledgeable in math, but are not as knowledgeable in science. In this sense, people can have varying levels of social skill knowledge and levels of use. Social skills are influenced by the behavior of others or our perception of the behavior of others to a greater degree than academic skills. It is, therefore, critical to attend to the issues of concern—the feelings, attitudes, and beliefs of students—on a daily basis to the greatest extent possible.

What Kinds of Social Skills Must People Learn in Order To Perform Successfully with Others?

Empathy forms the basis for developing many other social skills. It is critical for developing constructive communication, which is a necessary skill for successfully interacting with others. Constructive communication includes active listening–the ability to demonstrate body language and facial expressions that indicate attention, paraphrasing–repeating what was said in one's own words, questioning–the ability to ask questions that indicate a context for what was previously said, and clarifying–asking questions to improve one's understanding. Providing specific feedback to partners and group members helps each student develop thinking and communicating skills. Taking turns in a variety of leadership roles—e.g., team leader, timer, facilitator, equipment monitor, warm up leader, checker for individual and group understanding, encourager, feedback provider, recorder, and skills monitor—allows each person to learn to contribute in a meaningful way as a group member while also developing social skills. Social skills such as encouraging, caring, courtesy, positive disagreement, complimenting, kindness, fairness, honesty, and integrity will contribute to the ability to perform successfully with others.

There are many skills that help people interact successfully with others. The choices about specific social skills that will be emphasized for teaching in schools, churches, and homes will depend on the collaborative efforts and input of students, parents, teachers, community leaders, and spiritual leaders. It is important for people to know themselves well enough to identify their social skills strengths and weaknesses. This self-knowledge can help individuals construct personal growth plans. There are many strategies for developing social skills. Some are practiced individually, but most are developed as a result of working with others. When student interaction is planned and organized to create nurturing experiences, and to reflect on these experiences, students have a much greater probability of developing appropriate social skills.

How Do People Achieve the Social Skills Needed To Perform Successfully with Others?

Recent "brain-based learning" research has provided great insight into how the brain affects feelings, and how feelings affect behavior. Many of the thoughts, feelings, and emotional responses that people have come to believe are automatic can be controlled by understanding the processes in the brain that inhibit its full use, particularly in times of stress (MacLean 1990). A person's understanding of basic brain processes and the way that the brain filters information can serve as an excellent tool for controlling and self-monitoring behavior. It also provides a basis for understanding the elements of effective communication.

The ability to communicate thoughts, feelings, and understandings effectively provides the foundation for identifying, monitoring, and processing social skills. Effective communication requires abundant practice as well as feedback about how clearly thoughts, feelings, and understandings are shared with others. Social skills are learned by identifying and defining the skills, understanding them, and practicing those skills with others. Students may acquire social skills through role playing prior to practice, or through practice.

Let's examine three frameworks and the way that they can influence the learning of social skill concepts and interaction skills: cooperative groups, competition, and conflict resolution.

Cooperative Groups. Cooperative groups have predetermined steps for identifying the social skill to be practiced, ways for individuals to monitor the skill, and a way to evaluate it to see how well it was learned. One of the most effective strategies for practicing social skills during physical activity is to work with partners and cooperative groups. Working with a partner to solve problems and give feedback provides for the practice of a variety of social skills (e.g., active listening, paraphrasing, positive disagreement, caring, encouraging, and complimenting). Students' interactions with teachers also provide occasions for practicing a rich variety of social skills, such as getting to class on time (punctuality), being prepared (responsibility), listening attentively (active listening), and contributing to the success of the class (responsibility, caring, encouraging, courtesy). The social skills that students develop during school will affect their interactions with others in all areas of life.

Competition. While competitive experiences cause great anticipation for some, they can produce apprehension and anxiety in others. The effect of competitive experiences on social development has been identified by some as a necessary and natural part of preparing students for a competitive world. Qualities such as aggression and single-minded self-interest were thought to create "winners"—individuals who could beat out others to become "number one."

Alfie Kohn, in his book, *The Brighter Side of Human Nature: Altruism and Empathy in Everyday Life* (1990), makes the case for focusing on the side of human nature that is decent, caring, and concerned for the well being of others in social structures, and particularly in schools. Presumably, then, educators can change the nature of social expectations for individual success, and place greater value on qualities such as altruism and cooperation. The value of competition compared with other instructional strategies will continue to be debated for some time. However, when a teacher uses competition as a teaching strategy it is generally agreed that it is preferable to use it in combination with other teaching strategies.

Two examples that illustrate an appropriate method of focusing on social skill concepts within the context of competitive experience are downplaying or eliminating the score, and changing the scoring process to include points for appropriate use of social skills. Successful competition requires all students to be prepared to an appropriate level for the physical, cognitive, emotional, and motor demands of the activity. If students are adequately prepared and competition is producing anger, frustration, fear, name calling, aggression, cheating, or other forms of negative behavior, then additional instructional strategies may be required. These might include peer teaching, inclusion, and cooperative learning.

Creating an emotionally safe atmosphere that is conducive to prosocial behavior does not mean simply creating an environment where negative behavior is disallowed (such as having a "no put downs" rule). Safe competitive risks for all students can only occur in an environment where students nurture and care for one another. If the teacher pays daily attention to prosocial student interaction and models prosocial behavior, students will develop successful interaction skills.

Conflict Resolution. Routine practice of social skills increases the likelihood that the skills will be acquired. A process like conflict resolution provides another way to enhance social skill acquisition. Understanding how to resolve conflict involves recognizing the nature of conflict in relation to one's own beliefs. A person's beliefs and attitudes about conflict determine how that person will react when conflict occurs. If conflict is viewed by students as an opportunity to develop problem solving strategies and communication skills, and to learn more about themselves and others, it will be worthwhile. There are four situations in which conflict can occur: interpersonal (self), intrapersonal (between two or more people), intergroup, and between groups (Community Board 1993).

For the purpose of addressing resolution as a process, conflict is defined as two or more people who interact and perceive incompatible differences between, or threats to, their resources, needs, and values (Morton & Deutch 1973). What students do in response to conflict can lead to a consequence that is either negative or positive. For example, they may complain to someone else, cry, make jokes, smile even if it hurts, become visibly angry, pretend nothing is wrong, give in, or go to an authority. The choices that students make are critical, because the consequences of those choices can make their beliefs about conflict even stronger (Morton & Deutch 1973).

Fundamental to conflict resolution is the understanding that responses are conscious choices, and that individuals have complete control over them. Conflict will result in positive consequences and will de-escalate only if feelings are expressed rather than acted out, there is a decrease in emotion and perceived threat, disputants talk directly or use neutral third parties, and communication and problem solving skills are employed (Morton & Deutch 1973).

Major themes of conflict resolution programs include: active listening–the ability to paraphrase or summarize what is said to ensure accurate comprehension, cooperation–one person speaks while the other listens without interruption, and creative problem solving–individually or together brainstorming solutions and selecting the one that best accommodates the needs of both disputants (the win/win concept).

One of the most important aspects of conflict resolution is the use of "I" statements. "I" statements focus on the needs and feelings of the person with the problem. They provide a way for that person to communicate the consequences of a behavior, rather than just focusing on the behavior. "I" statements contain three parts:
1. I feel...
2. When you... or, when this happened...
3. Because...

"I" statements should be made in a nonthreatening tone of voice. Body posture and facial expressions should be open and caring. When people make "You" statements, such as, "You always yell at me," and, "You make me mad," they are not accepting ownership of the problem. Until each disputant owns the problem, it cannot be adequately resolved. Owning the problem is the ability of disputants to believe and say, "I did this..." and as a result, "this occurred." "I am responsible for my thoughts, actions, and feelings."

Another important skill in conflict resolution is the ability to paraphrase, or restate in one's own words what the other person said. This can be practiced within all pair, group, and team processing sessions. Teachers can model it when listening and responding to students.

The next step is reflection, or the ability of each person to state his or her understanding of how the other person feels. This skill can be practiced in partner activities that require students to depend on one another for safety and security. An example would be leading a student whose eyes are closed. After the pair walks for a period of time, they stop, and the person who had closed eyes describes how it felt to be led. The leader listens, then responds by describing the partner's feelings as he or she understood them.

In a real conflict situation, this skill is particularly critical to reaching the next step of validating the other person's issues and feelings while showing appreciation for his or her willingness to solve the problem. After validation, it is usually possible for disputants to generate several ideas for solving the problem and to agree on one.

Self-reflection is a critical component of monitoring one's own behavior and interaction with others. It is most beneficial to use positive self-reflection often, particularly when developing new social skills. Positively directed self-reflection focuses on what happened in the interaction that was worthwhile, while using any negative outcomes to determine what to do differently the next time. Self-reflection should not be used to dwell on mistakes or inabilities. This usually serves to decrease self-esteem and inhibit the growth of social skills (Bunker, Williams & Zinsser 1993).

Placing Social Psychology Concepts in the Curriculum

Integrating social psychology concepts into the physical education curriculum requires decisions about where to introduce aspects of each concept. In making placement decisions, it is important to remember that the skills do not occur independently of one another. Student needs as well as the appropriateness for the age and grade level also should be considered.

The table that begins on page 186 suggests placement of the concepts for grades K, 2, 4, 6, 8, 10, and 12. These grade levels were selected in order to remain consistent with the grade levels used in NASPE's National Standards. Teachers are encouraged to review the grade levels they teach and make necessary adjustments in order to meet the needs of their own students.

Integrating Social Psychology Concepts into Instruction

Social psychological concepts focus on the beliefs, attitudes, and perspectives of individuals and on the ways individuals interpret their interactions with others. In order to effectively instruct students and help them develop their own self and social skills, teachers are encouraged to first focus on themselves as individuals, and then on how they interact with students in their classes.

Modeling

Modeling appropriate social skills is more challenging than it sounds. When teachers participate in a process of self-reflection and make note of their own beliefs, thoughts, attitudes, and behaviors, they are better able to model appropriate social skills for students. Self-reflection helps teachers attain a clearer sense of one's personal identity. Personal identity is dynamic; that is, it has developed over time and continues to develop as one journeys through life. Identity is important because it helps to organize and guide interpretations and behaviors in all situations. One's personal identity as a teacher helps to determine how one perceives and interacts with students.

Personal identity is influenced by a sense of commonality with others. Affiliations or group memberships provide a sense of belongingness. For instance, "I am a physical educator, and I have something in common with all physical educators," or, "I am a basketball coach and I belong to a coaches association." These group memberships influence one's perceptions about teaching. Awareness of social group memberships and how these memberships influence one's life is helpful in understanding personal identity and its influence on teaching.

Modeling also is affected by teachers' attitudes toward students. Attitudes can be influenced by stereotypes, impressions, observations, and experiences. When teachers judge students, regardless of whether or not these judgments are accurate, they create expectations. And, students tend to live up to the expectations that teachers hold for them. For example, if a student is working hard, willing to try new things, and helping others whenever possible, the teacher probably will behave positively toward the student and the student will fulfill the teacher's expectations. The same holds true for the student who is viewed as a troublemaker. Teachers are more likely to treat such a student in a way that represents this view. And, most often, the student will fulfill the teacher's expectations.

Teacher beliefs and expectations directly influence their ability to model social skills in class, and they profoundly impact their students' sense of self and behavior. Teachers often find modeling social skills more challenging with students they perceive as low achievers. High expectations can promote positive self-esteem and self-confidence, and can promote more positive and constructive social behaviors. When teachers have high expectations for all students, they are more likely to consistently model social skills.

Table 1. Critical Student Concepts, K–6

Kindergarten	Second Grade	Fourth Grade	Sixth Grade
Social Psychological Concept I: How do people feel about themselves when participating in physical activity?	*Social Psychological Concept I: How do people feel about themselves when participating in physical activity?*	*Social Psychological Concept I: How do people feel about themselves when participating in physical activity?*	*Social Psychological Concept I: How do people feel about themselves when participating in physical activity?*
Safe and appropriate physical activity helps people feel good inside.	Safe and appropriate physical activity helps people to develop a sense of enjoyment and confidence.	Clarity and consistency in creating and following game rules gives people a sense of security.	Resting and deep breathing exercises can help people relax and feel calm.
Learning about the body and how it moves helps people feel positively about themselves.	Learning about the body and how it moves helps people feel positively about themselves.	Resting and deep breathing exercises can help people relax and feel calm.	Moving with control gives people a sense of self-discipline.
Succeeding in fun and challenging physical experiences helps people to feel capable.	Succeeding in fun and challenging physical experiences helps people feel capable.	Moving with control gives people a sense of self-discipline and helps to control impulsive and aggressive behaviors.	Working independently for periods of time helps students gain self-confidence.
	Understanding and following game rules helps people feel a sense of security.	Working independently on physical activities for short periods of time helps to develop self-understanding.	People's appreciation of their own uniqueness helps them to value the activities they do well.
		Determining realistic goals and strategies to achieve those goals helps people to realize success.	

Table 1. Critical Student Concepts, K–6

Social Psychological Concept II: How can people improve their sense of self through physical activity?	*Social Psychological Concept II: How can people improve their sense of self through physical activity?*	*Social Psychological Concept II: How can people improve their sense of self through physical activity?*	*Social Psychological Concept II: How can people improve their sense of self through physical activity?*
Using positive and kind statements such as, "Good effort!" "I like to move!" "I try my best!" "Look what I can do!" "I like to make up movement!" "Moving makes me smile!" and, "Yea, I did it!" helps people feel good.	Using self-encouragement when participating in difficult challenges develops perseverance.	Positive self-talk such as, "Good effort." and, "I enjoy playing and making up active games." increases self-confidence and one's ability to perform physical activities.	Self-praise can be developed by having people ask themselves what they did well in each effort/performance.
Learning from successes and mistakes helps people to improve skills while playing alone and with others.	Learning from successes and mistakes helps people to improve skills while playing alone and with others.	Mistakes and successes can be an important way to learn to set new goals and keep track of personal progress toward physical, social, and personal skills.	Perseverance through difficult physical challenges creates a sense of pride in accomplishment and effort.
Practicing and improving skills makes people feel pleased.	Practicing and improving physical skills helps people to develop a sense confidence about their abilities.	Practicing and improving skills helps people develop a sense of confidence about their physical abilities.	Continuously setting and achieving realistic goals related to physical activity develops a person's self-confidence.
	Accomplishing realistic physical challenges develops self-confidence.	Accomplishing realistic physical challenges develops people's self-confidence.	People learn to appreciate physical activity, enjoy participation, and achieve goals when challenged with difficult but attainable tasks.
		Participating in physical activities for the sake of the challenge provides opportunities for enjoyment and teaches appreciation for the experience.	Consistent use of self-evaluation when learning a new skill or activity makes it easier for people to recognize and appreciate the things they are doing well.

Table 1. Critical Student Concepts, K–6

Social Psychological Concept III: How can people continue to develop toward their full potential through physical activity?	*Social Psychological Concept III: How can people continue to develop toward their full potential through physical activity?*	*Social Psychological Concept III: How can people continue to develop toward their full potential through physical activity?*	*Social Psychological Concept III: How can people continue to develop toward their full potential through physical activity?*
Excitement helps people to try.	Openness to learning helps people want to be their best.	Practicing motor, social, and personal skills in many different ways helps people discover the ways that they learn best.	Achievement is directly related to the effort and motivation put forth.
People learn best in different ways—seeing, hearing, or doing, alone, with a partner, or in a group.	People learn best in different ways— seeing, hearing, or doing, alone, with a partner, or in a group.	Continuous challenges foster enjoyment, improvement, and the ability to persevere.	Practicing motor, social, and personal skills in many different ways helps people discover the ways that they learn best.
People can keep improving all the time.	Thinking about why a movement was successful helps people continue to repeat the movement successfully.	People develop a sense of pride in themselves when they are able to make decisions that match the agreed upon moral code.	Initiating positive interactions with others and asking for their support develops people's ability to influence their own success.
Playing fairly and honestly helps people to trust in and feel good about themselves.	Playing fairly and honestly helps people to trust in and feel good about themselves.	People demonstrate positive self-esteem when they are able to ask for the help and support of others.	Ethical decision making requires the development of integrity—a steadfast adherence to a clear moral or ethical code.
Reflection on why a movement was successful helps people continue to repeat the movement successfully.	Working alone and with others gives people the chance to become better thinkers.	Developing thinking skills requires concentration, time, and practice in all movement endeavors.	Initiating positive interactions with others and asking for their support enhances people's own success and progress toward self-actualization.

Table 1. Critical Student Concepts, K–6

Social Psychological Concept IV: How do people learn to understand and respond to individual and group diversity?	*Social Psychological Concept IV: How do people learn to understand and respond to individual and group diversity?*	*Social Psychological Concept IV: How do people learn to understand and respond to individual and group diversity?*	*Social Psychological Concept IV: How do people learn to understand and respond to individual and group diversity?*
Including everyone in an activity makes learning fun for all.	Moving safely while sharing space and equipment demonstrates understanding of the needs of others.	Learning about others includes listening thoughtfully to their needs and wants.	Welcoming differences and similarities in individuals helps groups function more effectively.
Moving safely while sharing space with others demonstrates understanding of the needs of others.	Boys and girls can learn to be partners and respect each other.	Including boys and girls and people with different languages, culture, or ability in groups helps everyone learn to participate positively with all kinds of people.	Respecting differences in others can be demonstrated by different levels of responses including tolerance, acceptance, appreciation, and celebration.
Learning new things about others is a good way to get to know people.	Caring about the needs of others is shown by being responsible for the safety and the feelings of others.	Learning about others is demonstrated by a willingness to consider their thoughts and feelings.	Learning about others involves the willingness to listen, paraphrase, and clarify thoughts and feelings of others.
Playing a variety of games and activities that are favorites of different people helps everyone to learn enjoyment.	Playing a variety of games and activities that are favorites of different people helps everyone to appreciate each other's differences.	Participating in a variety of cultural activities, movement experiences, and sports is a good way to build understanding of the cultures, abilities, and preferences of others.	Understanding and acceptance of diversity is strongly influenced by people's interactions and experience with others.
			Empathy is the ability to view a statement from another person's point of view.

Table 1. Critical Student Concepts, K–6

Social Psychological Concept V: What kinds of social skills must people learn in order to perform successfully with others?	Social Psychological Concept V: What kinds of social skills must people learn in order to perform successfully with others?	Social Psychological Concept V: What kinds of social skills must people learn in order to perform successfully with others?	Social Psychological Concept V: What kinds of social skills must people learn in order to perform successfully with others?
The ability to repeat what is said.	Taking turns being different kinds of group helpers allows everyone to learn many ways to help each other.	Encouraging and caring words and actions motivate people to keep trying when learning new or difficult skills.	Consistent use of encouraging and positive actions creates a safe and inviting place to learn.
Taking turns being the leader helps everyone feel special.	Using encouraging and caring words and actions helps everyone succeed.	Taking turns being a leader helps everyone develop self-confidence and responsibility.	Use of specific feedback helps people develop thinking and communication skills.
Using encouraging and caring words and actions makes everyone feel good.	Active listening is the ability to hear what was said and ask questions to build understanding.	Courteous and specific feedback develops people's ability to strengthen motor skills, social skills, and strategy knowledge.	Positive disagreement enables everyone to feel that their concerns have been heard and addressed respectfully.
Being honest and fair in all activities makes playing enjoyable.	Using courtesy and complimenting in all games and activities makes the activities successful.	Practicing empathy enables people to understand other people's points of view.	Paraphrasing is an important communication skill.
	Telling each other useful things about movement and social skills helps partners improve their skills.	Positive disagreement is an important skill for solving problems.	
		Student input regarding classroom behavioral expectations empowers students to meet expectations consistently and encourages peer accountability.	

Table 1. Critical Student Concepts, K–6

Social Psychological Concept VI: How do people achieve the social skills needed to perform successfully with others?	*Social Psychological Concept VI: How do people achieve the social skills needed to perform successfully with others?*	*Social Psychological Concept VI: How do people achieve the social skills needed to perform successfully with others?*	*Social Psychological Concept VI: How do people achieve the social skills needed to perform successfully with others?*
When people cooperate with others they work together in a game or activity in a way that everyone feels helpful.	Learning from mistakes takes courage and thought.	Using "I" statements and eliminating "you" statements when solving a problem helps to resolve the problem without assigning blame.	Developing thinking skills during the use of steps to conflict resolution will greatly enhance the person's ability to solve disagreements and prevent future conflict.
Telling someone to stop who says or does something that isn't wanted and letting the person know what is wanted are important steps in problem solving.	Learning a movement skill very well increases a person's desire to challenge those skills alone and with others.	Improving movement skill increases the desire to test skills alone or with others.	To successfully and enjoyably compete in an activity, people need to develop motor and social skills that match others in the activity.
Mistakes are a good way to learn to do something a different way the next time.	Practicing social skills when cooperating with others develops those skills while helping the group to be successful.	Collaboration is the process of working together, but not necessarily on the same goals or outcomes.	Personal challenge differs from competition in that it involves continuous improvement and setting new goals, regardless of someone else's performance.
Learning a movement skill very well helps people want greater challenges.	Using "I" statements when solving a problem helps to solve the problem without assigning blame.	Using the steps to conflict resolution enables people to work together to solve disagreements.	When people have the opportunity to alternate roles, give feedback, practice social skills, and contribute to the success of the group on a regular basis, they learn to be successful with people in any activity.
	Thinking about many ways to solve a problem and choosing the best thing to do for that problem helps the brain work better on future problems.	Learning from meaningful individual, partner, or group challenges helps the brain work better when solving future problems.	

Table 1. Critical Student Concepts, K–6

Understanding and strengthening the "thinking" area of the brain helps people better solve problems, learn from mistakes, and improve interactions with others.

Table 1. Critical Student Concepts, 8–12

Eighth Grade	Tenth Grade	Twelfth Grade
Social Psychological Concept I: How do people feel about themselves when participating in physical activity?	*Social Psychological Concept I: How do people feel about themselves when participating in physical activity?*	*Social Psychological Concept I: How do people feel about themselves when participating in physical activity?*
Student created movement games and dances help students develop a sense of purpose and meaning for physical activity.	Student created movement games and dances help students develop a sense of purpose and meaning for physical activity.	Community service and cross-age projects develop a sense of purpose and competence for physical activity.
Participating in challenging and culturally diverse physical activities develops positive attitudes and openness.	Participating in challenging and culturally diverse physical activities develops positive attitudes and openness.	Participating in challenging and culturally diverse physical activities develops positive attitude and openness.
Identifying behaviors that are supportive and inclusive of others in physical activity builds people's sense of self.	Working independently develops self-confidence.	Keeping the importance of winning and losing in perspective while participating in physical

Table 1. Critical Student Concepts, 8–12

People's appreciation of their own uniqueness helps them to value the activities they do well.	Keeping the importance of winning and losing in perspective while participating in physical activities and sports helps people maintain positive feelings about self and others.	activities and sports helps people maintain positive feelings about self and others.
Social Psychological Concept II: How can people improve their sense of self through physical activity?	*Social Psychological Concept II: How can people improve their sense of self through physical activity?*	Succeeding at increasingly more challenging physical activities, movement skills, and strategies creates a sense of accomplishment.
Physical activity is a means of self-expression.	Visualization of successful performance in a physical activity or movement may have positive effects on the actual performance.	*Social Psychological Concept II: How can people improve their sense of self through physical activity?*
People learn to appreciate physical activity, enjoy participation, and achieve goals when they are challenged with difficult but attainable tasks.	Providing abundant opportunities for people to record specific feedback regarding their performance enables them to grow.	Continually accepting new and diverse movement challenges leads to the appreciation of movement experiences, enjoyment of participation, and valuing of lifelong physical activity.
Consistent use of self-assessment when learning a new physical skill or activity makes it easier for people to recognize and appreciate the things they are doing well.	Pursuing multicultural and new activities and sports alone and with others allows people occasions to use self-encouragement	Opportunities to record specific feedback regarding performance enables individuals to grow and to construct achievable goals.
		Developing numerous strategies for preparing to excel in move-

Table 1. Critical Student Concepts, 8–12

The ability to set and achieve goals creates a sense of personal responsibility for one's own learning.	and positive self-talk while discovering more about their own abilities.	ment challenges—visualization, positive self-talk, relaxation exercises, etc.—can help people to be successful in any endeavor.
Social Psychological Concept III: How can people continue to develop toward their full potential through physical activity?	*Social Psychological Concept III: How can people continue to develop toward their full potential through physical activity?*	*Social Psychological Concept III: How can people continue to develop toward their full potential through physical activity?*
Initiating positive interactions with others and asking for their support enhances people's own success and progress toward self-actualization.	Ethical decision making requires the development of integrity—a steadfast adherence to a clear moral or ethical code.	Ethical decision making requires the development of integrity—a steadfast adherence to a clear moral or ethical code.
People who understand and apply knowledge of their own learning styles are more willing and able to adapt to a variety of learning styles.	Ethical decision making is a critical skill that is continuously challenged and cultivated throughout a lifetime.	Ethical decision making is a critical skill that is continuously challenged and cultivated throughout a lifetime.
Ethical decision making requires the development of integrity—a steadfast adherence to a clear moral or ethical code.	The ability to initiate positive interactions with others, ask for feedback, and formulate goals enhances self-confidence and self-actualization.	The ability to initiate positive interactions with others, ask for feedback, and formulate goals enhances self-confidence.
	Selecting appropriate learning styles to accomplish goals leads	A sense of competence is a critical component of self-actualization. It is developed through the

Table 1. Critical Student Concepts, 8–12

Social Psychological Concept IV: How do people learn to understand and respond to individual and group diversity?

Thoughtful reflection of past experiences and current interactions enhances understanding and openness toward others.

Empathy will enhance effective communication skills.

Inclusion is the act of taking in individuals as members of a group.

Participating in challenging and culturally diverse physical activities and sports builds understanding and appreciation of cultures, abilities, and skill levels.

to success and helps people become self-actualized.

Analyzing potential consequences when confronted with behavior choices increases the likelihood of making appropriate decisions.

Social Psychological Concept IV: How do people learn to understand and respond to individual and group diversity?

Participation in challenging and culturally diverse physical activities and sports builds understanding and appreciation of cultures, abilities, and skill levels.

Inclusion is the act of taking in individuals as members of a group.

Listening without judgment, paraphrasing thoughts and feelings, and clarifying for mutual understanding enhances people's ability to understand and appreciate others.

process of self-assessment, problem solving, and reformulating future actions.

Selecting appropriate learning styles to accomplish goals helps people become self-actualized.

Social Psychological Concept IV: How do people learn to understand and respond to individual and group diversity?

An increasing willingness to learn about others will include exploration of and participation in cultural and ethnic dances, games, and activities.

Empathy enhances effective communication skills.

Opportunities to practice inclusion greatly influences people's understanding and accommodation of similarities and differences among individuals.

Table 1. Critical Student Concepts, 8–12

Social Psychological Concept V: What kinds of social skills must people learn in order to perform successfully with others?

Integrity is the ability to adhere to a strict moral or ethical code.

Moral and ethical interactions with others in physical activity include the ability to hold one's self accountable to the rules and pre-determined standards of behavior.

Constructive communication, active listening, empathy, paraphrasing, questioning, and clarifying build shared understanding.

Using specific feedback in a caring and considerate manner helps to build a mutually nurturing environment for learning.

Social Psychological Concept V: What kinds of social skills must people learn in order to perform successfully with others?

Constructive communication builds shared understanding.

Distributed leadership enables all students to develop a sense of responsibility for self and others and to be perceived as a contributing member of the group.

Using specific feedback in a caring and considerate manner helps to build a mutually nurturing environment for learning.

Ethical decision making involves the culmination of a number of learned social skills, including empathy, respect for other people's property, honesty, integrity, and self-discipline.

Community service projects involving physical activity provide opportunities to learn about the needs of others and to practice social skills.

Social Psychological Concept V: What kinds of social skills must people learn in order to perform successfully with others?

Consistent practice of ethical interactions with others transfers to all interactions throughout a lifetime.

Constructive communication skills provide the tools for interacting positively and effectively throughout one's lifetime.

Distributed leadership enables individuals to experience a variety of roles within a group.

Improved communication skills increase content knowledge, improve oral speaking skills, and empower students to be more

Table 1. Critical Student Concepts, 8–12

Asking inquiring questions shows genuine interest in others as people.	*Social Psychological Concept VI: How do people achieve the social skills needed to perform successfully with others?*	successful in personal, social, and professional endeavors throughout their lifetime.
Social Psychological Concept VI: How do people achieve the social skills needed to perform successfully with others?	Steps to conflict resolution can be applied on a regular basis with or without the use of a mediator.	*Social Psychological Concept VI: How do people achieve the social skills needed to perform successfully with others?*
Steps to conflict resolution can be applied on a regular basis with or without the use of a mediator.	Cooperation, collaboration, and social skills practiced on a regular basis will increase a person's knowledge and ability to interact positively with others.	Steps to conflict resolution can be applied on a regular basis and rarely require the use of a mediator.
Continued attention to the practice and processing of social interaction skills in physical activity will make those activities more enjoyable, and skills critical to success in all areas of life will be developed.	A variety of physical activity choices and diversity of interactions can contribute to an individual's combined knowledge, experience, and attitude about lifelong physical activity choices.	Decisions about pursuing regular physical activity will be determined by an individual's combined knowledge, experience, and attitude about a wide variety of physical activities and the enjoyment level developed in relation to others in those activities.
Understanding of the "automatic," "emotional," and "thinking" areas of the brain will significantly increase people's control over their behavior in relationship to others.	Frequent self-reflection on interaction skills creates a deeper	Frequent self-reflection about interaction skills creates a deeper understanding that will allow people to continue to develop those skills for a lifetime.

Table 1. Critical Student Concepts, 8–12

Pursuing interests in a variety of physical activities and sports enables students to develop healthy and active recreation alternatives for a lifetime.	understanding that will allow a person to develop those skills throughout a lifetime.	Cooperation, collaboration, and social skills practiced on a regular basis will increase a person's knowledge and ability to positively interact with others in all social, academic, and professional endeavors.
	Increased understanding of the three parts of the brain: brain stem, limbic system, and neo-cortex helps people understand why they react the way they do in their interactions with others.	Increased understanding of the three parts of the brain: brain stem, limbic system, and neo-cortex helps people understand why they react the way they do in their interactions with others.

Effective Teaching Strategies

Beyond modeling, the teacher also must provide instruction on the concepts outlined in the previous section. Teachers are encouraged to move away from the traditional teacher-dominated model for teaching and adopt a more interactive, student-centered approach. It is also critical to create a positive classroom atmosphere where students feel safe to take risks and where mistakes are not feared, but welcomed as opportunities to learn.

Cooperative learning is a student-centered learning model that structures learner tasks in ways that allow self and social skills to be taught. It also encompasses higher order thinking skills. Cooperative learning is not simply higher skilled students teaching lower skilled students, and it is not the best or only way to teach. It is, however, the best way to teach some skills specific to social interaction. Five principles underlie successful cooperative groups (Deshon & O'Leary 1984):

- Equal distribution of leadership responsibilities (distributed leadership)
- Heterogeneous grouping
- Positive interdependence
- Social skills acquisition
- Group autonomy

Distributed Leadership. No leader is assigned by the teacher or chosen by the group. The teacher allows students to determine important tasks and the contributions that each student will make to the success of the group. These roles are continuously rotated throughout the week, month, quarter, etc., so that every student has the opportunity to perform all tasks. Some examples may include timer, facilitator, equipment monitor, checker for group understanding, encourager, feedback provider, recorder, and skills monitor (both social and motor).

Heterogeneous Grouping. Groups are formed at random or assigned in advance by the teacher. Groups should include both genders and a mix of physical capabilities, cultural and socioeconomic backgrounds, language/verbal skills, and cognitive and social skills. This kind of group diversity best reflects the real world and allows students the opportunity to learn and practice the skills involved in tolerating, accepting, appreciating, and celebrating differences.

Positive Interdependence. This is the opportunity for students to take personal responsibility while working with a group toward a common goal. The teacher can use one or more of the following strategies to ensure that everyone is involved in the learning: group accountability, common tasks, limited and shared equipment, and group projects. These strategies are often referred to as providing individual accountability, since they ensure that the most gifted or motivated student does not complete the entire assignment or activity alone.

Social Skills Acquisition. Cooperative learning is a particularly effective method for teaching social skills if the skills being taught also are modeled by the teacher. Social skills instruction is ineffective if the teacher tends to believe that students are "good" or "bad." Teachers may have expectations of how students are going to behave based on their appearance (e.g., tall and muscular, small, overweight), their race, their culture, a look, a feeling, who their parents are, socioeconomic status, gender, etc. Teachers also may listen to others who describe a student as "bad," "trouble," "incorrigible," or "unteachable." There is little mention of strategies to teach students social skills in undergraduate preparation. Therefore, whatever level of skills teachers have acquired has come from their own experiences with others, and primarily from their families. This creates two perceptions that can potentially inhibit social skills instruction: teachers may believe that their own behaviors/values are being questioned or criticized, or teachers may believe that families have the sole responsibility for teaching students to behave appropriately. Teachers who have these perceptions must address them before the process of teaching social skills can begin.

There are five steps to teaching social skills:

1. Introduce the social skill to be learned (e.g., caring, encouraging, courtesy) and provide a rationale for using it.
2. Role play what it is and (sometimes) what it is not.
3. Brainstorm the skill using a T-chart (students brainstorm what the skill looks like and sounds like).
4. Students and teacher monitor the social skill while students engage in a task that allows for performance of the skill.
5. Students and teacher process the skill and the task.

Group Autonomy. The teacher allows students to fail and learn from their mistakes instead of "rescuing" them by intervening at the first sign of trouble. Rescuing in this sense describes teacher behaviors such as getting students back on task, settling arguments, and offering solutions to student problems. It is important that the group members be given the chance to solve the problems that arise by themselves. They should be given a process to use and parameters in which to work out the issues before they ask for help. Teacher prompting and monitoring will encourage group self-sufficiency.

Each of the lesson examples in the box focuses on one social psychological concept. Each lesson uses cooperative learning strategies coupled with selected models for integrating concepts across curriculum. Teachers are encouraged to make age-appropriate modifications in order to meet the needs of their students.

The examples emphasize social psychological concepts, and therefore may reduce movement/motor learning time. These examples illustrate how the concepts may be used in class. The overall curricular emphasis in physical education, however, should remain on maximizing movement time and motor learning practice.

Integrating Social Psychology Concepts into Instruction

Example 1: Elementary School (Kindergarten)

Concept: Learning about the body and how it moves helps people feel positively about themselves.
Children at this age still engage in parallel play (playing side by side with minimum interaction) and strive to acquire body control while moving. The objective of this lesson is to help children learn that moving is fun and helps them feel good about themselves. One way to do so is to provide children with positive opportunities to explore moving their bodies safely and with control. In other words children would move without bumping into others or putting others in danger of getting hurt.
Teaching children the concepts of personal and general space is a good place to start. Personal space is that space immediately surrounding the body. General space is that space outside of one's own personal space.

Children should explore their personal space before they explore general space. Many teachers place poly-spots around the classroom, gymnasium, hard top, or field in order to help children identify their own personal space. As children come to understand the concept, the poly-spots are no longer necessary.

Providing a series of suggestions or asking open ended questions like, "How tall can you get?" are appropriate ways to enable children to explore their own personal space. For instance, as children stand on their poly-spots, the teacher suggests that they move their arms all around their bodies using different rates of speed at different levels (high, medium, and low). For example, the teacher may say, "Show me how you can slowly move your elbows to different places around your body." or, "Let's see you reach your hands high over your heads and stretch to a high level while standing on your tippy toes."

As children begin to understand the concept of personal space and exploring personal space with different body parts, the teacher can provide them with choices about moving in personal space. The teacher may suggest to children that they now choose a body part that they would like to explore and find different ways to move it around their bodies, using varied speeds and levels. From here, the teacher can encourage children to make shapes with their bodies, act out stories or songs, and/or simply explore further moving in their own space.

During this activity, it is most important to help children make the connection that moving their bodies is fun and helps them feel good. This can be done in a variety of ways. For example, the teacher may simply comment on the number of smiling faces (when culturally appropriate) that he or she sees during the lesson, and ask children to explain why they are smiling. Children may comment that they are having fun or that they feel good. Here, the teacher follows up by asking what is making them feel good, thus helping children realize that moving is fun and provides them with positive feelings.

Using other mediums to encourage discussion regarding this concept also is a good idea. For instance, the teacher can ask the children to draw pictures of themselves moving in their favorite ways. As children show their drawings, the teacher can ask them to explain how their favorite movements make them feel.

Example 2: Elementary School (Grade 4)

Concepts: Positive self-talk such as, "Good effort!" and, "I enjoy playing and making up active games." increases self-confidence and one's ability to perform.

Realistic challenges develop self-concept and self-esteem.

This lesson uses an inclusion style of teaching, meaning that everyone in class will have opportunities to experience success during the lesson. This strategy is helpful, particularly when teaching students to engage in positive self-talk, determine realistic goals, and take calculated risks. The inclusion style takes advance planning and good organization of the learning environment in order to ensure student success.

The lesson begins with the teacher stating the concepts and objectives for the day. Next, the students are asked to give examples of self-encouraging words and phrases. They discuss the positive, kind, and supportive things they can say to themselves while they practice jump roping skills. Teachers should consider using a T-chart to help students create a list of encouraging phrases and words.

The teacher should have the students jump rope and determine which skills they can do and which skills they would like to improve. With an idea of which skills they would like to work on, students can determine individual learning goals by answering the following questions:

1. What would I like to be able to do?
2. How will I achieve this goal?
3. What is my timeline for achieving this goal?
4. If this challenge becomes too difficult or unrealistic, what smaller goals can I set in order to experience success and continue toward the bigger goal?
5. If this challenge becomes too easy, what other goals will I find more challenging?

In a jump rope unit, the teacher can provide examples of rope jumping skills through videotapes, demonstrations, written explanations, and diagrams. In the inclusion style, students are encouraged to begin with skills they know they can perform and then identify new goals or challenges. For example, the student who cannot turn a rope and jump it at the same time may choose to lay the rope on the ground and jump over it. While students practice, they must engage in positive self-talk. Teachers should design opportunities—like writing in a log, answering teacher questions, and interviewing peers—to allow students to assess whether or not they have been successful in achieving their goals.

As students achieve their goals, they should describe their success and how it made them feel before setting new goals. If they do not reach their goals, they must determine why and set more realistic goals. Not reaching a goal should be looked at as a positive learning experience. Students should be reminded to use positive self-talk in these situations.

The inclusion model requires students to spend a lot of time working independently. Teachers serve as facilitators in this process. They help students make the connection between motor skill practice and developing a positive sense of self. They can use individual, small group, or whole class discussions, journals and worksheets, and feedback to help students develop positive identities and take responsibility for their learning.

Example 3: Middle School (Grade 8)

Concepts: Students can use physical activity as a means of self-expression.

Continuous challenges foster enjoyment, improvement, and the ability to persevere.

The ability to set and achieve goals allows students to develop a sense of responsibility for their own learning.

Fair play is an important concept for game play and for all interactions in life. In this lesson, students are involved in the process of establishing safe and realistic rules for game play. They will work with classmates in upholding those rules. Any physical activity, game, or sport unit can work in this lesson. Basketball is the example here.

Teaching the rules of a game can become rote and boring, especially if the process is teacher directed. When the rules of game play are taught using an interactive process, students learn to be responsible for themselves and to one another. Done well, the whole process can provide practice in worthwhile qualities such as honesty, integrity, respect, compassion, cooperation, and leadership.

The teacher first tells students that the purpose of the class is to modify the game of three on three basketball so that it is a cooperative effort between two teams. Next, the class is divided into heterogeneous groups of six. Students are asked to determine the contributions each student will make to the success of this group effort (distributed leadership). Tasks may include things like facilitator, timer, recorder, equipment manager, checker for group understanding, and social skills monitor. Teachers must remember to encourage group autonomy by refraining from rescuing groups too early, and to foster positive interdependence by sharing equipment and resources and holding each group member accountable for the completion of his or her tasks.

Each group of six modifies the game of three on three basketball so that it becomes a cooperative effort by both teams. Students are encouraged to modify the rules of basketball as they know it in order to achieve this goal. Students must ensure safety and inclusion of all players. Each member of the group is responsible for playing by the rules and acknowledging when they have committed a violation (honor code). Once each group has had the opportunity to play their modified game, they may make adjustments.

Students discuss this cooperative process during closure. Open-ended questions include: "What was it like to modify the game of three on three basketball?" "What did you like most about the lesson?" "What did you like most about the games that you made up?" "Can you describe how you played honestly and fairly?" and, "What did it feel like to play fairly?"

Students are guided to the realization that creating game play is part of taking responsibility for one's own learning. Cooperating, being honest and respectful, and taking leadership roles contributes significantly to developing one's human potential.

Example 4: High School (Grade 12)

Concept: An increasing willingness to learn about others will include exploration of and participation in cultural and ethnic dances, games, and activities.

Constructing for meaning allows students to develop a learning task that embraces their culture, heritage, interests, and experience. It stimulates creative and critical thinking skills, and it may involve research on the part of the learner. The teacher's principal roles are to provide appropriate primary resources (equipment, time, instructional materials, etc.), and to facilitate learning.

Students may work alone, in pairs, or in a group. They select a historical period that is of interest to them (e.g., the civil rights movement, the roaring twenties, modern pop culture, ancient Egypt, etc.), and research the significant movement and recreational activities from that period as a homework assignment. Any number of products can result from this research:

• Students can create a game, dance, or movement activity from the time period and teach it to the class. The class can describe the nature of the interaction skills involved in the activity, how these skills are learned through the activity, and their significance in the context of the culture from which they originated.

• Students can adapt games learned in class to incorporate the cultural, historical, or philosophical perspectives of their time period.

• Students can invent their own game or activity that incorporates motor learning concepts and principals, biomechanics, exercise physiology, or social skills.

• Students can invent a game or activity based on predicting what a particular culture and lifestyle might be like in the future, focusing on the social nature of the activity.

This kind of assignment lends itself to working together with the history or social studies teacher to develop a strategy for providing students with primary resources as well as helping them to develop their ideas. Teachers can decide together the kinds of outcomes they will require, the timelines and due dates, and what portions of the product will be used by and graded by each teacher.

Example 5: Elementary School (Grade 2)

Concept: Using courtesy and complimenting in all games and activities makes the activities successful.

Ask your students to brainstorm about the meaning of courtesy. Their ideas should be recorded and posted where they are visible to all. Students will then be asked to move a ball in various ways to the cues of the teacher. After several minutes of practice, have students think of as many ways as possible to be courteous when choosing a partner. Allow students to work with a partner if they wish. After several minutes, ask students to share their responses. Their answers may include:

- Say yes with a smile when someone asks to be your partner
- Be willing to be partners with someone besides your best friend
- Say "thank you" and "please" to your partner
- Don't leave anyone out, even if you have to make a group of three

Next, have students select partners. Give each student a task card with the following set of instructions written on it:

1. Say "thank you" every time the equipment is handed to you.
2. Say "you're welcome" when your partner says "thank you."
3. Hand your partner the equipment when it falls.

Give each pair of students one ball to share. While one child is performing to the cues of the teacher, the other is observing and making encouraging statements. After a few minutes, have the students switch roles. After they have each had a turn, they should stop and ask each other if they remembered to use the courteous statements and behaviors listed on the task card. They should talk about how it felt, then they should repeat the activity while trying to maintain or improve their courteous behavior.

At the end of the lesson, have students talk to their partners about whether they had the opportunity to use any of the other courteous words and behaviors listed on the class chart.

Example 6: Middle School (Grade 6)

Concepts: When students have the opportunity to alternate roles, give feedback, practice social skills, and contribute to the success of the group on a regular basis they learn to be successful with people in any activity.

The teacher divides students into heterogeneous groups of six, being careful to balance the groups with students having both higher and lower social skills proficiency. The students are given group identification names or numbers by a student monitor during warm-ups.

The teacher has a chart with the word "ENCOURAGE" written on the top, and "HEAR/SEE" underneath. After the teacher gives an example of a time when encouraging might be needed (e.g., a marathon runner is almost finished and can see the finish line but doesn't think that she can make it), the teacher then asks students to identify some other situations where encouraging might be helpful. Students brainstorm as many encouraging statements as they can. These may be things like: "You can do it!" "Keep going!" "Don't stop!" "Nice try!" and, "Way to go!" The teacher writes all of their ideas on the chart.

Next, the students brainstorm encouraging actions. These answers may include clapping, smiling, cheering, patting on the back, or giving a thumbs up or high five. After the chart is completed, the students are told that they will be practicing encouragement in the next two activities. They are told to listen and watch for it in their groups so they can share what happened at the end of the class. The teacher and/or selected students will also monitor as the students are performing, writing down encouraging things they say and do.

Each group of students creates two triads. In these triads, students perform the following tasks:

■ One student will practice the overhand throw, another will catch, and the third will watch and monitor the throw by referring to a task card that lists the following three critical elements:

1. Step forward with opposite foot from throwing arm.
2. Trunk twist starts with hips facing sideways in the direction of the throwing arm and ends with hips facing forward toward the throw at the moment of release.
3. Hand snaps downward during the release of the ball.

The student who is observing performs three tasks: gives the practicing student specific feedback on the three elements listed on the card, gives encouraging comments, and keeps track of the number of throws. The student who is catching also does or says encouraging things. After the practicing student throws six times, the students rotate. The activity continues until all three students have performed all three roles.

■ After students have practiced in their triads for a designated period of time, they will be asked to develop several ideas for a six-person game that uses the overhand throw and encouraging. After each group of three has had an opportunity to develop several ideas, they join the other half of their original group, share their ideas, and create and play their new game.

After playing the game, students are given three minutes to process their understanding of how they developed the ability to encourage and their use of encouraging during the game. They should use the following questions:

1. What did you hear or see that demonstrated the skill of encouraging?
2. How did it feel to have someone encourage you?
3. How did it feel to encourage others?
4. What did you do that helped you understand what encouraging others means?
5. What would you do differently next time.

At this time, the teacher should share some of his or her observations.

The first part of the cooperative learning model—self-esteem building—was the primary instructional focus of the lesson in Example 1. As mentioned earlier, self-concept and self-esteem comprise the foundation upon which self-confidence, improved social behavior, and achievement are built. The learning activity provides children with positive experiences that help build a positive sense of self. The feelings reinforced in this lesson that relate directly to positive self-esteem are:

1. Security. Children were given clear rules for participation and a clear definition of personal space. They knew what to expect and that it was safe.
2. Selfhood. Children were exploring their own space and moving in ways that felt comfortable to them. They were developing self-knowledge about the way their bodies move.
3. Affiliation. Each child saw that other children were working on the same thing, thus providing a sense of membership to the class.
4. Purpose. The purpose of the lesson was made clear. Children were practicing the concept of personal space and moving successfully. Not only did they come to realize that movement is fun and makes them feel good, but they also developed their own sense of self-empowerment.
5. Competence. Children gained a better understanding of how they move and a sense of accomplishment for moving appropriately in personal space.

Processing is the practice of evaluating what has occurred during the lesson or activity. It helps students to understand and internalize cause and effect, and it provides valuable feedback from peers and the teacher. Processing should not be used to provide a forum for blame when the group has not been successful, however. Students can be taught to use tactful statements, such as, "Our group did not complete the task because everyone didn't get a chance to share." Contrast this statement with, "Our group didn't work because Mary is so bossy." Processing is crucial to teaching social skills, and it also helps students to develop critical thinking skills.

Cooperative learning strategies are particularly effective because the learning occurs in the context of instruction, not as a separate unit, subject, or course. Teachers can select several social skills per year, and teach a new skill every four to five weeks, along with the regular curriculum. Teachers are encouraged to display, as visible reminders, social skill signs and posters. Teachers will decide how much time to focus on each skill based on the needs of their students.

Assessing Student Learning

When assessing student use of social psychological concepts, it is important to be clear and specific about what knowledge, behaviors, and actions will be appraised, as well as what assessment tools will be used. Teachers are encouraged to engage students in the assessment process as much as possible so they may bring application to their understanding of these skills. Several things should be considered:

1. What do you expect your students to know and be able to do as a result of the instruction?
2. How will you know it when you see it? What will the understandings/behaviors look and sound like at different grade levels? In different classes? What role will the teacher have in the assessment? What role will the students have in the assessment?
3. What criteria will be used for judging the students' knowledge, understanding, and use of the concepts?
4. What kind of feedback are you expecting to receive in order to make adjustments to the curriculum?
5. Are you collecting information that can help provide insight into the effectiveness of your personal interactions with students?
6. Are both formative and cumulative methods used consistently?

Following are some examples of ways to assess student knowledge and abilities regarding the social psychological domain.

Pair Share. The teacher gives task cards to each set of partners to help them monitor their ability to develop and use a social skill, such as courtesy, during the activity. At the completion of the lesson, each partner has 30 seconds to describe his or her own ability to use the social skill on the task card. He or she then describes the other person's performance.

Rubric. Rubrics are a means by which students can rate their own social skills and those of their classmates. Students work in groups of six to complete a task such as creating a new game incorporating the overhand throw. Then, students are asked to rate their team performance based on a specific rating criteria, or rubric. The teacher fills out a separate rating form for each team using the same criteria. The two are compared and discussed.

Sample Rubric

3   All students gave input into creating the game.
         All students used encouraging statements at appropriate times.
         Feedback provided by each student in the group was specific and clear.
2   Most students gave input when creating the game.
         Most students used encouraging statements sometimes.
         Feedback provided by most students was specific and clear.
1   Only a few students gave input into creating the game.
         Few students used encouraging statements.
         Few students provided specific or clear feedback.

Open-Ended Question Journal. Students keep a journal, or use paper distributed in class. The open-ended question journal enables students to reflect on self, social skills concepts, and experiences during class. The teacher can leave time for writing in class or assign journal writing for homework. The teacher and/or the students should determine an open-ended question for each writing assignment. Questions should relate to self-reflection, social skills, and lesson experiences. For example: "How would you describe your participation and contributions to the group in each of your assigned roles in today's activity?" "How did you feel about your contributions to the group?" or, "How you would modify your input in the future based on today's learning?"

Group Project. Group projects provide wonderful opportunities for students to work cooperatively. For example, after several weeks of school and numerous hours of teaching students elements of physical and emotional safety, the teacher decides to have the students create their own safety project. The teacher tells the students that they are going to develop the expectations for a safe physical education class for the kindergartners. Students are given time to work in pairs to think of as many behaviors as they can that make learning in physical education safe.

They will then be asked to describe how children learn these skills. After several minutes, the teacher asks partners to share their answers and record them on a chart. After everyone has had an opportunity to share, the teacher asks for clarification and consensus on the behaviors and methods of learning that the students have described. A group of students is assigned to redo the chart so that it is neat and clear, then all students sign the chart, and it is presented to the kindergarten class.

Checklist. As students are performing an assigned activity, they can be asked to self-assess, be observed by peers, or be observed by the teacher. Regardless of who does the assessment, a checklist is used. The observations work best if they are objective in nature and do not require any judgment on the part of the observer. Checklists can be modified to include specific behaviors.

Sample Checklist Items

OBSERVED

Frequently Sometimes Never

1. Student uses courtesy when asking for and returning equipment to others.
2. Student listens and can repeat what he or she heard a partner or group member say.
3. Student willingly chooses and welcomes partners of the opposite gender.
4. Student willingly accepts and welcomes individuals who are differently abled, or who have limited physical or cognitive abilities.
5. Student willingly invites and accepts partners and group members of different cultures and ethnic backgrounds.
6. Student contributes as a member of the group in whatever capacity assigned.
7. Student takes risks such as volunteering to demonstrate taking a turn when it is appropriate, answering questions, speaking in front of the class, finding own partner/group.
8. Student offers to help others.
9. Student is able to provide specific feedback in a caring and supportive manner to a partner or group member during an instructional task.
10. Student practices active listening during teacher instruction.

Portfolio. Social psychological concepts can be included as entries in comprehensive portfolios, or separate portfolios can be created specifically for social psychological concepts. A portfolio for social psychological concepts may document growth in understanding about social and/or interpersonal skills over time. Portfolios in the social psychological domain should reflect real life, challenging utilizations of concept knowledge and application, and/or synthesis of skills. Social psychological skills can be student self-selected, so that each portfolio contains skills specific to each student's developmental needs. What makes a portfolio different than a folder filled with completed assignments is the interactive process involved. When students create portfolios, they are actively engaged with content and their own learning. The steps for developing portfolios are quite specific, yet flexible, depending on student and teacher needs. The details of each step stated below may be determined by the teacher, the teacher and the student, or the student.

1. Determine the purpose of the portfolio (e.g., "Students will self-assess their understanding of how to develop social skills and their use of skills identified and taught throughout the unit, semester, or year.").

2. Determine what kind of student work will be included in the portfolio (e.g., "Students are to include a report that chronicles the development of their ability to understand and apply the social skill of accepting personal differences to their interactions with others in each game, activity, or skill throughout the unit, semester, or year."). Teachers and students establish criteria for evaluating the work.

3. Create timelines for completing each piece of student work. Make these timelines reasonable (e.g., "One reflection per week will be turned in to the teacher.").

4. Design ways to evaluate and provide feedback for student work, both during the process and upon completion. It is important to have checkpoints during the process where students can

have their work reviewed and discussed so they can monitor their progress. Evaluation during the process and upon completion may be conducted by the student, by peers, and/or by the teacher. For example, each student might receive feedback from a peer every two to three weeks regarding reflections and new understandings. The teacher can become involved if it appears that a student is having difficulty acquiring and/or applying the skill.

5. Build in opportunities for students to make sense of the learning process and share their finished portfolio with others. For example, students might have the opportunity to share their reports orally in small groups, and to discuss the learning they have used.

Concluding Comments

Every student in a physical education program has the potential to become a capable, caring contributor to the class, the school, and society as a whole. Why, then are some students unsuccessful?

We know that interpersonal and intrapersonal characteristics are shaped by a multitude of factors. At times it is tempting for educators to blame the environment, the family, the community, or society at large for challenging students. However, this view can prevent educators from embracing the challenge and taking responsibility for nurturing all their students. All students deserve the right to develop to their full potential. And, an essential attribute for successful development is a positive sense of self.

Teachers must believe that they have the power to nurture the sense of self in all students. The question that remains, then, is, "How?" The teachers' role in providing thoughtful, well organized environments where students feel physically and emotionally safe will depend largely on the amount of time, energy, resources, and self-reflection that they are able to expend. Integrating social psychological concepts across the physical education curriculum and into daily lessons invites the pursuit of personal and social lifelong learning for students and educators alike.

How Can I Learn More?
Workshops

Attend the following kinds of workshops, within the context of physical education if possible:

- Cooperative Learning
- English Language Learners
- Conflict Resolution or Conflict
- Social Skills Instruction Management
- Reciprocal Teaching
- Constructivism or Meaning-Centered Teaching
- Multiple Intelligences
- Multicultural/Diversity
- Positive Discipline
- Inclusion
- Authentic Assessment
- Tribes
- Class meetings
- Critical Thinking/ Higher Order Thinking skills
- Developing a Positive Learning Climate
- Project Adventure or Other Initiatives Courses

- Brain Compatible Learning
- TESA-Teacher Expectations and Student Achievement
- Building Student Self-Esteem
- GESA—Gender and Ethnic Expectations and Student Achievement

Books

Allen, A., & Gibbs, J. (1978). *Tribes–A process for peer involvement.* Lafayette, LA: Center for Human Development.

Bennett, B., Rolheiser, C., & Stevahn, L. (1991). *Cooperative learning where heart meets mind.* Bothell, WA: Professional Development Associates.

Glenn, S. H., & Nelsen, J. (1989). *Raising self-reliant children in a self-indulgent world.* Rocklin, CA: Prima Publishing and Communications.

Kuykendall, C. (1992). *From rage to hope, Strategies for reclaiming black and hispanic students.* Bloomington, IN: National Educational Service.

Lickona, T. (1991). *Educating for character: How our schools can teach respect and responsibility.* New York: Bantam Books.

Nelsen, J., Lott, L., & Glenn, S. (1993). *Positive discipline in the classroom.* Rocklin, CA: Prima Publishing.

Nicholls, J. G. (1989). *The competitive ethos and democratic education.* Cambridge, MA: Harvard University Press.

Rowan, F. F. (Ed.). (1994). *Programs with pizzazz: Ideas for elementary physical educators.* Reston, VA: AAHPERD.

Articles, Pamphlets, Reports, Papers, and Guides

Bredemeier, B., & Shields, D. (1984). Divergence in moral reasoning about sport and everyday life. *Sociology of Sport Journal, 1,* 348-357.

_____. (1986). Athletic aggression: An issue of contextual morality. *Sociology of Sport Journal, 3,* 15-28.

Bredemeier, B., Weiss, M., Shields, D., & Cooper, B. (1986). The relationship of sport involvement with children's moral reasoning and aggressive tendencies. *Journal of Sport Psychology, 8,* 304-318.

Deshon, D., & O'Leary, P. W. (1990). Social skills and processing in a nutshell, *Cooperative Learning, 10*(3), 35-36.

Duda, J. L. (1989). Goal perspectives and behavior in sport and exercise settings. In C. Ames & M. Haehr (Eds.), *Advances in motivation and achievement.* Greenwich, CT: JAI Press.

_____. (1989). The relationship between task and ego orientation and the perceived purpose of sport among male and female high school athletes. *Journal of Sport and Exercise Psychology, 11,* 318-335.

Hellison, D. (1993). The coaching club–teaching responsibility to inner-city students. *JOHPERD, 64* (5), 66-70.

McBride, R. (1995). *Conflict resolution resources for schools and youth.* San Francisco, CA: Community Board Program, Inc.

Nicholls, J. G. (1984) Achievement motivation: Conceptions of ability, subjective experience, task choice, and performance. *Psychological Review, 91,* 328-346.

Papaioannou, A. (1995). Motivation and goal perspectives in children's physical education. In S. J. H. Biddles (Ed.). *European perspectives on exercise and sport psychology.* Champaign IL: Human Kinetics.

Romance, T., Weiss, M. R., & Bockoven, J. (1986). A program to promote moral development through elementary school physical education. *Journal of Teaching Physical Education, 5,* 126-136.

Thill, E. E., & Brunel, P. (1995). Cognitive theories of motivation in sport. In S. J. H. Biddles (Ed.). *European perspectives on exercise and sport psychology.* Champaign IL: Human Kinetics.

References

Allen, L., & Santrock, J. W. (1993). *Psychology: The contexts of behavior.* Madison, WI: WCB Brown & Benchmark.

Borba, M. (1989). *Self esteem builders resources.* Torrance, CA: Jalmar Press.

_____. (1995). *Strengthening at-risk students' achievement and behavior, A resource handbook.* Bellevue, WA: Bureau of Education and Research.

Bunker, L. K., Williams, J. M., & Zinsser, N. (1993). Cognitive techniques for improving performance and building confidence. In J. M. Williams (Ed.), *Applied sport psychology: Personal growth to peak performance.* Mountain View, CA: Mayfield.

Caine, R. N., & Caine, G. (1995). Reinventing schools through brain-based learning. *Educational Leadership, 52*(7), 43-47.

Community Board Program, Inc. (1993). *Conflict resolution resources for schools and youth.* San Francisco, CA: Author.

Costa, A. (1995). *Teaching for intelligent behavior—Outstanding strategies for strengthening your student's thinking skills, A resource handbook.* Bellevue, WA: Bureau of Education and Research.

Cox, R. H. (1994). *Sport psychology: Concepts and applications* (3rd ed.). Madison, WI: Brown & Benchmark.

Deshon, D., & O'Leary, P. W. (1984). *A guidebook for cooperative learning: A technique for creating more effective schools.* Holmes Beach, FL: Learning Publications, Inc.

Duda, J. L., Olson, L. K., & Templin, T. J. (1991). The relationship of task and ego orientation to sportsmanship attitudes and the perceived legitimacy of injurious acts. *Research Quarterly for Exercise and Sport, 62*(1), 79-87.

Dweck, E., & Elliott, E. (1983). Achievement motivation. In E. M. Hetherington (Ed.), *Socialization, personality, and social development.* New York: Wiley.

Gallahue, D. L. (1993). *Developmental physical education for today's children* (2nd ed.). Madison, WI: WCB Brown & Benchmark.

Goleman, D. (1995). *Emotional intelligence.* New York: Bantuam Books.

Harter, S. (1978). Effectance motivation reconsidered: Towards a developmental model. *Human Development, 21,* 34-64.

Hellison, D. (1995). *Teaching responsibility through physical activity.* Champaign, IL: Human Kinetics.

Hewitt, J. P. (1984). *Self society: A symbolic interaction in social psychology* (4th ed.). Boston, MA: Allyn and Bacon, Inc.

Kohn, A. (1990). *The brighter side of human nature: Altruism and empathy in everyday life.* New York: Basic Books.

Johnson, D. W., & Johnson, R.T. (1994). *Learning together and alone: Cooperative, competitive and individualistic learning* (4th ed.).

Mac Lean, P. (1990). *The triune brain in education.* New York: Plenum Press.

Maslow, A. H. (1954). *Motivation and personality.* New York: Harper.

McPherson, B. D., Curtis, J. E., & Loy, J. W. (1989). *The social significance of sport: An introduction of the sociology of sport.* Champaign, IL: Human Kinetics.

Morton & Deutch. (1973). *Resolution of conflicts.* New Haven, CT: Yale University Press.

Mosston, M., & Ashworth, S. (1994). *Teaching physical education* (4th ed.). New York: Macmillan.

National Association for Sport and Physical Education. (1995). *Moving into the future: National physical education standards: A guide to content and assessment.* Reston, VA: Author.

Nicholls, J. G. (1984). Achievement motivation: Conceptions of ability, subjective experience, task choice, and performance. *Psychological Review, 91,* 328-346.

O'Block, F. R., & Evans, F. H. (1984). Goal-setting as a motivational technique. In J. M. Silva III & R. S. Weinberg (Eds.), *Psychological foundations of sport.* Champaign, IL: Human Kinetics.

Payne, V. G., & Isaacs, L. D. (1995). *Human motor development: A lifespan approach* (3rd ed.). Mountain View, CA: Mayfield.

Placek, J. (1983). Concepts of success in teaching: Happy, busy and good? In T. Templin & J. Olson (Eds.), *Teaching in physical education.* Champaign, IL: Human Kinetics.

Williams, J. M., & Leffingwell, T. R. (1996). Cognitive strategies in sport and exercise psychology. In J. L. Van Raalte & B. W. Brewer (Eds.), *Exploring sport and exercise psychology.* Washington DC: American Psychological Association.

United States Department of Health and Human Services. (1996). *Physical activity and health: A report of the surgeon general.* Atlanta, GA: Author.

Glossary

Acceptance: to receive with favor.

Active listening: ability to demonstrate body language and facial expressions that indicate attention.

Affiliation/belongingness: feeling of acceptance by others; includes feelings of appreciation and respect.

Appreciation: to greatly value over time.

Celebration: intense appreciation.

Challenge: a testing of one's abilities or resources in a demanding but stimulating undertaking.

Clarifying: asking questions to improve one's understanding.

Competence: relates directly to the achievement of goals and the recognition of success.

Competition: a test of skill or ability.

Cooperative groups: groups structured to promote positive interdependence and social skills acquisition.

Diversity: distinct characteristics of people.

Ego-oriented goals: focus on how one's abilities compare with others in the class or other settings.

Empathy: identification with and understanding of another's situation, feelings, and motives.

Integrity: adherence to a strict moral or ethical code.

Morality: a system of ideas about right and wrong conduct.

Paraphrasing: repeating what was said in one's own words.

Psychology: the study of behaviors and mental processes.

Purpose: positive reasons for living; leads individuals to a greater sense of self-empowerment.

Security: feeling comfortable and safe in an environment.

Self-concept: one's perceptions of one's abilities, behavior. and personality.

Self-esteem: a process used to evaluate oneself; it is influenced by how we think other people perceive us.

Self-talk: a cognitive process whereby individuals make statements to themselves, both internally and externally.

Selfhood: developing one's sense of unique individualism.

Social psychology: the study of how the thoughts, feelings, and behaviors of individuals are influenced by the presence of other people.

Social skills: those skills that help partners or groups complete a task and build positive feelings in the participants.

Sociology: the study of the characteristics of social groups and their relationships to other social groups.

Specific feedback: detailed, non-evaluative information about the performance, product, or outcome of a task or process.

Stereotyping: using insufficient or inappropriate information to label groups of people.

Student-centered physical education: an interactive learning process for students; together, teachers and students find experiential ways to link information and understanding.

T-chart: a charting method of identifying a social skill and brainstorming the visual and verbal attributes of the skill.

Task-oriented goals: focus on personal improvement and mastery of skills.

Tolerance: the ability to endure with patience.

Virtue: demonstration of behavior that is consistent with an established moral code for one's culture.

Chapter 8
Aesthetic Experience

By Judith B. Alter

When students describe something they admire as "awesome" they may be showing intuitive knowledge of aesthetic experience. However, that does not mean that such questions as, "How does aesthetic experience fit into a physical education curriculum?" "Why is it important?" and, "What is it, anyway?" are not valid. Because the meaning of the word "aesthetic" may be unclear to many students, substitute "appreciation," or "awe," or "wonder" when talking about aesthetic experience in movement.

What Is Aesthetic Experience in Physical Education?

Imagine, for example, watching a seventh grade student running in a race. Notice the student's running style, coordination, arm swing, and stride length. These features comprise part of the runner's technique or form. Notice the student's height, gender, hair color, running clothes, and facial expression. These features relate to the student's personal structure, or appearance.

Notice the speed of the student, the great distance in front of the other runners, and the pleasure or disappointment felt (by you, the onlooker) knowing that the student will win. These observations relate to the student's accomplishment. Now notice the elegant design and motion of the runner as he or she leaps through space. This attention to the entirety of all the features for only the pleasure of this unified focus constitutes the onlooker's aesthetic response to the running.

In the example above, the runner exhibits form, structure, and accomplishment—and these elements have aesthetic properties. The features combine into a whole when the onlooker appreciates the beauty of an outstanding young runner in action. Beauty is another term that describes exquisitely executed motor performance. It refers to the design of the body and the graceful running, elegant control, and effortless speed. The overall impact of the entire event can produce a powerful aesthetic experience.

Now imagine the response of the runner after winning the race. That young runner spent many hours practicing and training. The teacher comments that his or her stride and form were outstanding on that day. The runner—recalling the experience of the race—agrees with the teacher. The runner feels a rush of pleasure while contemplating how all those practiced components came together and united in the performance. That total recalled experience also is aesthetic: the totality of cognitive, physical/kinesthetic, and emotional appreciation are unified in that performance.

Judith B. Alter is associate professor of dance, Department of World Arts and Cultures, University of California at Los Angeles.

Though many elite athletes describe their outstanding performances in this way, each person's aesthetic experience also has unique features. Each person may have a different mode of experiencing self-appreciation: a visual image, a rhythmic memory, a kinesthetic/physical recall, a spatial picture, or a combination of some or all of these. Although these varied modes of recreating the experience can be difficult to articulate, teachers can guide students to use all of their senses to become self-reflective and, thus, able to appreciate their physical achievements as more than earning points or winning.

Aesthetic experience can be confusing because it is both a quality that can be observed and a special attitude people can feel. Said more simply, an object has aesthetic qualities in it, and people use their aesthetic attitude to appreciate these qualities.

Why Is Aesthetic Experience Important?

When students appreciate the aesthetic component of an activity they are better able to understand the goals for which they are striving when they are engaged in that activity. The kinesthetic sense—the muscle response—enables them to understand physical activity in themselves and empathize with it in others. British artist and dance educator Elizabeth Watts (1977), astutely points out that the word "esthetic" is the central part of the word "kinesthetic." She believes that the aesthetic quality of movement creates good feelings, and gives people the desire to repeat selected movements again and again to prolong these positive feelings. Students increase their ability to grasp the aesthetic features of movement in others when they have felt them in their own movements.

Aesthetic experience is a basic part of most physical activity, but teachers often concentrate on training students in skills and game strategies. And, they tend not to introduce the aesthetic component until the training progresses to the advanced level. When someone says, "Nice shot!" or, "Beautiful play!" it indicates appreciation for the quality of the action itself, as well as for the success of the action. These comments focus on how the student achieved the action, not only on what the student did. The special qualities that stimulate people to distinguish a well executed play from a beautiful one are often aesthetic qualities.

Aesthetic responses are stimulated by one particular person, action, or object that is seen as beautiful. These responses are evoked by something specific. Special qualities of a separate action, for instance, add up to make that one special lay-up shot much better than the others. Even though the specific shot is beautiful, it has properties that are found in other special shots that others players have made and will make again. Teachers and students can look for, articulate, and study these commonalties. Integrating the aesthetic dimensions of physical education activities into the process of teaching other dimensions, such as skills and rules, will greatly increase students' motivation for and pleasure in learning.

All human beings have aesthetic impulses and needs. People are satisfying those needs when they organize or arrange their rooms, desks, purses, and briefcases; clothe themselves in special ways; choose furniture; seek out beautiful places in nature; listen to music; and participate in special ceremonies. Anthropologist Ellen Dissanayake (1995) describes this impulse to put things in order as "making special" and "things done." "Making special" means to do something with care and focus that goes beyond what is necessary to accomplish the job. When students choose to wear colors in their clothes that contrast, yet go well together, rather than just putting on the first thing they find, they are using their aesthetic taste. The extra "thing done" in that instance is to take the time to choose, perhaps to hold up two or three combinations of shirts and pants to see which colors go best together. The aesthetic impulse, she explains, operates in most areas of people's lives, and has always done so. The impulse is part of making order out of the world's apparent chaos, and appears to be innately satisfying and positive. It is part of our attempt to take control of our lives, or of special times and experiences in our lives.

As they develop, children use this aesthetic impulse to understand themselves and their capabilities. When teaching physical education, it is the teacher's responsibility to point out the aesthetic component of various activities. And, it is the students' responsibility to pay attention to the qualities that trigger their aesthetic responses.

Cultural, generational, and regional differences in aesthetic criteria and the responses to them can be confusing. However, they also can widen and deepen students' understanding of aesthetic criteria. For instance, many students in the 1990s dressed in oversized clothes, pierced and tattooed their bodies, and wore unusual footwear such as untied tennis shoes or combat boots. The students who chose to conform to this fad adapted their aesthetic tastes to value this particular "look."

Ask students to identify and articulate the criteria they use when they choose to dress in a particular way. To answer this question, they will need to focus on the personal aesthetic decisions they have made and clarify their choices to others who do not understand or appreciate their "style."

As members of a diverse culture, students must be able to see, experience, describe, and appreciate the differences and similarities of culture, ethnicity, gender, and ability as they relate to gesture, movement choices, and patterns. This knowledge will help students meet the goals of Standard 6 of the National Standards of Physical Education: "Demonstrates understanding and respect for differences among people in physical activity settings."

Linking Aesthetic Experience to the National Standards

The aesthetic component of movement connects to Standard 7 of the National Standards for Physical Education: "Understands that physical activity provides opportunities for enjoyment, challenge, self-expression, and social interaction." This standard includes some elements of aesthetic experience, but does not address its central features: appreciation, awe, and comprehension of the total experience for itself. Enjoyment can come from meeting high aesthetic standards as well as from the fun that is central to many physical activities. And, while "challenge" is more often thought of as winning or surpassing one's own previous performance, it also can relate to reaching aesthetic goals.

Self-expression and communication frequently are associated with artistic and theatrical activities such as dance and mime rather than with recreational and competitive games and sports. Physical education activities can include these artistic disciplines, but without dance and theater specialists to teach them, they generally do not appear in the curriculum. Teacher preparation in the future must include the aesthetic component of movement. Such training can help teachers understand how this focus can enhance the enjoyment of all movement activities.

The curricular suggestions that follow include dance and mime activities in which aesthetic goals are embedded and which are evaluated primarily by aesthetic criteria. However, the main focus is on activities in which most physical educators have been educated and which normally are not evaluated or taught in this way.

Selected Aesthetic Experience Concepts

An overview of what students should know and be able to do after studying the aesthetic component of movement follows. It should be noted that the terms "component," "feature," and "dimension" are used interchangeably throughout the chapter to describe the parts of the aesthetic experience. Since movement is the means by which all of life's activities are conducted, the following concepts concentrate on movement in general. They highlight terminology that will enable students to analyze and discuss their aesthetic responses to all movement activities.

Guidelines exist to help teachers organize and sharpen the processes of aesthetic perception and reasoning. These broad guidelines apply to many activities such as art, dance, and film. They also work well for appreciating outstanding moments in physical activity. They are offered here as suggestions and jumping-off places for teachers and students.

In *The Intelligent Eye: Learning to Think by Looking at Art* (1994), David Perkins identifies six thinking "dispositions" that art, and by extension, other aesthetic experiences require and stimulate: sensory anchoring, instant access, personal engagement, dispositional atmosphere, wide-spectrum cognition, and multi-connectedness. In the first disposition, students encounter the activity with sensuous (of the senses) and imaginative perception. In physical education, the sensory anchor is most often the student in action or in a held position.

Instant access—being able to capture the moment—is more difficult to achieve when studying physical activity, because each instant goes by so quickly. Videotaping practice sessions can help preserve these instances. Continued repetition, so necessary in practice sessions, can provide access, although catching sight of the most outstanding action requires teachers and students to be alert.

Personal engagement requires special attention, focusing on the action, to see it in its fullest way. Personal engagement requires students to reflect thoughtfully with a receptive attitude. This takes time and patience. Personal engagement also requires experiencing and recognizing authenticity of focus in physical activity. Authenticity is evident in a student's energy level, intention, and clarity of action. Activities are not performed or executed in a passive, sloppy, or awkward manner; the student is concentrating completely.

By dispositional atmosphere, Perkins means that the mind-set of the class and teacher is one of appreciation. While it may be difficult to achieve, a "dispositional atmosphere" can enrich a competitive atmosphere. Paying attention to the aesthetic dimension of physical activity requires a generous and cooperative attitude along with the drive to do one's best. This positive attitude facilitates winning since it helps students focus on intrinsic action.

Wide-spectrum cognition is an advanced skill in understanding aesthetic experience. It helps students take in the unified whole or entirety of the action, not just one or a few of its parts. Students use this skill when they watch marching bands and drill teams create designs on a football field, or when they see flocks of birds or squadrons of airplanes fly in formation. Wide-spectrum cognition enables students to deepen their aesthetic sensibility. Students become sensitive to the how patterns and forms are organized. They sense the innate order of what they are perceiving.

Perkins calls the final disposition which encourages aesthetic thinking multiconnectedness. The idea here is to keep in mind all the parts of the event, such as the student, the situation, the goals, the level of development, and the physical and mental atmosphere. The sense that "everything just came together at that one moment" is the height of multi-connectedness. Students and teachers should look for these moments and articulate them. The best way for teachers to introduce these dispositions is to model them, call attention to them, and then have students use them in class.

Four major processes in physical activity provide occasions for developing aesthetic sensitivity. These can be defined as learning and training, participating and playing, watching, and reconciling different opinions about the aesthetic qualities of the event. These processes develop both internal and subjective and external and objective standards, and they foster discussion among participants about the validity of their aesthetic standards.

All the senses serve as receptors for registering aesthetic experience of movement activities. When watching a championship skiing competition, for instance, the observers' eyes receive the image of each skier coming down the slope. At the same time that the eyes introduce the image into the brain, the muscles identify with the actions of the skier. One entry point for the kinesthetic sense (which registers touch and muscle knowledge) is the eyes. Taste and smell enter the experience in a minor way with the memory of how excitement can lead to a dry mouth and the smell of sweat that comes from extreme physical exertion. Although snow sports do not generate a great deal of noise, skiing makes its own subtle sounds, and these also contribute to the appreciation of the beauty and grace of the skiers. Students learn to describe aesthetic experiences in words or drawings. They pay attention to their taste—what they like and dislike—and explain their preferences.

Participation in an event, whether at the elite or entry level, triggers personal aesthetic responses, especially if players are unsuccessful. Beginners can easily distinguish ineffective from effective plays or moves by using aesthetic criteria. They feel or sense that a beautiful play is easy and natural. Their muscles, eyes, ears—even their skin and nose—are concentrated and unified when they execute a beautiful play. This is how players learn what success feels like. This unity of senses helps players learn the "how" of performing at their highest, most beautiful level.

In the past 20 years, sports psychologists have been studying peak performance. They have interviewed many elite athletes about what they were feeling and experiencing when they were engaged in outstanding performances. These athletes report that while performing their best, they feel completely natural and at ease. They describe a sense of effortlessness. Their minds are so focused that they feel "egoless," unaware of themselves. This sense of total oneness is the height of aesthetic experience.

Psychologist and creativity scholar Mihaly Csikszentmihalyi describes this state as "flow." Fred Rohe describes it in his book, *The Zen of Running* (1974). Students must practice with deliberate focus for a long time to achieve this effortlessness and egoless sense. Once achieved, it can become a "positive addiction" and provide the motivation for lifelong participation in physical activities.

The ideas described here are organized around four basic concepts:
- Concept I: What are the aesthetic features of objects and people in the environment?
- Concept II: What are the aesthetic components of movement?
- Concept III: What are the characteristics of movement patterns?
- Concept IV: What factors help determine criteria for judging the aesthetic quality of movement in one's culture and other cultures?

These all fit together and operate as a unit.

What Are the Aesthetic Features of Objects and People in the Environment?

Students experience (sense and feel), see, and appreciate shape in anything that moves, organic or inorganic, apart from its functional goal. "Shape" here refers to the outline or form a person or object takes. "Movement" means both how something gets from one place to another (e.g., a tired person dragging his or her feet walking home) and how it stands in one place while moving the entire body or separate body parts (e.g., the way the branches of a tree sway and its leaves rustle).

To help students appreciate objects in their environment, teachers can have students identi-fy their shapes—i.e., square, rectangular, spherical, triangular, or cylindrical. How are these shapes spaced? Are they close to each other or far apart? Are they evenly or unevenly spaced in relation to each other? Are they behind or in front of each other? Are these shapes similar or dif-ferent in some ways?

Movement exploration lets students form their bodies into the different shapes they see around them and allows inexperienced students to participate at their own developmental level. Directed exploration works well for young and shy children; visual and observation skills improve as children mature.

What Are the Aesthetic Components of Movement?

Understanding the components of movement—time, space, effort, and flow—enables peo-ple to experience, describe, and analyze the aesthetic component of physical experience. By applying these concepts, people can focus on experiencing, seeing, and appreciating shape or design in stillness and in motion. The next dimension of this understanding of a moving shape is its location in space. The concept of "space" includes immediate (narrow, one's own space bubble, or personal space) and larger (in the room, on stage, on the playground) contexts. It also includes levels (high, medium, and low), directions (front, back, side, up, down, diagonal, and around), and pathway (the pattern of where the participants travel). People can see movement pathways when they watch basketball players advance down the court toward the basket or ice hockey players work their way toward the goal.

A more complex dimension of movement involves seeing, experiencing, and describing the concept of time in one's own movement and in the movement of others. The term "time" means time on the clock. The features of time include: rhythm–uneven and repeated sequences of sound such as that of the heartbeat; meter–evenly timed repeated sounds such as the clock tick-ing or feet walking at a slow speed; tempo–the speed of the sound sequence, such as feet run-ning at a slow, medium, or fast rate; accent–the sound that is emphasized more or is louder, such as the first syllable in the words basketball or soccer; and sound pattern–the overall design or the sound sequence, such as the sound of the basketball dribbled, passed, and dribbled.

The third component of movement—effort—refers to experiencing, seeing, and identifying the variations of energy used in movement. These variations are often called movement quali-ties. These include swing–what arms do when people walk; shake–what a wet dog does to help get its coat to dry; press–what a thumb and forefinger do to flatten a small ball of clay; clap–what hands do when applauding a good performance; and vibrate–what bodies do when they shiver with cold. Effort relates to the consistency and inconsistency in these movement qualities, such as when the wet dog stops and starts shaking itself at regular intervals with the same intensity to get dry (with consistency), or when the applause gets louder or softer at irreg-ular intervals (with inconsistency) during a slow baseball game. Sometimes the term "force" is used instead of "energy." Tension and ease, smoothness and choppiness, strong and weak are familiar descriptions of movement qualities that can hinder or enhance the performance of many physical activities.

The flow of movement is its "ongoingness," like the motion of a river or a bird flying. Flow can be rhythmic (like the regular flapping of a bird's wings or the waves on a shore), or it can have no rhythm (like a hum, one note held on a flute, or a ball rolling before it stops). Ice skating, roller blading, bicycle riding, swimming, and skiing are characterized by their flow. The ongoingness of those activities provides a particular aesthetic experience. The energy, time, and space covered may vary, and some activities may not have a large amount of flow in them.

What Are the Characteristics of Movement Patterns?

Experiencing, seeing, and appreciating movement patterns—symmetric, asymmetric, random, regular, irregular—is more complex than identifying the separate dimensions of movement. People walk in the street in random patterns using irregular strides, whereas members of a marching band synchronize the length and height of their stride in a regular unified pattern. A football team with its seven players on the front line, the quarterback directly behind the center player, the two halfbacks centered behind him and the fullback centered at the back creates a symmetric design. (A symmetric design is one that, if folded it in half, would be exactly the same on both sides of the fold.)

Once the football play is set in motion, the players break the symmetric design and move into asymmetrical patterns (ones that are not exactly the same on both sides). Play strategies in team sports utilize different types of patterns, formations, and designs. Teachers most often focus attention on how these line-ups and strategies function in games, rather than on the aesthetic component of the patterns.

Once students have mastered the concepts concerning the components of movement they can apply them to the more complex concepts that center on how and why the aesthetic component of movement functions. They will be able to experience, see, and appreciate movement that it is congruent (fits exactly) with its goal as being beautiful or elegant in design and in motion. For example, someone may make a goal in soccer but use an awkward kick. Although the movement was congruent and the points were scored it would not be considered beautiful. The same person might make a pass using perfect kicking form; that kick would be both congruent with its goal and beautiful.

People should be able to see their own movement, with its individual style, and discern when it is beautiful in design and motion and congruent with its goal. Videotape reviews of performance can facilitate self-observation. Students should identify the congruent movements based on their understanding of how function, skill, and form fit together.

Students should be able to synthesize the concepts of congruence with seeing, experiencing, and describing the expressive power of movement. Features of expressivity include balance–a combination of elements such as fast and slow or tense and relaxed to prevent monotony; contrast–combining distinguishable opposites such as loud and soft and wide and narrow to introduce interest; accent–the main point or points of interest; dynamism–a sense of liveliness or active involvement; "flow" in tempo; weight; dynamics of energy expenditure; and style, where the unique and individual structure and form are established and recognizable. Individuals should be able to analyze the aesthetic features of movement by studying the time, space, energy, pattern, congruence, expressivity, and style, and then connect them to see and appreciate the entirety of the movement.

What Factors Help Determine Criteria for Judging the Aesthetic Quality of Movement In One's Culture and Other Cultures?

As a final synthesis of their understanding of the aesthetic component of movement, students should be able to understand and develop criteria for making choices and judging quality.

These criteria depend on individual goals, experience, knowledge, and preferences and those of the culture to which the person belongs.

Most people intuitively resonate to their own personal aesthetic criteria while participating in or watching physical activities. They may not realize that their responses are an amalgam of personal, cultural, and learned experience. These multifaceted experiences influence learning even while students and teachers focus attention and effort on other dimensions of the activities, such as winning points and improving skills. Personal, cultural, and learned aesthetic standards interact with, and at times contradict, each other.

Personal aesthetic standards are often referred to as "taste." Others who disagree with those standards may dismiss them as unsophisticated or in poor taste. Personal aesthetic standards probably stem from students' earliest positive experiences with the persons, actions, or objects (e.g., the first "best" lay-up shot a person ever made or saw).

When teachers understand that initial learning can determine standards of taste, they can help students to articulate their existing aesthetic standards and enable them to develop and improve their taste as well as their abilities. For example, many young gymnasts and dancers think that hyperextended legs are part of "perfect" form. Teachers can help these students see that straight, aligned legs are beautiful even though they are not taut or stiff.

External aesthetic standards evolve from these same personal, cultural, and learned sources. These are more often written about and discussed than are the internal ones. When, for instance, a sports commentator raves about a superb play in a football game, the commentator will often state why he or she thinks the play is superb and describe the special qualities of how it was accomplished. Television and radio broadcasts of special events provide a public forum where external, recognized, and agreed upon standards are disseminated. Broadcasters frequently are former star players of the sport on which they report. They are able to combine their internalized standards from training and playing with expertise gained from observing and reporting on the game.

Sports broadcasters knowingly allow their personal preferences to enter into their judgment when reporting on games. Debates among sports experts are common on the air. Many sports fans listen and privately debate these public standards in the light of their personal standards.

Major disagreements among experts can challenge the established aesthetic criteria. Eventually, some new consensus emerges. Thus, over time, changes occur in aesthetic standards. Members of the public then compare their personal aesthetic criteria with updated ones. Evolving aesthetic criteria are evident in many areas in daily life such as fashion, car design, and, of course, the arts.

Placing Aesthetic Experience Concepts in the Curriculum

Before aesthetic concepts of movement can be integrated into the physical education program, decisions must be made about where to place them. The organization of these concepts in the table is developmental and can help teachers decide when to introduce them into their physical education activities. The basic concepts of the aesthetic component of movement relate first to concentrating on the parts: shape, movement through space and time with varying energies, and patterns; then integrating the parts into a whole; and finally determining criteria for evaluating them as a whole.

Student learning has the dual focus of recognizing aesthetic experience in others as well as in themselves. The understanding of aesthetic experience comes from being able to recognize it and focus on it. In the final analysis, words may not fully describe aesthetic experience, but when students excitedly shout, "Beautiful!" "Awesome!" or "Wow!" they are seeing and feeling it.

Table 1. Critical Student Concepts, K–6

Kindergarten	Second Grade	Fourth Grade	Sixth Grade
Aesthetic Experience Concept I: What are the aesthetic features of objects and people in the environment?	*Aesthetic Experience Concept I: What are the aesthetic features of objects and people in the environment?*	*Aesthetic Experience Concept I: What are the aesthetic features of objects and people in the environment?*	*Aesthetic Experience Concept I: What are the aesthetic features of objects and people in the environment?*
Shapes, patterns, and textures of objects in the environment stimulate movement responses.	Shapes, patterns, and textures of objects in the environment stimulate movement responses.	Shapes, patterns, and textures of objects in the environment stimulate movement responses.	Visual, kinesthetic, and aural stimuli for movement contribute to students' personal aesthetic preferences.
	Moveable entities stimulate movement responses.	Moveable entities stimulate movement responses.	
	Sounds made by people, animals, and objects in the environment stimulate movement responses.	Sounds made by people, animals, and objects in the environment stimulate movement responses.	
		Visual, kinesthetic, and aural stimuli for movement contribute to students' personal aesthetic preferences.	
Aesthetic Experience Concept II: What are the aesthetic components of movement?	*Aesthetic Experience Concept II: What are the aesthetic components of movement?*	*Aesthetic Experience Concept II: What are the aesthetic components of movement?*	*Aesthetic Experience Concept II: What are the aesthetic components of movement?*
The shapes and movements of people or things in the environment have recognizable aesthetic dimensions.	Terms such as level, direction, range of personal space, and pathway identify and clarify the aesthetic dimensions of one's own physical activities.	The rhythm of a movement affects its outcome; rhythm organizes movement.	The interacting components of movement (shape, motion, time, space, energy, and flow) vary with different kinds of movement.

Table 1. Critical Student Concepts, K–6

Aesthetic Experience Concept III: What are the characteristics of movement patterns?	Terms such as level, direction, range of personal space, and pathway identify and clarify the aesthetic dimensions of physical activities of others.	Meter and tempo affect movement activities.	*Aesthetic Experience Concept III: What are the characteristics of movement patterns?*
Variations of the same movement create a simple movement pattern.		Movement qualities, or many ways of using energy—whether they are carried out consistently or inconsistently—contribute to the aesthetic dimension of physical activity.	The combination of the basic elements of movement (shape, motion, time, space, energy, and flow) creates movement patterns.
	Aesthetic Experience Concept III: What are the characteristics of movement patterns?	Students' preferences for movement qualities influence their aesthetic perception.	Aesthetically carried out movement is congruent with its goal when the goal is achieved directly and efficiently.
	Variations of the same movement create a simple movement pattern.	*Aesthetic Experience Concept III: What are the characteristics of movement patterns?*	
		Variations of the same movement create a simple movement pattern.	
		Combinations of locomotor skills create movement patterns.	

Table 1. Critical Student Concepts, K–6

Aesthetic Experience Concept IV: *What factors determine criteria for judging the aesthetic quality of movement in our culture and other cultures?*	*Aesthetic Experience Concept IV:* *What factors determine criteria for judging the aesthetic quality of movement in our culture and other cultures?*	*Aesthetic Experience Concept IV:* *What factors determine criteria for judging the aesthetic quality of movement in our culture and other cultures?*
The practice and improvement of movement skills facilitates the development of aesthetic sensitivity to excellence.	The practice and improvement of movement skills facilitates the development of aesthetic sensitivity to excellence.	The aesthetic criteria for movement activity facilitate meeting the goals in the activity.
	Observation of peers and older students engaged in an activity develops aesthetic sensitivity to excellence.	
	Students' preferences for movement activities and qualities influence their aesthetic judgment.	

Table 1. Critical Student Concepts, 8–12

Eighth Grade	Tenth Grade	Twelfth Grade
Aesthetic Experience Concept I: What are the aesthetic features of objects and people in the environment?	*Aesthetic Experience Concept I: What are the aesthetic features of objects and people in the environment?*	*Aesthetic Experience Concept I: What are the aesthetic features of objects and people in the environment?*
Visual, kinesthetic, and aural stimuli for movement contribute to students' personal aesthetic preferences.	The aesthetic features—the parts and the whole—of a specific physical activity contribute to the overall appreciation of that activity.	The aesthetic features of a variety of movement experiences contribute to one's appreciation of those activities.
	The analysis and appreciation of the aesthetic features of the performance of others helps people articulate the aesthetic features they see and value.	The skillful execution of movement, and a description of this movement experience in words, drawings, sculpture, poetry, or on video demonstrate understanding of particular aesthetic features in many movement-related experiences.
		An amalgam of skill, talent, practice, expression, and intention contributes to different aesthetic experiences in and responses to movement-related activities.

Table 1. Critical Student Concepts, 8–12

Aesthetic Experience Concept II: What are the aesthetic components of movement?	*Aesthetic Experience Concept II: What are the aesthetic components of movement?*	*Aesthetic Experience Concept II: What are the aesthetic components of movement?*
The interacting components of movement (shape, motion, time, space, energy, and flow) vary in different kinds of movement activities.	The interacting components of movement (shape, motion, time, space, energy, and flow) vary in different kinds of movement activities.	The interacting components of movement (shape, motion, time, space, energy, and flow) vary in different kinds of movement activities.
Aesthetic Experience Concept III: What are the characteristics of movement patterns?	*Aesthetic Experience Concept III: What are the characteristics of movement patterns?*	*Aesthetic Experience Concept III: What are the characteristics of movement patterns?*
The combination of the basic elements of movement (shape, motion, time, space, energy, and flow) creates movement patterns.	Describing the congruence of aesthetic movement with its goal sharpens observation skills.	Games and folk dances from different areas in the United States and from other countries illustrate the aesthetic movement preferences of those regions.
All movement activities have expressive qualities that are understood kinesthetically. Football and wrestling manifest aggressive expressive qualities, whereas track and field events exhibit aggression in a more subtle way.	Criteria gained from observing congruence of movement with its goal in others facilitates self-observation.	
Describing the congruence of aesthetic movement with its goal sharpens observation skills.	Games and folk dances from different areas in the United States and from other countries illustrate the aesthetic movement preferences of those regions.	

Table 1. Critical Student Concepts, 8–12

Criteria gained from observing congruence of movement with its goal in others facilitates self-observation.		
Aesthetic Experience Concept IV: What factors determine criteria for judging the aesthetic quality of movement in our culture and other cultures?	*Aesthetic Experience Concept IV: What factors determine criteria for judging the aesthetic quality of movement in our culture and other cultures?*	*Aesthetic Experience Concept IV: What factors determine criteria for judging the aesthetic quality of movement in our culture and other cultures?*
The aesthetic criteria for a movement activity facilitate meeting the goals in the activity.	Taste, knowledge, and experience contribute to individual and personal aesthetic criteria.	Taste, knowledge, and experience contribute to individual and personal aesthetic criteria.
	Academic and professional criteria contribute to appreciation of aesthetic qualities.	Academic and professional criteria contribute to appreciation of aesthetic qualities.
	Student progress in achieving competency can be described in aesthetic terms.	Student progress in achieving competency can be described in aesthetic terms.
	Skillful execution of any movement for any purpose has identifiable aesthetic features.	Skillful execution of any movement for any purpose has identifiable aesthetic features.

Integrating Aesthetic Experience Concepts into Instruction

As the instructional concepts in the table illustrate, the aesthetic component of physical activity can be integrated into almost all content components and activities—physical and analytical—in the study of physical education. In fact, daily life offers many opportunities to highlight aesthetic features. People walking in the street, gesturing to one another, or sitting or standing together in groups are examples of daily activities that students can study, as both participants and observers.

Integrating Aesthetic Experience Concepts into Instruction

Example 1: Early Elementary (Kindergarten)
Concept: Shapes, patterns, and textures of objects in the environment stimulate movement responses.
Using guided discovery, children can imitate from the environment:
• Shapes of things, such as tables, chairs, rocks
• Patterns, such as shadows, fabric designs, writing on a page
• Textures of things such as sand, sweaters, paper.
These provide visual stimuli and source material for understanding the properties of things that contribute to the aesthetic dimension of shape in daily life.

Example 2: Early Elementary (Kindergarten)
Concept: Moveable entities stimulate movement responses.
Using guided discovery, children can imitate the shapes and movements of people, animals, and objects in the environment. These provide kinesthetic stimuli and source material for movement.
Using movement, drawing, sounds, or words, students can explore or experiment with their responses to shapes, motions, or patterns in the environment.

Example 3: Elementary (Grade 2)
Concept: Terms such as level, direction, range of personal space, and pathway identify and clarify the aesthetic dimensions of one's own physical activities.
One movement, such as running, can be varied using different levels, and it can be done in a small or a large area. Game sequences such as the hop and jump pattern of hopscotch can be done in many directions. Students can watch each other's experiments to see the many variations possible.

Example 4: Elementary (Grade 4)
Concept: Movement qualities, or many ways of using energy, whether they are carried out consistently or inconsistently, contribute to the aesthetic dimension of physical activity.
Students can look for out-of-the-ordinary qualities that cause them to pay special attention to the rhythmic pattern, dynamic action, unusual energy, and spatial design of actions or positions. When students pay special attention and notice unusual qualities they are developing aesthetic sensitivity. They can write about the qualities and can imitate them to experience the

various uses of energy they have observed. Then they can identify the obvious and more subtle movement qualities that help and hinder their own physical activities.

Example 5: Elementary (Grade 4)
Concept: The rhythm of a movement affects its outcome; rhythm organizes movement.
Simple movements such as pretending to throw a ball can be varied rhythmically. Movements in games, sports, or dance, or skills from any physical activity can be varied in tempo—i.e., regular time (seconds on the clock), faster, or slower. The sounds made by people, animals, and objects in the environment provide aural stimuli and source material to accompany movement.

Example 6: Middle School (Grade 6)
Concept: The combination of the basic elements of movement (shape, motion, time, space, energy, and flow) creates movement patterns.
Selected shapes, motions, or patterns in the environment provide sources for study and interpretation. Students choose a part of the environment on which to focus (such as a corner of the classroom, or a small area in the playground), and they study it. The purpose of this observation task is to discern patterns made up of the components of time, space, energy, and flow. Students then can apply these same observation skills to watching a game.

Example 7: Middle School (Grade 6)
Concept: Aesthetic movement is congruent with its goal when the goal is achieved directly and efficiently.
Watching videotapes of physical education activities enables students to study the congruence of their own and teammates' movements in games, practices, and even warm-up activities. Watching more skilled players allows students to observe the correspondence of movement with its purpose. Observing the harmony of movement with purpose in professional games helps students realize how congruence contributes to the aesthetic quality of sports activities and helps them to improve their own performance.

Example 8: Middle School (Grade 8)
Concept: The combination of the basic elements of movement (shape, motion, time, space, energy, and flow) creates movement patterns.
Students study videotapes of synchronized sports such as crew to identify repeated patterns and ball games such as soccer to see complex patterns. They gain improved proficiency in identifying these patterns by describing (in words or pictures) what they see. Students analyze the patterns in the different observed activities to determine the influence that time, space, energy, etc. have on the aesthetic impact of these activities. They demonstrate increasing understanding by describing (in words or pictures) these observations.

Example 9: High School (Grade 10)
Concept: The variables of time, space, energy, and flow comprise the components of movement.
The variety of motor activities in games such as volleyball and soccer, and dances such as

the waltz or polka, are sources for experiencing, studying, and writing about energy use, time, space, and flow in movement. Everyday movements like brushing one's teeth and activities such as climbing the stairs are sources for examining and understanding the various levels of energy use, time, space, and flow that students prefer to use. Their preferences help students kinesthetically identify (have muscle empathy) with other activities that use similar levels of energy. Watching classmates, more skilled players, and professional athletes in action provides students with opportunities to recognize and appreciate how energy level, time, space, and flow affect the aesthetic quality of physical activity.

Example 10: High School (Grade 10)
Concept: The analysis and appreciation of the aesthetic features of their performance and the performance of others helps students articulate the aesthetic features they value.
Students can inventory their physical activities, such as handwriting, keyboarding, bicycling, jogging, and dancing and note the activities in which they find aesthetic qualities. Students choose one small and one large movement activity to develop, improve, or change. They explain their choice in terms of space, time, energy use, and flow. Then they state their goals in aesthetic terms, such as improved form (i.e., shape or energy use), ease (i.e., flow, clarity, exactness or precision, beauty, or overall pattern).

Example 11: High School (Grade 12)
Concept: Folk dances from different areas of the United States and from other countries illustrate the aesthetic movement preferences of the different regions.
Students can dance and watch folk dances from as many countries as possible, paying attention to their similarities and differences. Students can watch modern dance, ballet, and jazz performances, paying attention to the similarities and differences among these dance forms and the integration of culture-specific dance movements into them.

Example 12: High School (Grade 12)
Concept: Games from different areas of the United States and from other countries illustrate the aesthetic movement preferences of the different regions.
Students choose games from three countries for in-depth study, relating the cultural, geographic, ethnic, social, religious, and economic context of these games to the movement choices in them. Writing a report about their findings gives students the opportunity to clarify their understanding of these subtle differences and similarities. Students teach one of these games to their classmates, relating the game to its cultural context.

Example 13: High School (Grade 12)
Concept: Taste, knowledge, and experience contribute to individual and personal aesthetic criteria.
The students can evolve the criteria by which to judge the aesthetic quality of what they see. To record the students' observations, have them describe, imitate, or draw what they saw. Students track how well they achieve their aesthetic goals for four to six months in one activity, evaluate, and then continue the tracking. This can build self-knowledge and help students maintain intrinsic motivation.

Next, students can compare their observations with other students to learn what they regard as special and identify what qualities they agree upon. After that, they can analyze what the differences depend on, and what parts of the activity these special features relate to. If this is a weekly activity, a record of the commonalties of standards of aesthetic quality will emerge and students can trace their own developing sensitivity to the aesthetic components of daily physical activity. Students can track their progress and periodically review their goals and achievements, revising them if necessary. These same guidelines can apply to movement in games, sports, dance, and daily life.

Videotapes of games early in the season and then later on provide tools by which students can study progress. Although aesthetic qualities occur more frequently at higher levels of skill, once students learn an activity they can begin to watch for aesthetically significant moments during their practice sessions.

Televised sports and dance events provide ready made opportunities for students to develop their aesthetic sensitivity as spectators. Watching elite performers play their best can help students discern the subtle differences between outstanding and excellent physical performance. Students can see the aesthetic qualities in well developed skills and form.

Watching professional athletes or dancers to spot their occasional awkward and careless movements also can help students pinpoint the relationship between a well-executed skill and its aesthetic quality. Such active and engaged spectator skills can enhance the students' sensitivity to their own progress and that of their teammates.

Supplementary Instructional Activities for Any Age

Poetry, short stories, photographs, paintings, and sculptures of sport and dance activities are good resources for teachers. They provide examples of how writers, photographers, artists, and sculptors have expressed their aesthetic responses to physical action. Bulletin boards in classrooms, gymnasiums, and dance studios should display photographs and drawings of sport and dance activities. Throughout the ages, artists have been fascinated by the dynamic action and intense energy displayed in sports and dance events.

When students study these works, they look at the activity through the eyes of the artists. Careful examination and analysis of just one or two of these paintings can help teachers and students increase their understanding of the special aesthetic features of physical activity. Ask questions such as:

• What is going on in the painting?
• What is the main focus?
• How is energy represented?
• How do the patterns of the various figures in the painting fit into the overall design of the painting?
• What mood is conveyed, and how is it conveyed?
• What shapes are repeated, not repeated, or varied?
• How do all these features fit together to make the whole more than the sum of its parts?
• Where have you seen some of these same features in real-life physical activity?

Questions like these can stimulate more specific questions and discussion.

Another tool for integrating the aesthetic component of movement into instructional activities has been examined by sports psychologists. They have demonstrated that mental rehearsal is successful in improving performance. The process of mental rehearsal requires serious practice, and does not work with everyone. For those who are able to use it, tests show that the muscles actually fire at a very low level. There is a physiological, kinesthetic effect.

In a and quiet relaxed setting, performers sit or lie down with their eyes closed and imagine their entire game experience, play by play, in the best form and at the highest level of skill. Aesthetic qualities of performance are an ideal focus for these imagined practices. (Day dreaming can actually be beneficial if it is purposeful and focused!)

Assessing Student Learning

When students can use aesthetic concepts to understand their own performance or the performance of others, the teacher has been effective in teaching about aesthetic features of physical education activities. Some of the techniques teachers can use to assess student learning are described below. They are considered in detail in *Moving into the Future: National Standards for Physical Education* (NASPE 1995).

Journal Writing. Regular written self-assessment exercises are useful tools for helping students revitalize their performance and understand the aesthetic component of physical education. The format of these exercises follow the guidelines used in authentic assessment methods. "What did I learn about … (e.g., space or time or expressivity)?" "What risks did I take when … (e.g., working on improving the regular rhythmic quality of my dribbling)?" and, "What would I change the next time I … (e.g., have an opportunity to practice my dribbling)?" are the three most useful questions to trace the development of understanding of concepts and skills (what was learned), experimentation with new ways of doing things (risks), and goal setting for improvement (revision).

Observations. Videotaping activity sessions is another way for students and teachers to refine observation skills and observe growth. When watching the videotapes, students can look for specific skills or plays. They can focus their attention on a selected aesthetic dimension. They can record their responses on a tape recorder and translate their ideas into writing or illustrations. Over time, such a record enables students and teachers to trace the development of comprehension and the execution of central concepts.

Student Projects. A more public assessment tool is a visual project such as a photo collage. Such a project will illustrate what students consider outstanding examples of athletes and dancers as well as everyday people engaged in motion. The examples can be arranged by theme. The students should articulate the criteria by which they chose their photos and explain them to their classmates. A display of these posters can help others grasp the aesthetic dimensions of physical activity.

Rubrics. No separate rubric for scoring the aesthetic component of physical activity is necessary. However, the aesthetic component can be woven effectively into the higher levels of achievement of other activities.

Concluding Comments

By integrating aesthetic awareness into the teaching of physical education, students' quality of life will be enhanced. Aesthetic awareness is the primary characteristic of a civilized way of life. Aesthetic awareness allows human beings to bring order out of chaos. Developing students' sensitivity about their physical education activities will transfer into other areas of their lives. Because the first sense of self that humans have is the physical self, when students work toward achievable aesthetic standards in their own physical activities, they are focusing on enhancing their body image, which is central to their self-image.

Since the reward in this pursuit is not winning or losing, earning points or breaking records, but is being the best—most beautiful—one can be, the internally motivated, self-powered goal can be unifying and satisfying. It can help students to empathize with and appreciate the great diversity of movement in their lives.

What if students cannot meet these goals, and then feel inadequate because they are not skillful in activities that require kinesthetic ability? Since the aesthetic component of physical education teaches the "how" of the activity, students know where they need to concentrate to improve. The focus is less on winning and more on continuing to work toward the sense of flow. The emphasis shifts from the end goal of the game or activity to the process and quality of the experience—engaging in the activity for its own sake.

How Can I Learn More?
Czikszentmihalyi, M. (1991). *Flow: The psychology of optimal experience.* New York: Harper Collins.
Dissanayke, E. (1995). *Homo aestheticus: Where art comes from and why.* Seattle, WA: University of Washington Press.
Gardner, H. (1991). *The unschooled mind: How children think and how schools should teach.* New York: Basic Books.
Glasser, W. (1976). *Positive addiction.* New York: Harper & Row.

References
Dinhofer, S. M. (1990). *The art of baseball.* New York: Harmony Books.
Kash, M. M., & Borich, G. D. (1978). *Teacher behavior and pupil self-concept.* Reading, MA: Addison-Wesley.
Lancy, D. F., & Tindall, B. A. (Eds.). (1977). *The study of play: Problems and prospects.* West Point, NY: Leisure Press.
Lieberman, J. N. (1977). *Playfulness: Its relationship to imagination and creativity.* New York: Academic Press.
_____. (1995). *Moving into the future: National standards for physical education. A guide to content and assessment.* St. Louis, MO: Mosby.
Perkins, D. (1994). *The intelligent eye: Learning to think by looking at art.* Santa Monica, CA: The Getty Center for Education in the Arts.
Rohe, F. (1974). *The zen of running.* New York: Random House.
Salter, M. A. (Ed.). (1978). Play: *Anthropological perspectives.* West Point, NY: Leisure Press.
Watts, E. (1977). *Towards dance and art: The relationships between two art forms.* London: Lepus Books.
Wingfield, M. A. (1988). *Sport and the artist, volume I: Ball games.* Woodbridge, Suffolk, England: Antique Collectors' Club.

Glossary
Accent: emphasis on sound, syllable, or part of a movement.

Asymmetric: when a design is not exactly the same on opposite sides when folded in half.

Balance: a combination of elements or features where one or more of the elements does not predominate.

Congruent: appropriate fit or harmony, correspondence.

Contrast: distinguishable differences.

Dynamism: a sense of liveliness or active involvement.

Meter: evenly timed repeated sounds, like the sounds of a clock ticking.

Pathway: the pattern where a participant travels in space.

Rhythm: uneven and repeated sequences of sound, like the sound of a heart beating.

Sound pattern: overall design of the sound sequence.

Style: where the unique and individual structure and form are established and recognizable.

Symmetric: when a design is folded in half, it is the same on both sides of the fold.

Tempo: metered speed of an activity.

Chapter 9
Pulling It All Together

By Bonnie S. Mohnsen

Throughout this book, the authors—having reviewed multiple national resources—have defined the important concepts students must know in order to meet the National Physical Education Standards and to live high quality lives in the twenty-first century. This chapter focuses on how to integrate the concepts from the various subdisciplines and standards into physical education learning experiences. Ideas for integrating these concepts with other subject areas also are provided. Sample learning experiences from a variety of instructional units serve to demonstrate the implementation process necessary to convey cognitive concepts to students while helping them to improve their motor skills and fitness levels.

Managing the Concepts

Looking at the variety of concepts identified in Chapters 2 through 8 at every other grade level may cause anxiety in many physical educators who typically teach an activity-based curriculum. Even those who are using a conceptual-based curriculum may be surprised at the number of concepts that have been identified. This section is designed to help physical educators deal with these concepts by providing a number of strategies for organization and instruction.

The first question to address is whether to include all of the concepts identified by the authors, or to select only a few. The concepts identified in each chapter are based on the authors' perspectives—along with input from reviewers and other experts—of what students need to know in order to meet the standards identified by the National Association for Sport and Physical Education (NASPE). However, it is the responsibility of each school district to establish its own local standards, concepts, and related curriculum. In districts where this has not occurred, resources such as *Designing the Physical Education Curriculum* (Melograno 1996), and *Teaching Middle School Physical Education* (Mohnsen 1997), will assist the reader in developing standards and curriculum.

When local standards differ from the National Standards, the selection of concepts also may differ. Even if the standards match the National Standards, local variables may limit the number of concepts that are addressed during each school year. For example, teachers who meet once a week with students are far more limited in what they can do than are teachers who meet with their students daily. Teachers should choose the concepts that are most critical for their own situations.

Bonnie S. Mohnsen is coordinator, Physical Education and Integrated Technology, Orange County Department of Education, Cosa Mesa, California.

Once the concepts are identified and sequenced, it may be helpful to assign them to one or more instructional units over a two year period. A concept may be taught in one instructional unit, taught again in another instructional unit, and reviewed in a third instructional unit. Or, the concept may be addressed in its entirety or broken down into parts that are addressed in different lessons or instructional units. What is important is that the teacher devise a strategy for teaching the concepts. And, the strategy and its implementation should be documented, along with the assessment of student learning.

While it is true that some learning occurs as a result of everyday experience, the teacher must provide learning experiences which insure that the concepts are learned. Discussing the concepts with the students is a good beginning. However, it is only through active learning that students make personal meaning out of the information. Active "hands-on" learning experiences include problem solving, creating, and exploring. The strategy of starting with an initial question, placing students in a variety of contexts in which to experiment with different answers, and allowing them to draw their own conclusions engages students in active learning. It is through these types of carefully designed learning experiences that physical educators will ensure that students understand the concepts and are able to demonstrate that understanding.

The actual learning experiences can be organized in a variety of ways. In the *Basic Stuff in Action* series (Bressan 1987, Kneer & Heitmann 1987, Lambert & Trimble 1987) the authors created a three-part organizational model (see Table 1) to describe the methods for including concepts in physical education instruction. Teachers can select one of these models or use a combination of all three.

The integrated model uses an activity-based curriculum (e.g., volleyball unit, softball unit, badminton unit) and integrates each concept throughout the different lessons. Some concepts are addressed in one unit, while others are addressed in several different units. For example, while teaching the overhand throw in softball, the teacher emphasizes the biomechanical concepts related to projectiles (biomechanics). The teacher reviews the projectile concepts again in the volleyball and badminton units. In order to address more than one concept, the teacher also relates the overhand softball throw to the overhand serve in volleyball and the overhand clear in badminton, emphasizing the concept of transfer of learning (motor learning). It is the inclusion of these concepts that enriches the learning activities and improves students' understanding of movement.

The segregated model brings in a one or two day lesson on a concept while the students are involved in a particular activity, such as gymnastics or dance. This is often seen with concepts related to exercise physiology. Once a week, the teacher focuses on exercise physiology and facilitates student learning of a particular concept. The concept may or may not be related to the unit of study. For example, the teacher might emphasize cardiorespiratory concepts during a dance unit, since dance is an aerobic activity, and flexibility concepts during a gymnastics unit, since gymnastics requires flexibility. On the other hand, the teacher may have sequenced the concepts for exercise

Table 1. A Three-Part Model for Including Concepts in Instruction

Integrated: One or more selected concepts taught within a lesson.
Segregated: One or more complete lessons on a concept which may or may not be related to the current unit of study.
Separated: Concept(s) taught as a unit of instruction.

physiology and may address them one after the other, regardless of the current unit of study.

The separated model identifies the concepts as the actual unit of study. The emphasis shifts from activity to the conceptual knowledge; however, this does not mean that physical activity does not occur. Rather, the activities are selected based on the concept(s) taught. For example, a unit may focus on projectile concepts and a variety of object handling activities (e.g., throwing a football, kicking a soccer ball, putting a shot) may be included in order to facilitate student learning of these concepts. Other units may include cooperation (subdisciplines of sociology and psychology), learning a new closed skill (subdiscipline of motor learning), the history of the Olympics (subdiscipline of historical perspectives), activities for the elderly (motor development), the beauty of sport (aesthetics), and health related fitness (exercise physiology).

Regardless of which organizational pattern is used, students should be able to demonstrate their understanding of the concepts. If the separated model works best for a particular learning environment, then the separated model should be used. If the segregated or the integrated model works best, then that one should be used. If a program is already based on an activity model, the concepts can be addressed as described, using the integrated model.

Integration with Other Subject Areas

Physical educators must first be true to their own subject area. They must ensure that they are facilitating student learning as it relates to the physical education grade level standards and concepts. In many cases, integration with other subject areas can facilitate this process. There are several educational models available for integrating information with other subject areas. The model shown in Table 2 is based on the work of Fogarty (1991), and is used here as a framework for integrating information between physical education and other subject areas.

The sequenced model encourages teachers to rearrange the order of their topics so that similar units in different subject areas coincide with one another. In the case of two related disciplines, teachers sequence content so that common subject matter is taught at the same time. In this way, learning in one subject area enhances the learning in another with very little interaction between the instructors. An example of this model is a health educator teaching a nutrition unit while the physical educator teaches a body composition or health related fitness unit.

In the shared model, teachers work together to look for common areas of curriculum. The focus here is on shared concepts, skills, and attitudes. This model extends the sequenced model, since it requires the teachers to plan overlaps in course content so that there is support for information from both subject areas and not simply a repetition of information. An example of this

Table 2. Interdisciplinary Models

Sequenced:	Topics are rearranged and sequenced to coincide with each other.
Shared:	Two subject areas with overlapping concepts are team taught.
Webbed:	A theme of interest is webbed in curriculum content and subject areas.
Threaded:	Major concepts are threaded throughout various subjects or units.
Integrated:	Several subject areas with overlapping concepts are team taught.
Immersed:	The learner chooses an area of interest and incorporates curricular areas within it.

Adapted from Fogarty, R. (1991). *The mindful school: How to integrate the curricula.* Palatine, IL: IRI/Skylight.

model is a movement education unit in which the language arts educator introduces a story and students illustrate the characters and their emotions through movement during physical education.

The webbed model is a thematic approach to integrating subject matter. Planning for instruction begins with a theme, and information related to that theme is integrated into different subjects. Themes that can cross various subject areas include transportation, patterns, space, and oceanography. In this model, the theme becomes central to the learning and the teachers provide information that supports the theme. Themes might include wellness, transitions, change, and space travel. In the space travel theme, physical education students explore the need for exercise in a weightless environment.

In the threaded model, the teacher selects concepts (e.g., social skills, multiple intelligences, technology) that are then threaded into the existing curriculum. This model does not require additional units; it simply requires that important concepts be revisited throughout the curriculum. Typical interdisciplinary concepts include writing across the curriculum and technology across the curriculum. The significance of this model is that the more reinforcement that occurs, the more likely students are to retain and use the concepts. An example might be the science educator addressing Newton's Laws during the first month of school and the physical educator addressing the application of Newton's Laws to various physical activities throughout the rest of the school year.

The integrated model is an expansion of the shared model. It represents a cross-disciplinary approach involving four or more subject areas. This model involves setting curricular priorities in each area and then finding the overlapping skills, attitudes, and concepts in the other areas. Again, the emphasis is on subject areas supporting one another, not the repetition of information in each subject area. An example is a health-related fitness unit in which the health educator focuses on personal health, the physical educator on conditioning and training, the science educator on the digestive system, and the math educator on word problems involving the input and output of calories.

In the immersed model, teachers select a concept and then design a project that requires students to select and study an area related to the concept. In this model, the learner integrates the concept with little outside intervention. This approach targets student interest areas. It also requires more time than most instructional approaches. Examples of interest areas include baseball, dinosaurs, robotics, and astronomy. In the robotics unit, students might explore ways to make a robot appear more human in its movement.

Implementing the National Standards and their Related Concepts

This section provides concrete learning experiences (one instructional unit from a yearly plan) for primary, upper elementary, middle school, and high school levels that address concepts from two or more subdisciplines (and standards) along with practice and/or participation in motor skills or fitness activities. Each instructional unit also contains interdisciplinary links.

In Chapters 2 through 8, the authors have provided ideas for teaching concepts in their subdiscipline. The purpose here is to illustrate how a number of different concepts can be addressed simultaneously in a logical manner related to the current curriculum and not simply "added on" indiscriminately. The following examples illustrate a variety of organizational and interdisciplinary models to provide the teacher with different options for addressing the physical education concepts. Remember, these are instructional units, and they fit into the larger structure of a yearly plan.

Physical educators will need to adjust these instructional units to coincide with their preferred teaching style and the specific learning needs of their students. Readers are referred to a number of books, including *Teaching Physical Education for Learning* (Rink 1993), *Teaching Physical Education* (Mosston & Ashworth 1986), and *Developing Teaching Skills in Physical Education* (Siedentop 1991) for more information on instructional styles, strategies, and behaviors. Although readers may teach at only one grade level, they are encouraged to read all of the examples, since the key to including concepts in learning experiences is understanding the process involved, and not simply following a few isolated examples.

Example 1

After reviewing the concepts and standards for kindergarten and first grade, the teacher uses a skill theme approach for developing a yearly plan. The instructional units for this approach typically include: introduction, space awareness, effort, relationships, traveling, chasing/fleeing/dodging, jumping and landing, rolling, balancing, transferring weight, kicking and punting, throwing and catching, volleying and dribbling, striking with objects, fitness concepts, and closure. Each of these units lasts from one to three weeks in a five-day-a-week program. For more information on the skill theme approach for teaching elementary physical education, readers are referred to *Children Moving: A Reflective Approach to Teaching Physical Education* (Graham, Holt/Hale & Parker 1993).

Once the instructional units are identified, the teacher decides which standards and concepts to address during each instructional unit. This may sound like a contradiction, but it is not. At this stage of the process, there is a continual shifting back and forth between selecting the instructional units and determining where the standards and concepts are addressed. Specifically, the distinct aspects of standards and concepts are assigned to one or more instructional units.

The traveling instructional unit consists of 12 one-day lessons (see Figure 1) that address the locomotor movements of walking, running, hopping, galloping, sliding, skipping, and leaping, along with the qualities of movement. Looking at the standards and concepts for first grade, the teacher decides to focus on Standards 1, 2, 5, 6, and 7 during this unit:

- Standard 1: Skill development in the locomotor movements (walking, running, hopping, skipping, galloping, leaping, and sliding).
- Standard 2 (Biomechanics): Lowering the body's center of gravity increases ability to maintain balance.
- Standard 5 (Social/Psychological): Safe and appropriate physical activity helps people feel good inside.
- Standard 6 (Historical Perspectives): Games that are played at school in modern times may have looked different long ago.
- Standard 7 (Aesthetics): Shapes, patterns, and textures of objects in the environment stimulate movement responses.

Looking at the instructional units for first grade, the reader may be thinking, "Shouldn't the biomechanical concept of lowering the body's center of gravity to increase stability be aligned with the balance unit?" The answer is definitely yes, but that doesn't prevent the teacher from also addressing the concept during this unit.

The next step in the process is to look for interdisciplinary links. This unit is ideal for integration with language arts. Students read a story—e.g., *Pretend You're a Cat* (Marzollo 1990), or any story that involves animals moving—that involves different locomotor movements. The reading is used during lessons seven through nine as students mimic animal movements. Pretending to be different animals provides students with the opportunity to practice different movements using dif-

Figure 1. Twelve One-Day Lessons That Address Locomotor Movements

Day	Motor Skill Focus	Conceptual Focus
1.	Traveling in space	
2.	Traveling in different directions	
3.	Traveling and freezing at different levels	Lowering the body's center of gravity increases ability to maintain balance.
4.	Traveling at different speeds	
5.	Traveling and changing force qualities	
6.	Traveling along pathways	
7.	Animal movements	Lowering the body's center of gravity increases ability to maintain balance.
		Shapes, patterns, and textures of objects in the environment stimulate movement responses.
		Safe and appropriate physical activity helps people feel good inside.
8.	Animal movements	Lowering the body's center of gravity increases ability to maintain balance.
		Shapes, patterns, and textures of objects in the environment stimulate movement responses.
		Safe and appropriate physical activity helps people feel good inside.
9.	Animal movements	Lowering the body's center of gravity increases ability to maintain balance.
		Shapes, patterns, and textures of objects in the environment stimulate movement responses.
		Safe and appropriate physical activity helps people feel good inside.
10.	Traveling activities (e.g., hopscotch, obstacle course)	Lowering the body's center of gravity increases ability to maintain balance.
		Games that are played at school in modern times may have looked different long ago.
		Safe and appropriate physical activity helps people feel good inside.
11.	Traveling activities (e.g., hopscotch, obstacle course)	Lowering the body's center of gravity increases ability to maintain balance.
		Games that are played at school in modern times may have looked different long ago.
		Safe and appropriate physical activity helps people feel good inside.
12.	Traveling activities (e.g., hopscotch, obstacle course)	Lowering the body's center of gravity increases ability to maintain balance.
		Games that are played at school in modern times may have looked different long ago.
		Safe and appropriate physical activity helps people feel good inside.

ferent qualities of movement (e.g., bears walk heavily, rabbits hop, horses gallop fast).

This unit also lends itself to integration with visual and performing arts, since the animal movements can be performed to music (e.g., animal walks or any music that contains a variety of rhythms). Science also can be integrated, since students can study stability principles during science and apply them during the traveling unit in physical education. History/social science is integrated into lessons 10 through 12 as students discuss with their parents how games they play at school were played differently by their parents and grandparents. Notice that the integration was not forced in any of these examples. Rather, it grew naturally from the instructional unit designed for physical education.

There are three major learning experiences (days 1 through 6, 7 through 9, and 10 through 12) in this unit. In lessons one through six, the students are improving their ability to demonstrate the basic locomotor skills (walk, run, leap, hop, skip, gallop, slide) while applying the components of movement (space, flow, energy, time). In kindergarten, students are taught the basic locomotor skills, and prior to this learning experience they are taught the qualities of movement. Since this is a review of the locomotor skills involving the application of components of movement, the teacher prompts the students with questions such as:
- Can you show me your body walking at a high level in general space?
- Can you show me your body sliding at a medium level?
- Can you show me your body running fast?
- Can you show me your body hopping lightly?
- Can you show me your body skipping in a zigzag pattern?
- Can you show me your body galloping forward?

In addition, the teacher addresses the biomechanical concept on day three while asking students to demonstrate the locomotor movement skills at the three levels (high, medium, low). After the students walk at each of the three levels, the teacher asks them to identify the level at which they felt the most stable. The teacher repeats this question after each movement. At the conclusion of the lesson, students discuss whether one level is more stable than the others.

In lessons seven through nine, a variety of environmental stimuli (music, stories, pictures) are used to assist students with their animal imitations. The teacher shows the students pictures of various animals from stories they have read and asks them to imitate that animal. Students select one locomotor movement skill and one component of movement to depict the animal (e.g., cows walk slowly, cats leap forward). The learning experiences provide students with an opportunity to continue to improve their locomotor movement skills and thereby increase their enjoyment of movement. Simultaneously, they discover stability concepts as they move at different levels.

During the next learning experience, the teacher asks students to pretend to be the animal in the picture, but this time they must move at a low level, then at a medium level, and finally at a high level. For the next learning experience, the teacher turns on music and has the students listen to the rhythm. Each time the rhythm changes, the teacher asks the students which type of animal might move to that rhythm and why. The teacher plays the music again, but this time the students move to the music, changing animals as the music changes rhythm. The teacher debriefs these learning experiences by asking students several closure questions:
1. What do animals who are not likely to fall down when running have in common? Guide the discussion toward being low to the ground. (Biomechanics concept.)
2. Did you enjoy pretending to be animals? Why? (Social/psychology concept.)

3. Why did you move the way you did when you were imitating a cat (or any animal)? How did you know how cats move? Guide the discussion toward the pictures, story, and music used during the learning experience, along with personal experiences. (Aesthetic concept.)

In lessons 10 through 12, the students participate in activities that help them practice the locomotor movements. These activities include hopscotch, obstacle courses, and Crows and Cranes. As each new activity is taught, students are asked to go home and ask their parents and other older relatives if they played the game when they were in elementary school, and if so, how was it played. This provides students with an understanding of how games have changed over time. Again, the teacher uses debriefing questions to reinforce the concepts addressed earlier in the unit. These might include:

1. When balance was important in the game, was it better to be at a high level, medium level, or low level? Why? (Biomechanics.)
2. Did you enjoy participating in the activities? Why? (Social/psychology.)
3. How are the games we play today the same or different from the games played by parents and other older relatives? (Historical perspectives.)

Example 2

Fifth grade teachers often continue with the skill theme approach to developing a yearly plan, but they may add a few activity-based units. The following instructional units comprise the fifth grade curriculum: introduction, fitness concepts, throwing and catching, striking with hands, striking with feet, rhythms, stunts and tumbling, striking with implements, multicultural-cultural games, dance, cooperative activities, and closure. Each of these units lasts approximately three weeks in a five-day-a-week program.

Once the instructional units are identified, the physical educator decides which standards and concepts to address during each instructional unit. For example, the cooperative activities instructional unit consists of 15 one-day lessons that specially address the social skill of cooperation as applied in movement activities (see Figure 2). Looking at the standards and concepts for fourth/fifth grade, the teacher may decide to focus on Standards 1, 2, and 5 during this unit:

• Standard 1: Development in the the six parts of skill-related fitness (balance, coordination, reaction time, agility, power, and speed).

Figure 2. Fifteen One-Day Lessons That Address Cooperation

Day	Motor Skill Focus	Conceptual Focus
1.	Skill-related fitness	
2.	Reaction Time (e.g., Knee Touch)	
3.	Reaction Time (e.g., Toe Touch)	
4.	Coordination (e.g., Circle the Circle)	Collaboration is the process of working together, but not necessarily on the same goals or outcome.
5.	Coordination (e.g., Booop)	Taking turns being a leader helps everyone develop self-confidence and responsibility.
		Collaboration is the process of working together, but not necessarily on the same goals or outcome.

Day	Motor Skill Focus	Conceptual Focus
6.	Balance (e.g., Stand Up)	Skills requiring balance can be improved with a visual focal point.
		For every action there is an equal and opposite reaction.
		Collaboration is the process of working together, but not necessarily on the same goals or outcome.
		Taking turns being a leader helps everyone develop self-confidence and responsibility.
7.	Balance (e.g., TP Shuffle)	Skills requiring balance can be improved with a visual focal point.
		For every action there is an equal and opposite reaction.
		Collaboration is the process of working together, but not necessarily on the same goals or outcome.
		Taking turns being a leader helps everyone develop self-confidence and responsibility.
8.	Speed (e.g., Shark Attack)	Collaboration is the process of working together, but not necessarily on the same goals or outcome.
		Taking turns being a leader helps everyone develop self-confidence and responsibility.
9.	Speed (e.g., Warp Speed)	Collaboration is the process of working together, but not necessarily on the same goals or outcome.
		Taking turns being a leader helps everyone develop self-confidence and responsibility.
10.	Power (e.g., Everyone Up)	Collaboration is the process of working together, but not necessarily on the same goals or outcome.
		Taking turns being a leader helps everyone develop self-confidence and responsibility.
11.	Power (e.g., Levitation)	Collaboration is the process of working together, but not necessarily on the same goals or outcome.
		Taking turns being a leader helps everyone develop self-confidence and responsibility.
12.	Agility (e.g., Courtesy Tag)	
13.	Agility (e.g., Dribble Tag)	
14.	Skill-related fitness	
15.	Skill-related fitness	

- Standard 2 (Biomechanics): For every action there is an equal and opposite reaction.
- Standard 2 (Motor Learning): Skills requiring balance can be improved with a visual focal point.
- Standard 5 (Social/Psychology): Collaboration is the process of working together, but not necessarily on the same goals or outcomes.
- Standard 5 (Social Psychology): Taking turns being a leader helps everyone develop self-confidence and responsibility.

The next step in the process is to look for interdisciplinary links. This unit lends itself to the web interdisciplinary model involving physical education, health education, and language arts and uses the theme of cooperation. In physical education, students participate in the cooperative activities. After physical education, students go to their health class where they debrief the activity in order to improve their cooperation skills. Then, in their language arts class, students write an essay describing the social skills they learned during the physical education activities. Science can also be integrated with physical education during this instructional unit as students study Newton's Third Law and apply it while participating in the cooperative activities. Notice again that in each of these examples, the integration was not forced, but grew naturally from the physical education unit.

In this instructional unit, students experience a wide variety of cooperative activities. (See Figure 3 for an outline of the unit.) Notice that two days are allocated for each aspect of skill-related fitness. Also, notice that only one activity is suggested. In reality, a class may address from one to four activities per lesson, depending on the length of time needed to accomplish each one. However, as discussed previously, it is not enough to introduce the cooperative activities and expect the students to understand the cognitive concepts associated with the sociology subdiscipline. Specific learning experiences must occur that provide students with "hands-on" learning opportunities.

The sociology concepts are first addressed on days four and five. The T-chart is a very effective strategy for introducing these concepts. On day four, the teacher sets up a T-chart (see Figure 3) with the word "collaboration" at the top. The students are asked to identify what collaboration looks like and sounds like. The cooperative activities throughout the unit provide practice in collaboration. During each lesson, selected students are asked to chart the number of times they observe a team demonstrating collaboration. This information provides feedback to the group and helps group members analyze their performance.

On day five, the teacher again sets up a T-chart, but this time with the word "leadership" at the top. The students are asked to identify what leadership looks like and sounds like. The cooperative activities throughout the unit provide different students with the opportunity to be a leader. At the end of each lesson, the teacher debriefs the activities with questions such as, "How did you feel being the leader?" and "How did collaborating with teammates help you in performing the cooperative activity?" in order to reinforce the two sociology concepts. Notice that

Figure 3. A Model T-Chart

Collaboration T-Chart

Looks Like   Sounds Like

the learning of social skills occurs simultaneously as students practice the skill-related fitness items and participate in the cooperative activities.

Although this unit focuses on the concepts related to sociology, there also are opportunities to address motor learning and biomechanic concepts. For example, on days six and seven, when the lesson addresses the skill-related fitness area of balance, it would be appropriate to include concepts from motor learning and biomechanics in the lesson. In terms of the motor learning concept, students are asked to accomplish the cooperative activity using a focal point and then not using a focal point. Students are then asked to discuss and summarize which scenario produced the best results.

From this learning experience, students are able to determine for themselves that a focal point is beneficial when participating in activities involving balance. In addition, since the concept of balance requires a state of equilibrium, the biomechanical concept, "for every action there is an equal and opposite reaction" can be addressed. At the end of each balance activity, students describe what happened during the activity and note the relationship between the action and its counteraction. Again, it is recommended that debriefing questions be used at the end of the lesson or as homework assignments so that students can demonstrate their understanding of the concepts. These might include:

1. What can you do to improve your balance? (Motor learning.)
2. What happened when someone accidentally bumped into you when you were performing the TP shuffle? Why did this happen? (Biomechanics.)

Example 3

Eighth grade teachers often use activity-based instructional units. The following instructional units comprise the eighth grade curriculum: introduction, square dance, project adventure, volleyball, softball, basketball, team handball, soccer, football, and closure. Each of these units lasts three to four weeks.

Once the instructional units are identified, physical educators must decide which standards and concepts will be addressed during each instructional unit. For example, the basketball unit consists of 20 one-day lessons that address the motor skills of stopping (two-step stop, jump stop), passing (chest, overhead, and bounce) and catching, pivoting, dribbling, one-handed set shot, lay-up, and rebounding (see Figure 4). Looking at the standards and concepts for eighth grade, the teacher decides to focus on Standards 1, 2, 5, and 6 during this unit.

Figure 4. Twenty One-Day Lessons That Address Basketball Skills

Day	Motor Skill Focus	Conceptual Focus
1.	Passing (chest, overhead, bounce) and catching	Motor performance can be increased by improving physical abilities and motivation to learn.
		Open skills are performed in unpredictable and unstable environments and should be practiced in variable conditions.
2.	Stopping (two step, jump stop) and pivoting	Motor performance can be increased by improving physical abilities and motivation to learn.

Day	Motor Skill Focus	Conceptual Focus
		Open skills are performed in unpredictable and unstable environments and should be practiced in variable conditions.
3.	Dribbling	Motor performance can be increased by improving physical abilities and motivation to learn.
		Open skills are performed in unpredictable and unstable environments and should be practiced in variable conditions.
4.	Combinations (pass, catch, stop, pivot, dribble)	Practice with increasingly complex interactions among teammates and opponents can help a person become a better player.
		Open skills are performed in unpredictable and unstable environments and should be practiced in variable conditions.
4.	Combinations (pass, catch, stop, pivot, dribble)	Practice with increasingly complex interactions among teammates and opponents can help a person become a better player.
		Open skills are performed in unpredictable and unstable environments and should be practiced in variable conditions.
6.	One handed set shot	Motor performance can be increased by improving physical abilities and motivation to learn.
		Open skills are performed in unpredictable and unstable environments and should be practiced in variable conditions.
7.	One handed set shot	Motor performance can be increased by improving physical abilities and motivation to learn.
		Open skills are performed in unpredictable and unstable environments and should be practiced in variable conditions.
8.	One-on-one strategies	Practice with increasingly complex interactions among teammates and opponents can help a person become a better player.
		Open skills are performed in unpredictable and unstable environments and should be practiced in variable conditions.
9.	Two-on-two strategies	Practice with increasingly complex interactions among teammates and opponents can help a person become a better player.
		Open skills are performed in unpredictable and unstable environments and should be practiced in variable conditions.
10.	Lay-up shot	Motor performance can be increased by improving physical abilities and motivation to learn.
		Open skills are performed in unpredictable and unstable environments and should be practiced in variable conditions.

Day	Motor Skill Focus	Conceptual Focus
11.	Lay-up and rebounding	Practice with increasingly complex interactions among teammates and opponents can help a person become a better player.
		Open skills are performed in unpredictable and unstable environments and should be practiced in variable conditions.
12.	Two-on-two strategies using lay-up	Practice with increasingly complex interactions among teammates and opponents can help a person become a better player.
		Open skills are performed in unpredictable and unstable environments and should be practiced in variable conditions.
13.	Two-on-two strategies using lay-up	Practice with increasingly complex interactions among teammates and opponents can help a person become a better player.
		Open skills are performed in unpredictable and unstable environments and should be practiced in variable conditions.
14.	Three-on-three strategies	Practice with increasingly complex interactions among teammates and opponents can help a person become a better player.
15.	Three-on-three strategies	Practice with increasingly complex interactions among teammates and opponents can help a person become a better player.
16.	Three-on-three strategies	Practice with increasingly complex interactions among teammates and opponents can help a person become a better player.
17.	Two basketball games from early history	Practice with increasingly complex interactions among teammates and opponents can help a person become a better player.
		Sport rules are influenced by societal events.
		Asking inquiring questions shows genuine interest in others as people.
18.	Two basketball games from middle history	Practice with increasingly complex interactions among teammates and opponents can help a person become a better player.
		Sport rules are influenced by societal events.
		Asking inquiring questions shows genuine interest in others as people.
19.	Two basketball games from later history	Practice with increasingly complex interactions among teammates and opponents can help a person become a better player.
		Sport rules are influenced by societal events.
		Asking inquiring questions shows genuine interest in others as people.
20.	Project	Sport rules are influenced by societal events.

- Standard 1: Application of locomotor, nonlocomotor and manipulative skills to basketball.
- Standard 2 (Motor Learning): Motor performance can be increased by improving physical abilities and motivation to learn.
- Standard 2 (Motor Learning): Open skills are performed in unpredictable and unstable environments and should be practiced in variable conditions.
- Standard 5 (Social/Psychology): Asking inquiring questions shows genuine interest in others as people.
- Standard 6 (Motor Development): Sport rules are influenced by societal events.
- Standard 6 (Motor Development): Practice with increasingly complex interactions among teammates and opponents can help a person become a better player.

The next step in the process is to again look for interdisciplinary links. This unit lends itself to integration with history/social science. Many eighth graders study United States history during the 1800s in their history/social science classes. Therefore, students can learn about the history of that era during history and then participate in basketball, which was invented during the same period, during physical education. Students can consider why basketball was invented during the 1890s, what social factors influenced its development, and how the game has changed during the last 100 years.

Notice that this integration with history/social science only works because basketball is an appropriate activity for eighth graders. It would not, for example, be appropriate for second graders. As the students trace the development of basketball throughout its 100-year history and speculate about how the game may change during the next 10 years, language arts or visual/performing arts can be integrated into the unit. For example, students might choose an essay format or a video or model format for their project.

In this instructional unit, students have the opportunity to review and practice the basic skills related to basketball in a variety of games. As the teacher introduces the motor skills related to basketball, the students will observe a wide variety of skill levels among their peers. This provides the teacher with an opportunity to discuss the motor learning concept, "Motor performance can be increased by improving physical abilities and motivation to learn." At the end of each lesson, the teacher can ask students to use a rubric to assess their performance. Then, using the data on the students' previous experience with basketball that was collected on the first day of the unit, the teacher—and later the students—can analyze the relationship between previous experience and current performance on a motor skill related to basketball.

At the beginning of the basketball unit when the individual motor skills are being reviewed and practiced, the teacher can address the other motor learning concept, "Open skills are performed in unpredictable and unstable environments and should be practiced in variable conditions." This concept can initially be addressed through the drills and activities for practicing the various skills. It is imperative that the teacher point out how he or she is setting up the drill to ensure that open skills are practiced in variable conditions. Later in the unit, students should be asked to create their own drills and activities to ensure that they understand the concept.

This instructional unit takes students from two on two basketball, to three on three basketball, to basketball of the 1890s, to basketball of the 1990s. Throughout the unit, the teacher addresses the motor development concept, "Practice with increasingly complex interactions among teammates and opponents will help you become a better player." by first setting up isolated skill practice, then combined skill practice, one-on-one situations, two-on-two situations, three-on-three situations, and then finally game situations. Debriefing questions will determine student understanding of this concept. These might include:

1. Are you getting better at playing basketball?
2. Why do you think you are getting better at basketball?
3. What would happen now if you stopped trying more complex drills and activities?

The last two concepts are addressed specifically during learning experiences at the end of the unit. Even though students teach their games to one another during days 17, 18, and 19, the project is actually assigned early in the unit to provide students with sufficient time to gather information and determine how they will present their games. The project uses a cooperative learning structure known as "coop coop." Each group of five students investigates the game of basketball at various points throughout its history. Each student has a specific responsibility that is unique from the others. In addition to learning the rules and strategies of the time period they are researching, each group must determine the influence of societal events on the game rules.

During the presentations, the other groups are encouraged to ask questions for clarification before playing the game for a brief period. This activity should be debriefed each day with questions such as:

1. How did it make you feel when someone asked a question? Why? (Sociology.)
2. How did it make you feel when no one asked a question? Why? (Sociology.)
3. What were the major reasons why basketball changed during the time periods covered in today's lesson? (Historical Perspectives.)

Example 4

In many states, high school physical educators are required by law to provide either a year, semester, or quarter course on health-related fitness. Often, a high school physical education textbook containing information on health-related fitness—e.g., *Fitness for Life* (Corbin & Lindsey 1990), *Looking Good and Feeling Good* (Williams et al. 1995), or *Moving for Life* (Spindt et al. 1991)—is central to the course of study. In other states, high school physical educators provide a quarter course on health-related fitness, but they also address one or more of the following areas: team sports, individual/dual sports, self-defense, tumbling and gymnastics, dance, and/or aquatics. Students may be required to participate in one unit related to each of these content areas in some states, and they may choose the courses they will take in others.

Once the instructional units are identified, teachers decide which standards and concepts to address during each instructional unit. For example, the health-related fitness unit consists of 45 one-day lessons (see Figure 5) that address the health-related fitness components (cardiorespiratory endurance, flexibility, body composition, muscular strength, and muscular endurance). Looking at the standards and concepts for tenth grade, the teacher decides to focus on Standards 2, 3, and 6 in addition to Standard 4, which is the focal point of the instructional unit:

• Standard 3: Participate daily in physical activity which sets the stage for a lifetime of activity.
• Standard 2 (Biomechanics): A change in the moment arms of the involved muscles or the resistance forces can increase or decrease the relative difficulty of an exercise.
• Standard 6 (Motor Development): Females who participate in vigorous regular exercise can lessen the effects of age-related diseases like osteoporosis.
• Standard 6 (Motor Development): Young adults already past their growth spurt may be able to use longer or heavier equipment to improve their force or power.

Figure 5. Forty-Five One-Day Lessons That Address Health-Related Fitness

Day	Fitness Focus	Conceptual Focus
1.	Introduction to Physical Fitness	
2.	Introduction to Physical Fitness, day 2	
3.	Introduction to Physical Fitness, day 3	
4.	Introduction to Physical Fitness, day 4	
5.	Introduction to Physical Fitness, day 5	
6.	Components of Fitness	
7.	Components of Fitness, day 2	
8.	Components of Fitness, day 3	
9.	Components of Fitness, day 4	
10.	Components of Fitness, day 5	
11.	Goal Setting	
12.	Goal Setting, day 2	
13.	Guidelines	
14.	Guidelines, day 2	
15.	Principles	
16.	Principles, day 2	
17.	Evaluation of Activities	
18.	Evaluation of Activities, day 2	
19.	Flexibility	
20.	Flexibility, day 2	
21.	Flexibility, day 3	
22.	Flexibility, day 3	
23.	Cardiorespiratory Endurance	Females who participate in vigorous regular exercise can lessen the effects of age-related diseases like osteoporosis.
24.	Cardiorespiratory Endurance	Females who participate in vigorous regular exercise can lessen the effects of age-related diseases like osteoporosis.
25.	Cardiorespiratory Endurance	Females who participate in vigorous regular exercise can lessen the effects of age-related diseases like osteoporosis.
26.	Cardiorespiratory Endurance	Females who participate in vigorous regular exercise can lessen the effects of age-related diseases like osteoporosis.
27.	Body Composition and Nutrition	
28.	Body Composition and Nutrition	
29.	Body Composition and Nutrition	
30.	Body Composition and Nutrition	
31.	Body Composition and Nutrition	
32.	Muscular Fitness	Muscular strength is improved by performing isotonic, isometric, or isokinetic exercises every other day. Young adults already past their growth spurt may be able to use longer or heavier equipment to improve their force or power.

Day	Fitness Focus	Conceptual Focus
		A change in the moment arms of the involved muscles or the resistance forces can increase or decrease the relative difficulty of an exercise.
33.	Muscular Fitness, day 2	Muscular strength is improved by performing isotonic, isometric, or isokinetic exercises every other day.
		Young adults already past their growth spurt may be able to use longer or heavier equipment to improve their force or power.
		A change in the moment arms of the involved muscles or the resistance forces can increase or decrease the relative difficulty of an exercise.
34.	Muscular Fitness, day 3	Muscular strength is improved by performing isotonic, isometric, or isokinetic exercises every other day.
		Young adults already past their growth spurt may be able to use longer or heavier equipment to improve their force or power.
		A change in the moment arms of the involved muscles or the resistance forces can increase or decrease the relative difficulty of an exercise.
35.	Muscular Fitness, day 4	Muscular strength is improved by performing isotonic, isometric, or isokinetic exercises every other day.
		Young adults already past their growth spurt may be able to use longer or heavier equipment to improve their force or power.
		A change in the moment arms of the involved muscles or the resistance forces can increase or decrease the relative difficulty of an exercise.
36.	Stress	
37.	Stress, day 2	
38.	Consumer Issues	
39.	Consumer Issues, day 2	
40.	Consumer Issues, day 3	
41.	Program Design	
42.	Program Design, day 2	
43.	Program Design, day 3	
44.	Program Design, day 4	
45.	Program Design, day 5	

- Standard 4 (Exercise Physiology): Muscular strength is improved by performing isotonic, isometric, or isokinetic exercises every other day.

The next step in the process is to look for interdisciplinary links. This unit lends itself to the web interdisciplinary model involving physical education, health education, science, and math using the theme of wellness. In physical education, students learn about health related fitness, in health education students study personal health, in science students study the muscular/skeletal system, and in math students graph their fitness improvement throughout the unit. Again, this interdisciplinary model works well because it includes content that should be addressed in tenth grade physical education, health education, science, and math.

As stated earlier, a fitness instructional unit is often required by state law. The intent is to ensure that students understand the various concepts related to health related fitness. In some situations this will be a review of information presented previously; in other situations this will be new information. One of the tenth grade concepts identified by the authors of this book is addressed during a unit on cardiorespiratory endurance, while the other three concepts are addressed during the muscular fitness lessons (see Figure 8).

In addressing the first concept, "Females who participate in vigorous regular exercise can lessen the effects of age-related diseases like osteoporosis," students work in groups to research the benefits of good cardiorespiratory endurance for various groups of people. One group of students is assigned females over the age of 50. The students use the Internet, books, and interviews to answer the research question. Students then share their findings with the rest of the class.

The learning experience related to, "Muscular strength is improved by performing isotonic, isometric, or isokinetic exercises every other day," is taught through a cooperative learning structure known as a jigsaw. In a jigsaw experience, students work in groups of four (home groups), and select one aspect of information to study in detail. Detailed information includes frequency, intensity, time and type variables related to muscular strength development. The students read about their topic and then meet with students from other home groups who have the same topic (expert groups). If groups are larger than six people, then the teacher forms double expert groups (e.g., two groups meet together to study frequency). Each expert group discusses the information and prepares a presentation. The intensity group is also given information related to the "use of levers as a means of increasing the intensity of an exercise," and, "young adults already past their growth spurt may be able to use longer or heavier equipment to improve their force or power."

Students then meet back with their home groups to share their presentations on the variables related to muscular strength development. The students demonstrate their ability to apply the first two concepts by creating a personal plan for improving muscular strength at home. The teacher reminds the students that the use of levers is an effective technique for increasing resistance when weights aren't available. Students demonstrate their ability to apply the last concept by writing an essay that addresses the following question, "Why should an individual wait until high school before beginning a strength development program?"

In order to ensure understanding of the process for addressing the concepts in a variety of lessons, the reader should now return to each lesson, look at the list of concepts for that grade level, and determine if and how any additional concepts can be addressed during each instructional unit. This will provide good practice before beginning to adjust current lesson plans.

Concluding Comments

The concepts outlined in Chapters 2 through 8 provide the knowledge base or content to ensure that students have sufficient information to demonstrate the National Physical Education Standards and live high quality lives in the twenty-first century. This chapter provides several examples of learning experiences that bring together concepts from various subdisciplines and standards, and shows how they can be integrated with other subjects areas. These examples serve as models that teachers can use to create their own learning experiences. It is important to remember two points when doing so: incorporate one or more National Standards or concepts into each learning experience when feasible, and identify the link between the learning experience and the related concepts and the National Standards.

Resources

Animal walks. (9107 or 9107C). Long Branch, NJ: Kimbo Educational.

Marzollo, J. (1990). *Pretend you're a cat.* New York: Dial Books for Young Readers.

References

Bressan, E. S. (1987). *The basic stuff in action for grades K-3.* Reston, VA: American Alliance for Health, Physical Education, Recreation, and Dance.

Corbin, C. B., & Lindsey, R. (1990). *Fitness for life.* (3rd ed.). Glenview, IL: Scott, Foresman and Company.

Fogarty, R. (1991). *The mindful school: How to integrate the curricula.* Palatine, IL: IRI/Skylight.

Graham, G., Holt/Hale, S., & Parker, M. (1993). *Children moving: A reflective approach to teaching physical education.* Mountain View, CA: Mayfield.

Kneer, M. E., & Heitmann, H. M. (1987). *The basic stuff in action for grades 9-12.* Reston, VA: American Alliance for Health, Physical Education, Recreation, and Dance.

Lambert, L. T., & Trimble, R. T. (1987). *The basic stuff in action for grades 4-8.* Reston, VA: American Alliance for Health, Physical Education, Recreation, and Dance.

Melograno, V. J. (1996). *Designing the physical education curriculum.* Champaign, IL: Human Kinetics.

Mohnsen, B. S. (1997). *Teaching middle school physical education.* Champaign, IL: Human Kinetics.

Mosston, M., & Ashworth, S. (1986). *Teaching physical education.* Columbus, OH: Merrill.

Placek, J. H., & O'Sullivan, M. (1997). The many faces of integrated physical education. *Journal of Physical Education, Recreation, and Dance, 68*(1), 20-24.

Rink, J. E. (1997). Teacher education programs: The role of context in learning how to teach. *Journal of Physical Education, Recreation, and Dance, 68*(1), 17-19, 24.

Rink, J. E. (1993). *Teaching physical education for learning.* St. Louis, MO: Mosby-Year Book.

Siedentop, D. (1991). *Developing teaching skills in physical education.* Mountain View, CA: Mayfield.

Williams, C. S., Harageones, E. G., Johnson, D. J., & Smith, C. D. (1995). *Personal fitness: Looking good, feeling good.* Dubuque, IA: Kendall/Hunt.

Spindt, G. B., Monti, W. H., & Hennessy, B. (1991) *Moving for life.* Dubuque, IA: Kendall/Hunt.

Glossary of Games

Booop

In fours.

Form a circle and join hands except for person with balloon or beach ball.

Person with balloon tosses it in the air and then joins hands.

The objective is to keep the balloon in the air while hands remained joined.

Circle the Circle

In fours.

Form a circle and join hands with hula hoop around a pair of joined hands.

Pass the hula hoop around the circle without letting go of joined hands.

Courtesy Tag
Whole class.
Each person has a scarf.
Everybody is it.
When someone is tagged they must go down on one knee and give their scarf to the tagger.
Players may have no more than two scarves in their hands at one time.
Players with two scarves may give one of their scarves to a player who is down.
The player receiving the scarf must say thank you.

Crows and Cranes
Game is played on a large rectangular area.
Students are in two groups.
One group is named crows, the other is named cranes.
Groups form parallel lines facing each other, approximately two yards apart in the middle of the area.
Teacher calls out either "crows" or "cranes."
If the teacher calls out cranes, the cranes turn and run away from the crows, who chase them.
Any crane tagged before reaching the end line joins the crows.
If the teacher calls out crows, the crows turn and run away from the cranes.
Any crow tagged before reaching the end line joins the cranes.

Dribble Tag
Whole class.
Each student has a flag or scarf tucked into their waist band.
Each student is dribbling a ball (hand or foot dribble).
The objective is to take other players' flag while protecting one's own flag.
Play continues until all flags have been taken.

Everyone Up
In fours.
Sit on the ground facing each other so that soles of feet are touching the adjoining person.
Hands are tightly grasped to the adjoining person.
The objective is to stand up.

Knee Touch
In pairs.
Standing facing partner.
The objective is to touch your partner's knees while preventing your partner from touching your knee.

Levitation
Group of eight in a circle with one person designated as the person to be lifted in the center.
Person to be lifted lies down on back.
Group kneels around the person.
On signal, the group lifts the person up overhead.
Return person to the ground.

Shark Attack
In groups of four.
Each group has a hula hoop which they must hold onto while running.
On the command "Shark!" the group puts the hula hoop down on the ground and everyone in the group gets in the hula hoop.
The last group to get in looses their hula hoop.
On the command "Release!" each member of the group that lost their hula hoop must join another group.

Stand Up
In pairs.
Sit on the ground, back to back.
Bend knees and link elbows.
The objective is to stand up together.

Toe Touch
In pairs.
Standing facing partner.
The objective is to lightly tap your partner's foot with your foot while preventing your partner from tapping your foot.

TP Shuffle
Two groups of four.
Each group stands on a horizontal telephone pole or a raised curb facing the center.
The objective is for the two groups to change ends of the pole without touching the ground.

Warp Speed
Group of eight in a circle.
One person holding a fleece ball.
The group establishes a tossing pattern, so that everyone in the group tosses and catches once.
The group practices the pattern in order to complete the pattern as quickly as possible.

Index